KEYS TO A
SPIRITUALLY-BASED LIFE
FIFTY TENETS OF A NEW FAITH

M A STREET

Copyright © 2013 M A Street

All rights reserved.

ISBN-10: 1482316099

EAN-13: 9781482316094

The key to a spiritually-based life is the steadfast belief in the eternal perfection and divine goodness of God— and that this goodness, which is also called grace, is apportioned the same to all people.

ONE

What is Spirituality?

Is it necessary to believe in God, by whatever name, in order to have a spiritually-based life?

The quick answer is *yes*. The term *spiritual* implies there is a part within us that seeks to move beyond our internal limitations, as well as an external force we can access and derive energy from.

Any desire to move beyond our current physical and psychical forms to discover greater understanding of the divine would be considered spiritual.

Most of us believe a part of us all seeks *more*. Call it conscience or consciousness, a piece of ourselves, through awareness, prods us to be better human beings—to know more and experience more; to traipse into different areas of wholeness and satisfaction, beyond our egos.

To seek the *spiritual*, whatever we think it to be, is the first step in a spiritually-based life. We cannot find a thing unless we believe it exists.

At some point, we may see life as a pilgrimage, a diurnal journey into a more expansive way of seeing, feeling, hearing, living. We may wander or take a straight course. Eventually, and for whatever reasons, we find a course to take.

The success of all spirituality is defined by the course one chooses to take.

Ironically, the yearning for spirituality is a part of our human evolution. As we grew from mere survivors into clans then into societies, our individual natures also grew to realize a better, more enlightened way exists for us. We wanted to be *more*. We wanted to be *better*. We wanted to understand the *why* of things. This became far more than mere intellectual curiosity. It became a thirst.

Thus, we began to seek, and the *more* we sought, the *more* we found, and so we continued to seek and find—to become *better*.

All keenness, all comprehension, generates *more*. Human intelligence breeds yearning, and every hunger persists until satiation.

The eventual evolutionary conclusion to *better*, no matter how remote or unattainable, is *perfection*.

Perfection is the terminus for all spiritual practices. Perfection, though technically an end, and fixed, is never fully manifested to us. Through spiritual growth, we become more alert to its boundless dimension and innumerable facets. Through spiritual growth, we learn of greater potential.

To believe in *perfection* is the second step in a spiritually-based life.

To understand the true concept of *perfection*, to believe in a source without blemish, without weakness, without corruption of any sort; to embrace the belief in perfection in contrast to our own humanity and its foibles, is to seek the ultimate spiritual source.

The ultimate spiritual source is to be called *God*.

The only possible *perfection* is God.

To believe in God as the only possible source of perfection, is the third step in a spiritually-based life.

What is Spirituality?

We also know it is impossible for any human being to ever achieve perfection. No matter how much we grow in faith and practice—no matter how successful we are in reaching that part within us we call our spiritual selves—or any relationship outside ourselves to the *divine*, there is always going to be *more*, and there will be times when we are discouraged by the distance between ourselves and the divine.

Yet those desiring a spiritually-based life will *always* reach for *more*. This, too, is the bliss of persistence.

Though our poor human brains cannot accommodate perfection, they do allow us to recognize the *more* as an *ideal*. Then the reality of *more* expands. There is *more*, and *more*, and *more* after that—as long as we continue. As long as we continue, progress is insured. As long as we continue, we discover.

Spiritual growth is infinite, just as the path between ourselves and God is infinite. Comfort and enjoyment can be found in realizing we are moving farther along the path. Consistency is often more important than distance.

To deny the possibility of perfection is to deny God.

Rationally, one only has three choices:

All human growth is achieved by our own internal resources and limited to self-contained attributes.

Or…

We believe God exists.

And…

We believe God is either perfect or imperfect.

If we believe in *the perfect God*—that God is the only source of perfection, of the divine—that to seek the divine is to seek God—to find the potential of perfection is to find God—we are drawn to another conclusion.

Nothing imperfect can truly be divine.

Also, nothing we discover in humanity can be wholly divine.

Our imperfection is what brings us to seek a more spiritual basis for our lives. The recognition of *lack* in ourselves, without self-castigation, is the drive to find the *more,* and acquire the *more.* So once we believe in perfection, and God as the perfect source, and have the desire to pursue such a source, we must then believe in the reality of a connection between ourselves and this source.

To believe in the connection to *perfection* is the fourth step in the spiritually-based life. Should we merely believe in perfection in the abstract, we cede the potential for a connection. Should we grasp perfection and embrace it, we are better able to understand what God is, and what this means to us.

The beginning of such a connection begins with understanding what part is within and what part is without.

Within, we have a seed capable of imagining the ideal. We seek, we encounter new revelations, we experience epiphanies, and we are sustained—all the while accepting that parts will always remain out of reach. We *conceive* perfection without ever becoming perfect, just as we consider the vastness of the heavens without fully understanding their intricacies. We may *recognize* perfection without ever truly *knowing* it.

Without, is *perfection,* the divine. We must learn how to communicate with the divine, to be nurtured by the divine. We shed the skins of our past. We *see* and *feel* perfection and want to bridge the gap as much as we are able.

Call it the spirit, the soul, higher consciousness or any other term, a unique part within us moves us toward the supreme and allows us to find it. Everyone is capable of finding God. Everyone is capable of finding the nurture of God.

God is the **source.** We are the **receptacle.**

So, we *can* find the *perfection of God* without ever being perfect. We can find in ourselves near-limitless capacity. We can find states of joy that continue to expand even as we think there can be no more.

That is the wonder of perfection—to draw ever nearer and always receive more—the more of a perfect God.

Is it possible to be a *good* person and not believe in God? Probably. There are those who can maintain a sense of equity and justice, and who can be altruistic without believing in a higher power or the concept of perfection. Some may even strive to be better people, and believe in the growth of cognizance without believing in God. They can believe all goodness is within and can be developed. They can believe everything necessary for humankind to rise above its current predicaments can be generated from within. This is limiting, however, because *within* is limiting. Within is only us. Eventually, everything self-generated will be used to a greater degree than can be replaced, and will begin to cannibalize itself.

> **No one can truly access the depth of the spirit—that part which is drawn toward the penultimate ideal—without believing it exists. To believe in the existence of the ideal, to forever be alert to the possibility, to feel the tug toward a superlative we are incapable of creating with our own resources, is to be a spiritually-based person.**

Further, to not believe in God is to deny any possibility for the reception of *grace*, the manifestation of God in us. To disavow God is to cede all potential for wholeness beyond our corporeal selves, and what we are capable of producing on our own.

Grace is the divine energy we receive from God. Grace is the oasis along the path, the reward of the sojourn. Grace is the unseen endowment of goodness we cannot generate within ourselves. And as our belief solidifies, and our faith is rewarded, we find the oasis immediately, always within reach.

Grace is perfection bestowed upon all who believe.
Grace is perfection bestowed upon all who seek it.
Grace is the power and the richness of God given to us.
To believe in perfection, to believe in the perfect God, to seek and receive grace, and to truly become *more* with ever-increasing potential is to define a spiritually-based relationship with God.

TWO

What is God?

Since the first primordial thought of the earliest sentient version of ourselves, we have sought to describe God. Every culture has named it. Every prophet and teacher has sought to interpret God's nature. And every person who has felt the power beyond the face of humanity has struggled to understand it.

God is eternal perfection and divine good.

Very few believers would disagree with this. But how this is defined and manifested is what creates the paradoxes that confuse and distress us.

Why?

Because in reality most traditional interpretations do not describe a *perfect* God at all.

To many, God is an all-powerful *creature* endowed with omniscience and omnipresence. It is a god of machinations and mystery, an elaborate god beyond our understanding, a god of authority and jurisdiction. It is a god of passions and inventions, and an instrument into the inner workings of humanity.

What many believe God to be is actually a demigod. In other words, a *superhuman* God.

What does this mean?

A demigod, or superhuman God, by its own implication, would still possess *human* characteristics. God would have thoughts, emotions, personality, will. God would be subject to stimuli and be required to make decisions. A superhuman God would possess an awareness of humanity and an authority to act. This God would have *business* and the impetus to function in a human manner.

This God has a superhuman consciousnesses, its power manifested in its relationship to us. It acts or refrains from acting for its own inexplicable reasons. It is oblique and incomprehensible, and we are left to interpret its actions or inactions.

No matter how wise or how potent this may seem, or how intoxicating these *godlike* attributes are, these are not true *Godly* qualities. Ultimate power, as we understand it, is ascribed to a god of motive and desire, of rule and consequence. Perceived capacity has been interpreted as *godliness,* yet without much thought to true divinity. We are lesser versions of God, and God is a greater version of us.

Nearly every major faith system on earth looks to such a God. Despite the enormity of such a deity, and the differences between major faith systems, God has always been a master, a lord, an uncreated creation capable of everything.

It has always been sufficient that God is superior in every way to the human condition.

Yet far-better-than-we-are, in any capacity, is not the same as divinity. If certain insects were sentient, would they not look at us in much the same way? If our pets, or any lesser creatures on this planet possessed the ability to reason, would they not see us as *god?* Is God simply a superbeing?

Many tales have been written about so-called primitive cultures believing in the divinity of more-progressive humans. Much lore is given to the premise of superior, even alien, species in our sphere of existence. This version of *better* deals with exceptional knowledge, and not true divinity.

We readily admit none of these is God. Are we afraid to go the next step?

An eternally perfect God would have no corporeal traits. Perfection can have only one trait—divine good.

So what does *eternal perfection* and *divine good* actually represent?

Eternal perfection would mean there can be no humanity—in any sense—in God, even those traits we may find desirable. In true perfection, there can be no conscious influence, no self-awareness as we know it, no mental states as we understand them, no sensations or sensibilities. God could possess no ego, no emotion, not even thoughts and ideas. There would be no cause, or even capability to *think* or *act*.

Eternal perfection would be the *antithesis* of humanity in every positive sense. It would be the complete and total absence of all things mortal, transient and *imperfect*, no matter what value we may place on them.

Divine good is transcendent good, incapable of anything else. This would not be goodness in any kind of active sense, but a revolutionary, intrinsic goodness that is constant, immeasurable, and beyond our imagining. Divine good is infinite purity. Divine good is such that a pinprick of light would illuminate the entire universe, and still be as a mere atom to all matter contained therein.

Divine goodness is not even part of human potential, but rather a condition every spiritually-based person aspires to, because even a mote of it can enlighten our former selves beyond recognition.

The most powerfully perfect expression in the universe could only be goodness.

Good-ness is the complete and utter absence of all human resemblance, regardless of its potential nobility.

Good-ness is a true divinity devoid of all conscious expression.

Good-ness is the only outcome of perfect *god-ness*.

Perhaps because of our human-ness, which is inescapable, we have sought to give God aspects we can more easily fathom, rather than reaching beyond ourselves to explore God's true nature and function.

Perhaps so few of us, past or present, have allowed ourselves to look at God in any other way beyond our own meager human reflection of what we conceive as potency, and the function of such potency.

Perhaps we have become so ingrained with concepts we are unwilling to doubt, by fear or faith, we cannot overcome any initial resistance that might evolve should we allow it. We are simply reluctant to ask any question we are not mentally and spiritually prepared to consider at any level.

But at the very least, let us ask the question:

What if God is simply an everlasting source of constant and consistent goodness we are able to absorb and use to grow our spiritual selves, resulting in more godly behavior?

What if God is the only fixed, constant, unchangeable, and divine part of the universe as all things beneath continue to evolve?

God is its own supreme and unlimited source, requiring nothing, expecting nothing, desiring nothing, doing *nothing, yet imparting everything; and we may have failed to understand the* true simplicity *of the divine.*

Have we never thought it odd we have assigned so many imperfect and strictly human characteristics to God?

Are we reflections of God, or have we conceived God as a greater reflection of us?

It may be comforting to believe in God as a fatherly figure who watches over us, guides us and protects us. It may even provide some sense of order amidst chaos in believing there will be a reckoning when we falter.

Yet in attributing this kind of *personality* to God, we are actually establishing limits to the prospect of perfection, and are therefore restricting the possibilities of intimacy with the divine.

If our God is indeed perfect, then what we traditionally attribute to God is wrong. If our God is *imperfect*, then there cannot possibly be perfection at all. God cannot be both. Either our God is flawed or our perspective of God is flawed.

When we begin to view God as perfection with no recognizable traits save good, we are liberated to reach further into our own spiritual resources and become more of what we are capable of becoming, through the genuine God.

When we begin to seek *perfection* instead of submitting to and ennobling *imperfection*, we give ourselves opportunities to grow beyond our previous understanding, to grow beyond inconsistencies, no matter how long held.

When we begin to believe more for us exists in a perfect God rather than an imperfect one, we see possibilities we have ignored or never conceived. We are not reduced to contemplation. We are not bound to muddle. We do not have to puzzle over the *why* of things. Our comprehension is clear, so all our actions are more clear. We are more effective because we allow the true God to be more effective.

When we understand what God really is, we can then become more of God's likeness, without succumbing to conventions that fail us.

Our task is to go beyond our human prejudices and seek to envision what real perfection actually is.

And what we receive in return is diluted only by our own imperfection, which can be vastly improved upon, and not by the perception, acknowledged or not, of a less-than-perfect God. We do not waste spiritual energy, nor exhaust ourselves in what we have believed is spiritually energy—within and without.

When we are able to set aside all notions of a divinity laden with mortal characteristics, then and only then can we grow in proximity to the true nature of the divine.

THREE

What is God's Nature

So if we are to alter our very definition of God to *perfection*, then we must also alter what we perceive as God's *nature*.

Obviously, the true God would have no nature, in the conventional sense. But as the concept of perfection may have been abstract or even alien to us, our beliefs as to God's *personality* must also change—even beyond the premise that a perfect God would have no personality.

Why?

> **As infants in faith we have committed so many preternatural aspects to God's nature we will be required to dismantle them, transition them to aspects of perfection and goodness, and do so with a sense of profound enrichment.**

Suppose we, as enlightened people, regardless of our previous or current beliefs, dug a well and put a spigot in some remote corner of the world where the indigenous peoples were not so informed, and had never been exposed to such a thing.

If we revealed such a marvel to them, we might then be considered *God* until we clarified the situation.

And what if we did not reveal this to them at all?

One day, members of the tribe would walk past and see the small pool of water at the base. They would drink. They may even see water dripping from the spigot. They would call this a *miracle*, a sign, a portent. Yet eventually the water would dry up.

So they would pray, perhaps even thinking they were being tested or punished. They would pay tribute and even make sacrifices.

But the water would not return. And in their misunderstanding they might even ponder the mysteries of God, so they could better grasp God's nature.

If they understood the true nature of the well, there would be no mystery.

In traditional faith systems, many also believe:

God is in control. (Everything is in God's hands).

God has a plan for each of us.

Things happen for a reason.

We are to surrender to and obey what we believe to be God's will.

Our lot in this life has been predestined.

These are parts of our well, our *divine enigma*, explained as *divine mystery*.

So again we return to the reality of perfection:

Authentic perfection simply does not think in the human sense, and therefore cannot have a will in the human sense, nor can it make any decisions in the human sense.

In fact, a perfect God cannot be proactive at all, in the human sense.

How does this translate?

Let us consider what many of us have believed to be elements and indications of God's true nature.

God is in control.

Control implies desire and need to seek a balance and a result. No matter how beneficial this could potentially be to us, these are not attributes of *perfection*. These are things of human creation. Even as we seek equity, justice, and goodness of every sort—even as *we* seek the means *through* God for a more divine state, they will remain the province of humankind. Perfection has no such need and no such role.

God has a plan for each of us.

How thrilling, how secure it makes us feel to know we have a part for us to play in some vast, orphic system. Understandably, especially in times of struggle, we believe God has some purpose for us beyond our current awareness.

Perfection does not conceive or plan. It cannot. The human mind does. Even if it sounds harsh, a perfect God has no motivation for a plan. Even more obviously, awareness, as we know it, precludes the possibility.

If we believe God has prescribed an endgame for any of us, we revert to faith in the *imperfect.*

If we believe all our behaviors are part of some complex puzzle with a moral at the end, we may also find this to be true—but it is not God.

If we believe our disappointments are a part of some divine process, we may be comforted—but this is not God.

Things happen for a reason.

There *are* reasons for everything. There are physical laws and the decisions we make. Everything has a result and consequence. Cause-and-effect directs many aspects of our lives.

But perfection has no cosmic sense of checks and balances, because that would require conscious creation, just as in any *plan*.

God has some reason is also a frequent rationalization when there are imperfect results, wrought by human decisions and human hands. This relieves us of responsibility.

The *reasons* are ours. Eternal perfection does not allow for contemplation, preparation, execution or consummation.

When we believe in a divinity that has *secret* reasons for every outcome, we yield to the *imperfect God.* Thus, the true God escapes us. It may bring us solace at times, accepting that the idea of a greater purpose for every disaster, but that purpose is not God's, except as we interpret it.

We must surrender to and obey God's will.

Obviously, if we believe in the perfect God, God can have no will.

But more than this is the strictly human desire to interpret God's will, sometimes with vastly contrary and punitive results.

Are there rules and ethics attributed to God that help prevent chaos and enrich our lives? Of course. Our earliest ancestors learned that. And if God *were* a conscious being, no doubt there would be principles of behavior for us.

In goodness, we will know what *should* and *is to be* done in order to have a more spiritually-based life.

But the perfect God has no all-enveloping ambition for any of us.

The perfect God can have no *will*.

We will learn *we* set the tone.

We will take to heart what God is.

Certain other *divine* attributes have been passed down through the ages.

God is omnipotent, omnipresent and omniscient.

God *is* omnipotent and omnipresent. Just not in the ways convention describes.

God is the most powerful force in the universe, through eternal perfection, but without conscious effort to wield any authority. No decisions need be made through any sort of divine awareness.

God is everywhere because *grace* is always proximate to our desire for it at all times and in all places.

We will learn what this means and the incredible benefits available to us.

We must acknowledge God is not looking over our shoulders nor alert to our behaviors.

Omniscience is a faculty attributed to *the* universal source. It is logical, given any description of the *ultimate*.

However, we return to the premise that perfection has no real awareness. It needs none. Perfection is its own self-contained totality.

All true *knowledge,* great or small, must contain elements of recognition. We see, we learn. God neither sees nor learns.

When we believe God is *aware* of us, we cannot help but believe such awareness *must* lead to action.

We need to be cognizant of the true God.

Let us consider a simple premise.

God simply is. And it is we who suffer and falter by failing to understand God's nature, not the reverse.

Does this prospect cast us into a downward spiral of despair and massive crises of faith? It doesn't have to be that way.

God is the one true source of eternal perfection and divine good. That is its sole purpose. What that should mean is there is boundless spiritual energy for us to tap into, to create a sense of joy, to help us heal in times of stress, to grant us peace, and to share with those we encounter. This is far greater comfort than believing in some sort of arbitrariness that defies understanding in the guise of infinite wisdom.

In one of the earliest recorded religions, people looked to the sun as God. They beseeched the sun for fair weather and good harvests. When fair weather and good harvests prevailed, they thanked the sun. When there was drought, or flood, or famine, they believed somehow they had offended the sun. They made offerings and did penance.

Now, most of us see this as primitive. We realize the sun is the star that nurtures our planet, but has no metaphysical function. We realize nothing created by human hands is *perfect.*

So why do we persist in believing God is something other than what God is?

Because we want to give the responsibility to someone or something else, even as we believe there are ways for us to reach out and receive.

We may actually *need* God to be in control, to make decisions and right wrongs

Perhaps by better understanding God's true nature and God's true function, we come to better understand the role of God in our lives and the role *we* play in a vital relationship with God.

We must learn the absolute reliability of God in a whole new way.

If we accept God's nature as described, we then know what our roles are in the spiritually-based path.

And if we stop to consider all the implications, the true nature of God opens us to even greater blessings. We are **all** deserving, we are **all** equally capable, and **all** of us share the same access and the same capacity.

Those who determine how fruitless it is to believe in a God contrary to its own likeness begin anew at the same place. Those who do not sacrifice the abundance available to them.

FOUR

Divine Intervention?

Divine intervention is the last vestige of belief in a proactive God.

To declare such a belief to be irrational is not cynicism, nor a means to indicate *rightness* or *wrongness*.

It is, in essence, a plea. A plea for the rational to take hold so the spiritual will not be impeded. A plea to engender more fruitful time and effort so we do not build our spiritual lives upon the unreal, or place our trust in the arcane. A plea for us to *become* because that is our prospect, and not because we are afraid.

Nearly every faith system believes it has a fairly clear understanding of how God functions in this world—God makes decisions and acts upon them.

Of all the conventional canons of God, divine intervention possesses the greatest allure.

The reason is obvious. How many times in our lives have we needed guidance from a higher sphere of comprehension? How many times in our lives have we needed solace when no human touch would do? How many times in our lives have we yearned for relief, or understanding, or justice?

How many times in our lives have we needed a miracle?

The possibility of divine intervention often preserves us, especially in times of great stress.

However poignant, this inevitably leads to an acceptance of *divine intervention* in matters great and small, in times of need and suffering, and when we are incapable of managing whatever situations we have created, or are experiencing those not of our creation. Our perspective is shaped by desire for relief.

We, or someone we love is suffering and we ask God to right the situation.

Is there any real harm in this?

In a fundamental sense, there is. When we understand God has no hand in adverse events, we may also understand God cannot undo the results of these events, *except in us*.

We must also accept, even in intense pain, *divine goodness* is available to us in *perfect form*, and not in some last gasp hope for resolution.

The foibles of divine intervention have three parts:

First, nearly all people accept the *likelihood* of divine intervention is slight.

This is defensive. We believe in the *possibility* but not the *likelihood*. We see what we consider to be evidences from afar, happening to others, and it provides a measure of hope it *can* happen.

Second, we have come to believe divine intervention is an accurate measure of *our faith*, and its absence results from the absence of faith.

When we ask and do not receive it is because our faith has faltered and that has made the difference. We accept responsibility, not for the condition itself, but for the result. While we may have contributed to the condition, the result stems from some mystical rationale we have adopted.

So we more easily accept our own lack of faith than the proper faith that would help us heal.

Third, and paradoxically, we have learned to accept God has said *no*—the result may not be entirely due to our lack of faith, but God has reasons beyond our understanding.

This helps us reconcile ourselves to the helplessness we feel at times of tragedy. Again, God has some unique purpose far beyond our grasp.

This is a shortcut through the intolerable.

The belief God is a source to aid us in all things is sound. Strength through divinity is available to us. God's power *is* available to us.

Yet the prospect of divine intervention has actually supplanted God. God is no longer God. God is a superhero capable of rescue if all the right words are spoken, all the right planets are in alignment, all the right submissions are in place.

No matter what anyone believes God's role to be, God is to be a God of faith. We cannot prove the improvable or name the unnamable to the satisfaction of anyone who chooses not to believe. And it is this *unbelief* in the guise of faith that stunts the growth of every spiritually-based person.

Perhaps the answer, at least in part, lies in our more rational selves. And if we believe in God's nature as described, it becomes easier. When we are in the midst of crisis, it is almost impossible to think rationally. To think rationally in the midst of crisis is not even the goal.

The goal is to return to the rational as quickly as we can, and not let false hope shroud our becoming.

So let us consider these things *rationally*:

First, to believe God has reached down to assist anyone is to deny the reality of perfection, no matter how we are inspired when we believe, or how we long to believe.

We simply cannot assign any decision-making processes to the *perfect* God. Perfection has no self-consciousness of purpose and function. These cannot exist in *perfection*, only in the human condition. More importantly, there is no way to make these traits *perfect*.

Second, even if there was some way a perfect God could maintain such knowledge, under what circumstances would there be intervention into the order of our world?

We all naturally realize every person has *free will* and the ability to choose. This is a fact, yet also a premise some use as a reason God would not intervene in certain matters. If God chooses not to intervene, it is because of the choices we have made.

Why then are we so apt to believe God would arbitrarily do so?

We have natural disasters such as storms and floods. Perhaps we cannot prevent them, but who is responsible for protecting ourselves against them? History has recorded wars, plagues, famines and epidemics. Who can eliminate them or mitigate them? We have had holocausts and terrorist attacks, and all manner of unspeakable cruelties of human beings to one another. Whose hearts created them, and whose hearts can alleviate them?

There are horrible accidents and even more horrible illnesses. We may not understand them. Even *scientific* reasons will not alleviate our pain nor help us cope.

It may even seem more damaging, more heart-breaking in the short run to *know* God will not intervene. But eventually we will return to the conclusion this is because of God's nature, and not because of the who, why and what of events.

Finally, believing in divine intervention translates to the reality God has helped some and not others, again for reasons beyond our knowledge, and being favored above others distinguishes them from anyone else.

Even if we ignore the obvious in God's nature, it will still clamor a capriciousness in human affairs in the guise of transcendental enigma.

Consider the events of September 11, 2001, in the United States, which everyone knows. A horrible tragedy created by the minds, hearts and hands of men.

Ask the following questions as they relate to what you believe God's nature to be, especially concerning divine intervention—

1) Were some spared and others not because of a higher calling?
2) Did God intend those who perished to perish and not others?
3) Was some cosmic lesson such as punishment or the absence of the *right* faith to be learned from the experience?
4) The men who executed the plan believed they were acting according the will of God. God did not intervene, so were they right?
5) Who had the power to stop such an act? Who lessened its blow? Who sought peace in its aftermath?

To believe in the perfect God is to answer *no* to the first four questions, and to answer *ourselves* to the fifth.

Let us humbly contemplate what we truly believe regarding divine intervention.

Is the fact some live and some die all part of a *master plan?* Do we believe that such disasters are a part of God's retribution? Do we allow ourselves to justify such things because what we believe is different from what others believe?

Even more dangerously, do we truly want believe God would reach down and save us if we tried to destroy ourselves and this world? Or destroy this world *himself* for our digressions?

Again, it is time for us to consider God is simply not proactive in the workings of this world, because it is impossible for perfection to be so.

Perhaps there is no greater truth to be found. All the events and occurrences in our daily lives are not controlled by any otherworldly source. Things such as physical laws, natural laws and our own evolution into introspective people is *reality*, and nothing from *beyond* is going to alter or undo that All change for good or ill is in *our* hands, because that is not God's role in our world.

Perhaps it is time we consider there are no prayers, no magic words, no spells or potions we can use will alter the course of evolution. Our decisions will make the difference.

Perhaps the truth of God is not a mystery at all. The conventional ways we believe God to behave, and the manner in which we try to communicate with God creates these *mysteries,* because of their ineffectiveness and seeming indiscretion.

Belief in divine intervention reinforces that God is subjective-- that God selects some and rejects others, that God is involved in human affairs as a matter of course, or in some subjective and cryptic way.

Only when we allow God to be God can we conceive our own spiritual potential and do what needs to be done.

FIVE

What Is Our Faith?

So, if God is not in control of our world, does not intervene in human affairs, and will not reach down and save us if we err, provide miracles when we need them, or punish us if we stray too far, what's the point?

What good is such a God to us?

The good is with our understanding of God's true nature and role we are able to build a vital and potent relationship that serves us and others more effectively because we will no longer be distracted by the imperfect.

God is still the most positively powerful force in the universe. And grace is the progeny we all may share equally. We need never again concern ourselves with the abstract, knowing the concrete. We will devote ourselves to the authentic and not to the arbitrary.

Everything operates according to its function. Though we may wish and hope and pray, and even *believe*, sometimes desperately, that God serves as our Master, our Shepherd, our Lord, wanting all things contrary to the manner in which a thing works can only lead to frustration and disappointment.

We cannot *will* the nature of something, especially God, into an entity that acts contrary to its nature. We can rationalize all things as the hand of God, and perhaps even find a sense of satisfaction in that, but we will surely find it lacking.

We find this lacking because it can be no other way. No matter how strong our faith in *god*, if we expect anything counter to a different reality of God, we will come up empty. We will find ourselves mired in age-old practices and beliefs that cannot serve us. This will lead us to frustration, despair, and a kind of hopeless faith in the fanciful. We cannot wish, hope, or even pray our way to what is not. We cannot wish upon a star and alter certainty. We cannot *create* anything contrary to certainty and have it work for us.

A molecule of water is comprised of two hydrogen atoms and a single oxygen atom. There are other forms of liquids, and molecules can be corrupted, but once that composition is altered, it ceases to be water.

We simply cannot drink oxygen without hydrogen. If we try, we will thirst to death. Water is what water is, just as God is what God is.

Remember our story of the well? Remember the tribe that did not understand? How easy it is for us to know we simply turn the tap. Once anyone turns the tap, the well operates according to its design and function. Once understood, the mystery is no longer a mystery. It is no longer lore, but axiom.

What then is our relationship to God to be?

We must believe God is the *only* source of divine good, and that is God's *only* function.

We must believe this *good* is tangible and the only true source of spiritual energy available to us.

We must believe we can access this good and draw it in, and no limit to its abundance exists except within ourselves.

We must believe, by dedication, this good is available to us in every moment and under every circumstance—and the timing is not of God's choosing, but ours.

We must believe *grace* exists solely for us to claim, regardless of who we are.

We must believe this grace does not have to be earned.

Finally, we must believe whatever good we receive, in whatever increasing portion we can accept, cannot be stored or held, but must be imparted to others in order to flourish or remain divine.

Our human mind, which gives us the capacity to open our souls to the perfection of God, is also the instrument of our doubts and emotions. It doesn't matter why. It only matters that it is. Our mind is the *only* impediment to God. Any and all obstacles will be of our creation and our own disposition.

What we fail to realize is in God there is already an inherent solution for us, an eternal, unbiased solution.

Grace exists for us in far more abundance than we could ever conceive or receive. It is up to us to claim it. And our failures are not because of God's *judgment*, but because we have failed to understand what God is, how God works, and our role in this relationship. This is the sole key in all human-God links.

What matters are our endeavors, and the enrichment of our souls for the purposes prescribed to us as the spiritually-based creatures we should be. What matters is a unique approach to the spiritually-based life.

We must move far beyond all interpretation of events to the authenticity of God's unchanging goodness.

And as we realize all that is available to us, we then understand what we must do.

The first part is commitment.

We know how difficult commitments can be. We know the first requirement of any commitment is *desire*. We cannot be truly committed to anything unless we truly want to be. Our commitment must be steadfast even in the face of our own disbelief. Our commitment must be steadfast even in the face of the worst of our human traits. Our commitment must be steadfast no matter the events we face.

We will waver and falter. We will doubt and suffer. But as long as we believe enough to return, we will never be lost.

The second part is faith.

We must believe in divine good and that it is ours to have—it is our birthright because we all have the seed of God within us, as evidenced by the consciousness and introspection that is ours and ours alone, which enables us to communicate with God. No one is any more or any less deserving than any other.

We must believe and accept that divine good is as real as the physical world around us. The force or spiritual energy of divine good gives us peace and purpose. It creates in us the potential to be our better selves. It is all we have in the materiality of God. It is also all we need in the materiality of God, and nothing else exists without it. Without faith in divine good, God may as well be a phantom, an abstruse creation of our imaginations.

Later we will examine methods of communion and receiving, but first we must accept divine good as a verifiable and accessible power that can alter us.

The third part is purpose.

We must understand and accept that *we, as spiritually-based people,* are how God intervenes in human lives. When we receive grace, we become the hands of God. When we receive grace, we may *believe.*

We must accept nearly every ill described in the history of human existence to the
present day could have been alleviated or mitigated by spiritually-based people. All responsibilities have been ours just as all remedies have been ours.

We must understand God does not touch us to become whole. We become whole by touching God.

On any bright, sunny day, the sun is what it is and does what it does as a part of a natural order. We determine if we want to step into its light, or avoid its heat—to praise it or curse it—to participate in its offering or not.

As truly spoken in nearly every faith system, God is the light of the world. What is often missing is that the light is constant and unchanging, and we must bend and move beneath it. The light does not seek us out or follow us. We look and discover the light, and all its sustenance.

It is the same as all separate conditions of belief: the nature of perfection vs. our own imperfect humanity. Perfection exists whether we use it or even acknowledge it. It exists solely as a nurturing force. It does not select who receives it and who doesn't. It does not label us saint or sinner. It is up to us to know its goodness.

We, on the other hand, make these judgments, internally and externally. We place limitations on what we are able to receive, or whether there are feelings of worthiness, or whether what we feel is real. *We* ascribe aspects of the human condition to it, not the other way around. *We* make God flexible and prone to enigma. *We* create the sense of how little we can do to alter the world around us in any cosmic sense. *We* make the decisions as to what is purposeful or what is vain.

If we accept what God's true nature is as opposed to ours, common sense, if nothing else, should tell us that it is the imperfect which establishes any barrier to the perfect. All other practices are part of the human condition and purpose, and have no basis in the genuine absoluteness of God. These are what we have created and upheld.

God is *the* source, the enduring and everlasting and infinite wellspring. The nature of grace is unlimited and untainted.

All we must do is learn to drink. We turn the tap....and drink.

Then, and most importantly, we will learn that all we receive must be distributed in some form or fashion. We become pools beyond the wellspring, and we must commit this divine water to others before it stagnates or evaporates or becomes diluted by the lesser aspects of our humanity.

To become a spiritually-based person is to understand and accept these things are as they can only be.

SIX

How Do We Begin?

So what then is the basis for spiritual growth as a part of the spiritually-based life? What do we do to have a vital relationship with God in accordance with God's true nature? What are the true *keys?*

Once we realize and accept how God works, what wondrous opportunities are then at our disposal!

The pure, perfect, and inexhaustible fountainhead is open to us and all we have to do is learn how to access it. Divine good is ours and we are able to partake until we are full. And then we are able to return time-and-time again to refill ourselves. This is the true glory of the perfect and eternal God.

Incredibly, we find our capacity also increases beyond anything we have ever imagined. The more we use the cup, the bigger the cup itself becomes. We are not just filling ourselves, we are *expanding* ourselves.

The soul is not a fixed shape or measure. The soul is fluid, malleable, far-reaching. That is the path to perfection, to the *more*, the *better*. Unlike our muscles, our senses, even our brains, our souls can burgeon and extend more quickly and more readily than any mortal element. We outgrow our former selves like a toddler outgrows clothes. We may grow unaware of the transition until we take a pause and look back.

Is it truly so simple? Yes. But s*imple* and *easy* are entirely different concepts, and not interchangeable.

At times, the most simple is the most difficult. Such tasks as walking, riding a bicycle or learning to drive are relatively simple in hindsight. Yet most of us struggled to learn. Perhaps we even know someone who has fallen ill and temporarily lost such ability and have witnessed the difficulty for them to re-learn.

We can all remember the seeming impossibility of the more intricate functions we now take for granted.

Why is such a simple practice not easy for us?

For the same reason the evolution of anything is such a slow, arduous process. We are habitual, and yes, even lazy, in spiritual matters. We are so easily distracted, and so averse to unfamiliar territory. We doubt so quickly, and *believe* so grudgingly, even when the benefits are so obvious and rewarding.

We are habitual in all the wrong ways. Routine makes it easier for us to do what we do not wish to further explore. We save our curiosity and satisfaction for those things that stimulate us, and our energies for those things that bring us pleasure. We pigeonhole our spiritual selves into certain time frames, certain practices.

Yet we do not consider our access to the great God of grace is achieved in the same manner. Our energy focused upon God is what brings us to revelation. Our satisfaction and pleasure is nearly instantaneous. Our joy in being may grant us a place of amity we have so long sought and only provisionally found.

But we must begin. And in order to *do*, most of us will have to *undo*.

First, we have to alter most of what we have ever believed about divine nature.

We must understand God does not care who or what we are. God does not even care if we believe or not, in the literal definition of the word *care*. We must accept God as God is, and not what we want God to be.

We must remove our egos from acceptance. We must not be sensitive about these novel, yet essential differences. If we cannot overcome the concept that God is our elder who wants to sit us upon his knee and stroke our hair, then we will not be able to stir. If we cannot envision even greater possibilities with a God of perfection, though forever nescient, we will not advance. Unfortunately, we cannot carry multiple persuasions of such depth and magnitude to any sound end.

We cannot have it both ways.

Until we accept as fact the fundamental nature of God as *indifferent* majesty, we cannot proceed, nor hope to progress.

We must accept and take to heart that God is God and we have the capacity to consume. *That* has to be enough. *That* has to be our reality.

Unless we alter our viewpoint and accept the real nature of God, we are destined to fail. We see this failure manifested in every single woe around us, and in every single woe in the world.

Every form of strife, every want, every unmet need, every disappointment or disillusionment, every doubt, every unbelief, every act of aggression, every dissonance, great or small, every element of lack that finds its way to our senses is a result of the ignorance of God's true nature.

Our beliefs in God as an *active* distributor of grace will hold us back.

If we genuinely accepted God's true nature, and applied ourselves to these principles, the nature of the world would change. Even the worst of our humanity, and the certainty of lapses, would still prove resistant to every form of antagonism. Our mere awareness would serve, at least in part, to thwart our lesser inclinations. We would move to a greater *knowingness* of what we are and are not to do.

This is not a fantasy of a world in song, hands held in rings of naivete. This is *the* foundational premise to become our potential.

Secondly, we must realize, and whole-heartedly accept nothing can keep us from Grace except ourselves.

We have already been exposed to this, but now it must be taken to heart.

God will not tap us on the shoulder. God will not invoke itself in our desperate times of need. God will not manifest itself in any way shape or form without our bidding. God will not whisper in our ear.

Without our faith, without our spiritual action, without our consuming desire, God may as well remain in the dominion of invention, for God cannot serve us otherwise. In whatever environment or condition, *nothing unused actually works.*

This has all been previously advanced. No matter the richness, the purity, the sheer gratification and luxuriance of infinite good, as well as the undeniable desire for it, unsought grace is as impotent as *abracadabra.*

We do not *wish* a thing into existence. We seek and find the thing that already exists, where it has always been. Where it will always be past, present, and far into the future—doing what it and it alone can do.

Discipline lies in the search, and reliability in the discovery.

Thirdly, we must learn to take, to receive.

What good does it do us to *know* and not *do?*

We cannot retreat to the old ways. Even in our failures, we must return to the reality of God and what we must do.

As in the story of the well, even when we know to turn the tap and let the water flow, we must also prepare a vessel to capture it or else it spills on the ground. Once it evaporates, it is gone from us.

It always exists for us. It is ready whenever we are. Yet should our container have a hole, it serves no worthwhile purpose for us. Pouring it on our heads, hands and feet may temporarily make us feel better, but we will remain unquenched.

We seek according to design. We receive according to our aptitude.

How Do We Begin?

What remains undiscovered to us? Wealth, station, overt happiness, peace-of-mind? These are whims. But the undiscovered God is a tragedy for us. Like a wanderer in the desert, who does not know to uproot the plant is to find sustenance, or the traveler lost in the cold, who does not know to bury himself in the snow is to find warmth, the one who chooses ignorance over encounter, thirst over absorption, is lost.

We are *lost* simply because we have failed to discern the markings on the map.

What then is the process?

The process has three simple parts: to *believe* in divine good, to *absorb* divine good, and to *dispense* divine good.

The practice of our relationship to the divine can be described as the **Three A's.**

We **acknowledge** God as the source of divine good—a real and potent force of perfect spiritual energy readily available to us, and ours to claim.

We **absorb** divine good into ourselves through encounters with God. We take it in and it permeates all we are.

We **act** upon divine good by communicating it in every aspect of our lives, and then by disseminating it in every way possible, and to everyone we encounter.

We come to understand and accept and *believe* there is no other way.

Nothing is more simple or profound.

The effort is simple, the result profound.

Yet it remains the duty, privilege, and effort of each individual seeker to reach, to connect, to receive.

SEVEN

Acknowledging God

Even after deep and abiding acceptance of God's true nature, there will always be sufficient cultural gravity to draw us back. There are also many *mental* and *emotional* impediments due to unfamiliarity.

As previously illustrated, nearly everyone believes God is divine. Most also believe God is the sole, true source of divine good. However, once we make a distinction, we will discover just how sensitive others are to long-held mindsets. So, it is a benefit that each of us must learn these steps individually.

What we accept as the meaning of *perfection*, and how that translates to God's nature, will not readily be accepted by those who believe in a proactive God. Simply too much discomfort lies in the prospect to change the outlook of many. It is not our purpose to change the minds of others. Our purpose is our own. Our purpose incorporates *all*, but our transformations are singular.

We understand, and embrace, that the fruit of perfection is divine good.

Divine Good is the supreme wholeness. Divine good is the utmost of what we can imagine. If we think about everything we have ever witnessed we called good or perfect—and we can all remember *perfect* days or *perfect* events—then we can begin to understand how such a wholeness exists on an eternal scale, and one multiplied beyond our scope. We take our highest and greatest points-of-reference and compound them as much as we are able at this point in our experience.

It may seem redundant, or even pointless, to refer to a level of divinity we cannot possibly record, but understanding we can never outreach it is critical. It exists for us and we are to discover and accept it. That we are able to grow in grace until the day we die is important for us to believe.

Practicality, if nothing else, makes this desirable. We want good for ourselves and our families. We want good things to happen to us. We want our surroundings to be as free of tension and contention as possible. We want more tranquility in our environments. We want as much as possible about us to be *good*.

But there is a difference between creation and recognition. We recognize much we seem unable to reproduce. We have it within us to create good. We have the capacity to make decisions that enhance every environment in which we participate, enrich the lives of everyone with whom we come in contact. We usually know the difference between something serving the *common good* and something more egocentric.

Yet we do not always recognize (or acknowledge), goodness existing beyond us. We do not always appreciate the efforts of others, or understand what is *of* God and what isn't. As we've discussed, we tend toward cultural prejudices, just as we tend to stay near the surface of things. We don't always want to delve deeper. We don't want to question the periphery of experience. We prefer to allow things to be as good for us as we can create, and then cope with misfortune as best we can until it passes.

Even as we do this, some part of us inherently understands either we are excluding God from the process, or retreating to the premise God is already *involved* in everything. Reaching may be difficult for us.

Always…always…we must delve deeper.

How is this to be changed, and how are we to grow?

Faith—and to *acknowledge*, even with trepidation, our understanding and acceptance of God's true nature will not be an easy transition. To understand and accept the task and responsibility for communication as ours will not always elevate us, especially if we are in dire need. Would that God might reach down and transform us.

What we may fail to see is in the certainty of God's nature lies enormous benefit. When *we* reach, there is no time and place. We do not have to wait for God to act. We do not have to wonder when the answer will come. We do not have to ponder what God is doing.

True faith is *always* a positive force. Good (God) is available to us always, consistently and unfailingly.

Obviously, even when we believe, this will be easier at certain times and on certain occasions more than others. It's easy to have faith when all about us is thriving. It's harder when something happens to distract us. It's easy to have faith when we are in a positive frame of mind. It's harder when we are embroiled in conflict. It's easy to have faith when all the tumblers seem to be in place. It's harder when our confidence is shaken, or events cause us to be uncertain despite our best efforts.

Our faith must be that good is available in limitless abundance. This does not mean our hearts and our environments will be magically transformed. This means we will open our souls to the power of good and receive it, and are worthy of it. Our faith allows us to claim it. And as we claim it, we grow. As we learn to claim it, the process becomes second nature to us. Without it, the spiritually-based person cannot grow.

Our faith understands good comes to us in calm, not in pleading or emotional blood-letting. Good does not come to us in desperation. Good does not come to us when we are wracked with pain and confusion. Good does not come to us because we *need* it, though we certainly need it. Good does not come to us when we *demand* it. Good comes to us because we *want* it.

Our faith knows true good is not putting a positive spin on the tragic or intolerable. Horrific things happen. Loss and injustice happen. There may even be crushing blows that tear us heart and mind. At times, we will be unable to express our faith because as human beings we are endowed with natures that have evolved since the first of us drew breath. We will have doubts. We will still wonder where God is. We may still find ourselves absent of faith because we have been torn by external circumstances.

True faith is returning to the belief.

We must reinforce our understanding the power of good can only come to us through *our* bidding. We can learn how to let good in so the eternal seed within us can grow. Soon, this will begin to supplant so many of the lesser imperfections that influence us or control us. Soon, none but the greatest tragedies will shake us to the point of unbelief.

Our faith becomes so deeply rooted no event or series of events can ever completely undo it; we will always return to it. Moments, hours, days, weeks, months—the absence of faith is always ours, not God's. We will know the sooner we return to it, the sooner divine good is ours.

Our faith becomes so compelling we never stray without knowing our way back. We *always* know where it is.

And so…

— — — — — — — — — — — — —

I acknowledge God is the ultimate source of divine good and grace is abundantly available to me at this very moment, and always.

— — — — — — — — — — — — —

When we can wholly accept *perfection* is impersonal, we can acknowledge God's goodness and grace without any disappointments. Our relationship to God *is* special and unique because *we* are special and unique. God recognizes us without naming us. God is ready to fill us whenever we are ready to receive.

Always remember, again and again, God will never withdraw. *We* will.

When we can state this, silently or aloud, and have no doubt, we begin the first step toward receiving grace.

Acknowledging divine good is believing, steadfastly, and with all our minds, the following is true:

1) I **know** God is the one true source of divine good.
2) I **know** divine good is available to me at this very moment.
3) I **know** I can have divine good in limitless abundance.
4) I **know** I will receive divine good in whatever portion my openness to it allows me to receive.
5) I **want** to receive divine good to be an increasingly whole person.

Again, how we wish the *simplicity* of acknowledgment was the same as the *ease* of acknowledgement.

Accept that there can be no other way, and nothing within or without us will alter that fact. No matter what occurs about us, only our assent and practice of these principles can lead us back.

Suppose a single bridge separates one place from another. We can wait on one side. We can view the bridge as rickety and unsafe. We can ponder if another bridge would make more sense, even though we see none.

We can move part of the way and hover. We can debate within ourselves the wisdom of crossing. We can turn around and go back. We can rationalize anything—what we are seeking is not really there—we don't need to cross in order to find what we seek—the place beyond the bridge will somehow find its way to us.

But as time passes, and life is spent, the geography does not change. It is eternal. It is fixed and immutable. It is there, and what lies beyond the bridge will *always* be absent from us unless we cross.

To believe is to acknowledge. Failure to believe and acknowledge is to allow our grace to remain unclaimed.

It is a first step. But as we all know, without a first step, there can be no forward motion.

I believe and acknowledge God is the ultimate source of divine good and grace is abundantly available to me at this very moment. I come to claim grace as my own.

EIGHT

Absorbing Grace

To **absorb** grace should be as easy as absorbing the sun's rays. Sadly, it isn't. In fact, if we do not believe or acknowledge grace, we will never be able to take advantage of it. We will be like driftwood on the sea, allowing external circumstances to determine where we are. Likewise, opening a channel to divine good should be equally easy. Again, it isn't, and there are many reasons for this. Conventional forms of worship and prayer do not teach us how to receive divine good. The entire concept may be foreign to us. Not even certain forms of meditation guarantee success. Why? Because even in spiritual optimism, these methods are focused upon our more ego-based interiors. These are about *us*, not our relationship with the divine. If we find an inner pathway and do not take the next step—to God—we have only salved ourselves.

However, let us recognize the absolute certainty of this single proposition. We simply *cannot* proceed without this step. No matter our intellectual capacity or earnest efforts, we have no faith until we are able to absorb grace.

We have both external and internal distractions. We are called upon to deal with outward distractions nearly every moment of every day. People depend on us or make demands of us. Life can be very chaotic. Even when we are alone, and stillness is about us, our minds are elsewhere, thinking of many things that make our lives chaotic. Releasing these things and opening ourselves is difficult.

We are constantly inundated with external stimuli. We cannot move beyond our four walls without having to cope with the lesser aspects of the human condition. We find ourselves going where we really do not want to go, doing things we really do not want to do, even being who we really do not want to be.

1) **We must seek stillness and calm.**

Call it prayer or meditation, we *must* find calmness. If there are distractions we cannot put aside, we must stop, for nothing will flow through a clogged passageway. We cannot force it. Often the time and place is not of our choosing, but rather those unexpected times when we find stillness. Whether we seek such times, or such times find us, once such a time is upon us, and whenever or wherever that may be, we must take full advantage. Many disciplines can help in this process, including other forms of meditation as long as we know these are steps, and not the destination.

We must do whatever it takes to find such stillness.

We must find outward calm to help bring about inward calm.

2) **We must be open to receive.**

Our first attempts may be halting or even unproductive. We do not build our faith and our ability to receive by self-hypnosis, mantras or ritual. We can only receive through genuine contact. There are no magic words or phrases or charms. We do not have to put ourselves into a trance or chant. If any of these things help us focus, great, but again, we cannot open the channel by force. It must come through calm.

We must also have purpose as to what we are seeking. We are seeking the divine good of eternal perfection. Most of us have never done this. We may seek to calm our thoughts or our emotions, but now we are moving far forward. This is preparation for what we desire, not the end result.

We have all had what we may refer to as *peak experiences.* These are things that occur which cause us to feel all is right with the world, things are as they should be, the true potential within us has opened.

It may be a first kiss, or the first time we held our child, or some incredibly beautiful vista we've seen, or the simple warmth of the day—or some unexpected pleasure. An external stimulation is almost always what reveals the concept of perfection or near-perfection to us. These feelings do not last, of course. They cannot. They exist as emblems of the *highs* in our lives.

Remember how you felt during those moments of eternal promise. Remember the rapture that captivated you.

All things that have impacted us positively can help us open ourselves to receiving divine good.

These can be entries to the passageway.

These same feelings and the results they produced in us enable us to open ourselves. Rationally, it should be easy. Rationally, we should be able to convince ourselves this is the only means to be in the presence of God, and we are about to receive the most profound and astounding thing in all existence—the divine, eternal, goodness and grace of God.

Even so, we cannot talk ourselves or even think ourselves into openness. We must *feel* it, and feel it fully.

Why is *feeling* important? Isn't true calm the absence of feeling? Isn't this contrary to the concept of a dispassionate God? Isn't our goal to rid ourselves of toxic feelings and hyper-emotionalism?

Feeling matters so purity is not lost.

This is God, remember. We are not seeking to simply cleanse ourselves of prevailing stress or worries. We are not seeking communion with the outer edges of our consciousness or the great unknown. We are not seeking to subdue our lesser selves.

When we approach divine good with a glad and willing heart, grace is transmuted into the kind of peace and contentment and rejuvenation we might call love.

Think of something you have learned to do by rote—a song, a prayer, a poem—and the difference when it was really *felt* in the beginning, but which soon became a recital. Consider a passage of a sacred text, or a national anthem, or even the words *I love you* to someone very important to you.

Can you honestly say you are reminded of the same *feeling* as the first time you did this?

That is the difference purity makes. It may serve us adequately in our daily lives, but it will not serve us in approaching God.

There are other tools we can use.

Sometimes a special piece of music can move us to a place where we are not so distracted.

Sometimes it is in the first moments of a new day before the day itself claims us.

Sometimes we find ourselves unexpectedly alone and at peace.

> **Most of us know our brains continue to process what we are thinking about when we go to sleep, consciously and subconsciously. What better way to imagine the fullness of God as when we put our heads down to rest? What better way to open the channel to absorb grace?**

When we are finally still, and have a gentle heart, all thoughts turn to God. Whatever perfection is to us, there our serenity is. There we find God.

This is just a step. God is the next step. Only our belief in God allows us to absorb the divine.

Once we are *there* within, we *reach* without.

3) **Receiving and absorbing.**

Perhaps this seems like two steps, but it is a single continuous process, the same as drinking water and quenching one's thirst is the same continual process, or the flow of electricity and its output is the same continual process.

We are receptacles of divine good. Divine good does not originate within us. Divine good exists beyond us and only by opening ourselves to it can we receive. Within and without are like two magnets moving closer to the natural attraction.

No matter the path we take to get there, once we get there we will *know* it. We will feel it, and it will be like no other feeling we've ever experienced. It is the part of *perfection* we may have experienced before but didn't know exactly how it came to be or what is really was. Our minds turn only to God.

God is here. The grace of God is available to me.

When the channel is open, we will begin to feel the flow.

I accept the divine good that is available to me.

Make no mistake, when divine good begins to flow into you, there will be no doubt as to what it is. It is as standing in a field on a cloudy day, eyes closed with the face tilted skyward. Suddenly the sun emerges and we know what it is without seeing, as it bathes us in warmth and light.

It is as a peaceful dream in which we are the only player and nothing comes between us and *perfection*.

It is as a bend in a mountain road, and we look outward into the valley feeling the immensity of life surrounding us, or on a shore where we can gaze out across the sea into the unseen horizon.

In solitude we can realize the vastness beyond us and open ourselves to it. We've experienced so sparingly the epiphany of calm, and now we truly know what it is, where it begins, and how we might receive it more consistently and deliberately.

To experience any elevation in spirit without rational cause is to receive divine good.

The clearer the channel, the stronger the flow. Good will come to us in whatever measure we can allow. We must always take heart. As we begin the process, distractions will occur. How could they not? But once the channel is open it will not close until some part of us tells it to, whether consciously or unconsciously.

A trickle of good to a willing soul is more powerful than any intellectual or physical strength we could muster on our own.

The great thing is that once something is done successfully, it can be done again, more readily, more easily, more efficiently and more effectively.

I feel divine good flow into me.

When the breath of God is upon us, and we feel it inflate us, and course through us, we let it flow. We feel it fill us, change us, alter our perspectives as to what our capacity and purpose should be. There will never be any doubt again that we have received.

We *must* want it. We *must* seek out opportunities for practice. And we do have to remove as many conscious and unconscious obstacles as we can. We simply find ways where we can put aside as many distractions as possible at any given time

Through practice, we learn to open the channel more naturally and more effectively.

We only have to be successful **once.** As with any other practice, from the mundane to the sublime, once it occurs, we *know* it is genuine, we know it can be accomplished, and we know what the results can be.

As we become more proficient, and our practice more frequent, something astounding happens. We discover not only does the channel open wider, it opens more easily. When we realize the channel is always there, even as we deal with the realities of the day, we discover the residual humanity which comprises so much of our conscious thought and daily activities is slowly replaced by a constancy of good.

Our points-of-view change. Things around us that seemed threatening before, testing us, are no longer so threatening. Things we viewed as unpleasant are no longer so. Things we viewed as trials are easier to cope with.

We will begin to crave this relationship, not in any base, human sense of the word, but we will seek more frequent opportunities for communion. Our interior composition will be reformed, negative thinking will diminish, stress and drama by others will become less potent. Our internal lives move toward a consistent peace.

Here's a challenge. Make a list of everything that happened today you interpreted as having a *negative* impact on you. Put the list away. Return to the list after you've experienced fifteen or twenty occasions to receive the power of divine good. See if most of them seem trivial now, or have been resolved.

This does not mean there will not be setbacks. Illness, troubles at work, issues in relationships, family matters, financial difficulties, etc., are all real problems that need to be addressed. There will be times when the world itself seems ready to explode. There will be times when we suffer grave losses and terrible hurts. This does not mean our humanity is erased.

Be patient.

It is difficult, perhaps impossible, to try to schedule when we turn to God for grace. As intoxicating as it is, and as desirable as it is, we will still find time tends to slip away from us. Obviously, if we can find a way to receive our good every day, it is an enormous benefit. On occasion we will find the perfect time and the perfect frame of mind, and may lose ourselves in grace for ten, fifteen minutes or more.

At other times we will open the channel successfully only to find our minds wandering, or some other complication after only a minute or so.

If we continue our practice, however often we can, and as long as it remains genuine, good will manifest *itself*. Yes, it will manifest itself in our attitudes. Yes, it will manifest itself in our coping skills. But more importantly, it will manifest itself as an implement of the divine and we will be able to better separate conditions of the world from the divine substance that should be.

Again, the greater the frequency, the easier it becomes. The easier it becomes, the more we are able to receive.

We will become true children of God. We will become true beneficiaries of grace.

Whenever we find the process at an end, for whatever reason and for this occasion only, we acknowledge again.

I know divine good is in me now. I am blessed.

It is a uniquely personal thing. We may meditate in groups, pray in groups, worship in groups, but we cannot ascend to grace in groups. The moment will never be quite the same for two separate individuals, much less a group.

If we engage in any practice that does not always work for us, then we can spend all of our time and energy focusing on the practice which is supposed to help create calm, and forget what the ultimate objective is: God's perfect spiritual nourishment.

We find the way that allows us to open ourselves and receive.

NINE

Dispensing Divine Good

As we participate in the cycle of *good*, the practice becomes like breathing—good comes in, good flows out. Even if we falter or suspend our effort, we can always return to it. The grace of God is unchangeable.

Generating goodness without supply, without spiritual fuel is impossible. Nothing is self-contained.

The divine goodness of God is always flowing and our souls should be like rivers, always open at both ends. It is a part of our faith and its function to move outward, to allow it to flow onward. Then we can become more fully replenished.

This begins the moment we learn to receive divine good, and grows as our experience grows. The good we accept on any level must lead to a familiar, habitual tangible expression of it or our faith is not real.

We must also acknowledge and understand *good* cannot exist within us without being rendered.

Good cannot be held. Good will stagnate and decay like the water in a pond when the spring beneath it stops flowing. Even in perpetual practice, good simply cannot remain dormant. Spiritual energy cannot remain undiluted in confinement, and we will struggle, wondering why we cannot achieve any real sense of internal well-being. We may actually be successful in absorbing grace that seems incomplete and transient.

If the reception of divine good does not inspire us toward a desire to serve, then what we believe we have received is not divine good.

This third step is vital to our spiritual well-being.

If we are compelled to seek this energy we are likewise compelled to practice it. It is a simple rule of cause-and-effect. The glory of a spring is not merely that it produces fresh water, but also that it opens a conduit for more water to flow.

Grace is not usually an impetus to make radical changes in our lives. It isn't designed to be. In the story of Saul's conversion in the Christian Bible, he is struck by light and must change everything about him.

This is not what happens to us. What happens to us is that our outlook changes. We see need we did not see (or want to see) before. We see the potential for service we previously ignored. We see the possibility to inject kindness into tense or hostile situations. Grace inspires and we act upon such inspiration.

We do not become missionaries. We become emissaries, modest and without pride or desire for recognition.

We must **act**.

We must understand we are the conscience and consciousness of God.

We must become custodians of the good we've received. This is not an achievement. This is a process that leads to a new interior culture. Once the channel is opened and reopened, and we truly feel the good and see the truth in its measure, we then become emblems of faith, to show its existence and value to everyone we encounter. We do this wordlessly, without passion or pretense, with no claim to our fitness or anyone else's fitness or *unfitness*. This is display in the purest sense, to exhibit the entirety of our faith that all are worthy to reap the same benefits as we are, and to be done without any expectation of gain.

We are to be kinder. We are to measure our words so no criticism or judgment is revealed. This is a natural part of our relationship with God. Of course we cannot eliminate our humanity, but if we have not been so moved by the practice, then something is awry and we must renew our efforts.

In every action, whether it's something as simple as letting someone else take a parking space or as complicated as reconciling with someone we have not been able to bear, we are to be living examples of the divine good we've received in every facet of our lives. We are to express our joy at the substance of our faith in every action we take, everything we say or do. We convey the *more*.

We all have ingrown personalities, formed when we were very young and evolved into what we are now. Nothing can change this except the gradual evolution spawned by the consistent filling of our souls.

To receive divine good is to be an enabler of divine good, proof positive our faith is genuine. This is perhaps the most difficult of all, because we will all be required to provide action we are unaccustomed to, to those whose past actions may have hurt us, or whom we do not agree with.

This is a marker of the validity of our practice. If we are not changed within, compelled toward these things, then we must begin again, for we have not truly received divine good.

If our attitudes toward all our fellows does not compel us toward compassion and outreach, we are fooling ourselves into believing God dwells within us.

We realize no faith system or ideology that emphasizes *self*, regardless of the noblest intentions, has a truly spiritual basis.

Self is the primitive in us our ancestors sought so desperately to shed.

Knowing we are receptacles of a divine good that cannot be stored, we also know we are able to receive more and more with practice, and it will permeate every cell of our being.

Again, we are not bowls with finite depths and hard edges. Our spiritual selves are lithe and expansive, stretching to receive more with every intake.

We must become hands-on, especially to those in the midst of troubled circumstances. Stop now and recall someone in true need who crossed your path and you did nothing.

Divine good is more than inspiration. It is animation.

The reason we did nothing in the past will be altered by the inpouring of divine good.

Again, being human and carrying with us the lesser vestiges of our humanity, this will not be easy. The requirement to act is something even more unfamiliar to us. We may be unaccustomed to outreach. We may want to mind our own business. We may deceive ourselves into believing things will work themselves out in due course. We may even be insecure or afraid.

But we assist.

If we are comfortable asking someone what they need, we ask. If we are not, we still find the means to serve.

In many instances, the need is obvious. And at times these needs will be simple and temporary.

A person parked alongside the road with a hood up has a disabled vehicle. Do we stop and see if they need assistance? Someone walking on an egress or some other place where walking is not normal may need a ride. Food banks need supplies. Homeless shelters need clothes, blankets or gift cards. Our neighbors and peers need to know we *desire* to help, and are available to be called upon in time of need.

We are to offer help to anyone who crosses our paths in whatever measure we are able. That is God. That is what Godliness is.

It is impossible to quantify our efforts. Too often practices become stale and uninspired when they are scheduled or made routine. Yet we must also challenge ourselves to do what is ours to do. We must distribute what we have gained.

> *So, suppose we strive to devote three hours per week to outreach. Suppose at the very least we seek to share the divine goodness we were not required to earn, and set a modest standard for ourselves.*

Does employing such a goal infringe upon the purity of what we receive? Perhaps. We may find we have gone too long without a visit to God. We may not always be in the proper frame of mind, or frame of *spirit*, to honor such a commitment with a whole heart. We may find the real world persistently and aggressively calling to us.

Regardless, we do this so we do not forget. We do this so at the very least we honor the God of grace, and the grace we have received. We do this to remind us of our practice, to acknowledge, absorb, and act.

Have we ever experienced a time of need and did not know where to turn? Have we ever desperately wished someone would reach out to us?

Would such a meager amount of time have made a difference? Of course.

Suppose we live in a community with twenty thousand people. Half may be young, or infirm, or in need themselves. Suppose out of the ten thousand remaining, a tenth believed in this premise we have described.

That would mean three thousand hours of service to the common good per week. That is over four months' worth of dedicated service every week.

Of course playing such numbers' games is contrived. This is not our function or purpose. It is merely an exercise in possibility. It also should serve to show we do not have to be great to do great things. In the calm of our individual selves we come to know God. And in the smallness of ourselves our spiritually-based largesse compels us toward goodness for its own sake.

Beyond this, if we so tune ourselves to imbibe the perfect and eternal grace of God, this largesse cannot help but expand demonstrably.

And by dedicating ourselves to a *minimum* of time, the cycle returns to the beginning—

—the undenied, undeniable, and immeasurable grace of God.

TEN

Spiritual Law?

Nearly every faith system defines certain *spiritual laws* that affect and govern our behavior. The concept of reaping what we sow and Karma are two similar examples. We are cosmically rewarded or punished based upon how we act. Another is that if we ask, we will receive. Our faith in the certainty of reciprocity will be rewarded. Others are elegantly listed in the Ten Commandments of the Hebrew Bible. And, of course, the implied result of noncompliance is suffering.

These are delicious ideas. They imply balance. Something or someone beyond us is in control. Also, there are entitlements to be had for dedication to certain premises and woe should we fail.

From the most fundamental of Judaic principles to the most airy prescripts of so-called New Age or retrospect ideologies, there is a shared pretext: spiritual cause-and-effect is at work in our lives.

Of course this returns us to the same presumptions of most other faith systems; either God is at work, or we may somehow manipulate divine energy to do our bidding. These are contrary to God's nature and are counterproductive in the spiritually-based life.

There *is* spiritual cause-and-effect. If we receive grace we become more spiritually attuned. There are countless interpretations and elaborations, but, essentially, there is nothing more.

We have already broached certain aspects of why such beliefs are attractive. First, these help us quantify and rationalize when misfortune comes to us we do not understand, or did not create for ourselves. Surely there must be some lesson to be learned or else such adversity would not have come to us. Either our faith is being tested or else we are being punished.

Secondly, through what may be deemed *successes,* we enjoy the elevation of believing we have found favor with God.

The problem is these concepts are simply not accurate, not in a cosmic sense nor in a mathematical sense. When we look at our world, we know this is not true. People suffer who are innocent. People starve and endure illness who have done nothing to deserve it.

People who seem to contribute little appear to thrive. We do not condemn nor resent them, but neither are we blind to it. They are *special* because God *wants* them to be special. Obvious danger lies in this thinking.

There is only one immutable spiritual law.

God is the only source of limitless divine good and we can absorb it in whatever capacity we are able, whenever we choose.

That's it. There is no other behind-the-scenes activity in any spiritual sense.

Of course physical laws also govern our world, such as gravity, energy, mathematical forms, etc. These are used to help us understand the basic rules of cause-and-effect. Certain things are not going to change just because we want them to, or because some otherworldly entity decides they should.

Spiritual Law?

Some decisions are *always* going to produce certain ends, and the results of our decisions cannot be avoided when it comes to natural or physical laws.

If we are running late and we ignore a traffic signal, and another car is on our path, what's going to happen? If we fire a loaded gun directly at someone, what's going to happen? If we do not take care of our bodies, what's going to happen? If we consume poisonous substances, what's going to happen? If we swim out into the sea until we can swim no more, what's going to happen?

At other times, it seems we are able to avoid consequences. If we have a near-miss it may appear to be divine intervention. If we are supposed to be in some place at some time, and we are able to avoid something that would have held us up, it may seem providential. If we find ourselves in any danger zone, and manage to escape unscathed, God has *blessed* us.

If we are spared the worst this does not mean God had a hand in it. It means we were lucky, and should strive not to make such decisions again.

There are times when good fortune lays its hands on us—when we are operating on all cylinders and nothing seems to be out of place. We may earn this, of course. But it would be naïve to believe we always make our own luck.

Unearned misery and unearned serendipity are both parts of our world.

The people who inhabit our world make billions upon billions of decisions each day, from the infinitesimal to the profound, and these combine with the laws of the *corporeal* world to create *reality*.

Even the seemingly inexplicable has a reason whether we probe deeper or not. A tornado that destroys one building and leapfrogs over another has an explanation based upon physical law. If we continue to believe God overrides physical laws, or exempts certain of us from them, we are denying reality.

People win at games of chance and against mathematical odds, but even so, there is a structured forethought to the game itself…if no one ever won, no one would ever play.

Remember:
God does not make decisions that affect our lives. We do.
There is validity to spiritual cause-and-effect in a very broad, very general sense. Goodness creates goodness. Harm creates harm. The only mitigating factors come from spiritually-based people. It is *we* who can prepare, alter, thwart and allay. It is we who can praise, reward, embellish and enrich.

More, this is a spiritually-based acceptance of our responsibilities in this sphere of existence.

Our spiritually-based action can alter outcomes on a spiritual level. The people who suffer or hunger or thirst are experiencing this simply because not enough spiritually-based people have worked to remedy these conditions.

Predictability and unpredictability are parts of the same process. A cruel accident which claims the life of one but spares another is strictly the result of physical law and human decisions and good fortune. An illness which claims the innocent is a result of the same thing, or there may even be a genetic reason for it.

If we understand the one immutable spiritual law and the true elements of our faith in the spiritually-based life, we then understand what we are to do to accomplish a better order to the true nature of things.

First, we must understand the impact of the decisions we make within the framework of the laws that govern our world.

We must not behave recklessly or carelessly. Sometimes, someone's Karma, or reaping what has been sown, is a result of *our* poor judgment or lack of response to someone in need, even if they *err,* creating an environment where they have to deal with the consequences alone, or in disproportion to questionable decisions they have made. If we deny care to someone in need, what's going to happen? Every action has consequences. Therefore, conscious action should contain whatever measure of *divine good* we have received.

Secondly, we must promote good.

We must generate and spread good so it is transmitted into the decisions we make and the decisions of others. Again, and in a broad, general sense, good creates good. If we do not harm someone they are less likely to harm us. The complications we have created—political, social, economic—are what make the simple difficult. Anyone on the spiritual path knows almost instinctively when they stray. Our language and behavior under stress are prime examples. The less harm we do, the less harm there is.

Thirdly, we must take responsibility for and command of the concept *everything happens for a reason.*

Perhaps the *reason* is a part of our shortcomings on behalf of ourselves and others, especially when it is less than what we ourselves were capable of providing. We must strive to rectify our contributions to poor outcomes and provide whatever remedy we can. We do not seek to punish—ourselves or others—or rationalize catastrophes in any broader sense than that human beings make decisions.

Even when nature provides a devastating event such as a major storm or flood or fire, all beyond our control, *we* are responsible for preparedness and the after-effects.

We **choose** if we are going to believe in the power of divine good. We **choose** if we are going to illustrate good. And we **choose** if we are going to administer good.

Fourth, we must cooperate with physical laws and the laws of nature.

We contribute to pollution, knowing the results. We contribute to substandard housing and sanitary conditions, knowing the results. We contribute to poor utilization of natural resources, knowing the results. And we shake our fists at heaven or lower ourselves to self-righteousness when certain ends come to pass.

There are also those suffering because of defects passed down through countless generations, or cruel acts of nature, or poor decisions, and we must resist any consideration of *reasons* for these beyond an opportunity to act with understanding.

We must respond to those facing difficulties only with good, without finding fault in any of the reasons that contributed to these difficulties, even if self-inflicted. Do we treat an addict differently than we would a child who has suffered a terrible illness or accident? To inherit divine good is to make no distinction. Do we treat the perpetrator of an event differently than its victim. The spiritually-based life expects to us render care to both.

To truly participate and benefit from divine good, we must make no such distinctions or we can never claim the real potential of wholeness for ourselves.

There is no *havingness* without *givingness*. There is no real good to be done unless we seek to provide the wounded with whatever is required without judgment or opinions.

The only divine purpose in any hardship is to give those of the spiritually-based life the opportunity to practice our faith in divine good.

Good exists for all. Good is readily available to all. Practice builds our faith in this, and our application of this faith. When good is dispensed in concrete remedies all those involved are enriched.

Imagine the outcome if this was practiced! Slow, even haltingly at times, with many setbacks, what would our communities, our nation, our world be if everyone believed and practiced divine good, without judgment, knowing how events and conditions are truly shaped—by physical law and human decisions.

Imagine our world if we understood this is the only design God has for us.

How differently would we act, and what wondrous effects our contributions to *the whole* would be.

ELEVEN

Rules to Live By?

All faith systems share the same heritage—the belief in *the divine source.*

As faith systems evolve, altering and enhancing their beliefs, the manner in which they seek God also evolves. All faith systems define what is necessary to believe in order to maintain a relationship with God. These are elements, tenets, principles, doctrines, commandments—in essence, rules. Most have grown to encompass aspects of the material world in addition to those of the spiritual world.

Every faith system has guidelines. Every faith system has processes.

Inevitably, some of these *rules* have evolved into warnings: **if you *do* this (or *don't do* this) there will be consequences. Or you cannot truly have a spiritually-based life unless you adhere to these conditions.**

Of course actions have consequences. Jump from too great a height and bones are broken. Set yourself on fire and you will be burned. Dive headlong into shallow water and you will injure yourself.

Yet there are also *warnings* inherent in most faith systems. If you do not do *this* you cannot truly *belong*.

Again, God's true nature has been ignored. *Conditions* for communion with God have been established. Inevitably, a conclusion has been advanced that unless these conditions are met, one cannot find the *true* path. Without the *true* path, one will suffer.

Our faith has conditions, too, though exceedingly simple and obvious. If one does not go to God, one cannot receive grace. If one does not reach out to others, the potency of grace is diminished. The only punishment is self-imposed.

This is not to say that warnings have no merit. Self-destructive behavior leads to self-destruction.

But we must also understand rules are always human creations, and are limiting. We must understand they serve two purposes.

First, these *warnings* serve to galvanize people to a doctrine, so that strength-in-numbers can be applied. The more people who believe a thing, the more powerful it becomes.

Secondly, these *warnings* serve as a means to insure order and cooperation. There can be no dissension among believers.

What we must examine, without any judgment as to the propriety of another's faith system, is what we, as spiritually-based people, are to glean from these.

Don'ts and *can'ts* are negative by nature. *Do not* and *can not* always throw up a barrier, often with disastrous, yet predictable, results. We human beings cannot resist peeking beyond a *do not* or *can not*, even to our own harm. There is an attraction to rebellion. There is an attraction to the taboo.

Not to say every *do not* or *can not* is lacking merit. The Five Precepts of Buddhism hold great wisdom, and two of them deal with sexual behavior, alcohol and drugs in a practical sense, which other faith systems do not. The Seven Pillars of Islam are universal. (Incidentally, in the Nizari interpretation, *Jihad* means to be an adversary of vices, such as intolerance, anger, lust and judgment, and not as a response to someone else's behavior.)

Do not's and *should not's* contain life lessons, and caution us against deleterious behavior—the same way public signs do.

Still—and in some way—all of us upon the spiritually-based path have at one time or another acknowledged that *do's* are more potent than *do not's*. We have thought through the concept that our behavior is more important than what we seek to avoid or object to.

Actions speak louder than words.

But in many instances, where *warnings* have invariably evolved into *objections*, no matter how long-held or valid, these carry with them the potential of distraction from our true purpose of receiving and sharing God's good for us.

They establish a source of focus that is of the worst of our human emotions and not of our spiritual natures. Obviously, any *warning* as to the potential of damaging behavior is sound and should be treasured. Also, some of these have long strayed from caution to chastisement, and enforced by brethren in the name of God, and not God *himself*, which serves to dilute both the initial belief in an intercessory God, and establishes the right of leadership to execute certain judgments in accordance with a God, who by their own definition, should need no such assistance.

The reason for this is obvious, though often ignored, rationalized or even subverted.

All lore, all philosophical lexicons, all sacred texts, contain cultural by-products that can distract from the simplicity of our relationship to God.

First, they relate to traditions and mores of the past.

If a single plant or animal were available for food, neither would be unacceptable. (No one living by the sea would ever claim healthy fish were forbidden). If only a handful of materials were available for clothing there would be no restrictions on what to wear. If social systems had evolved where all were truly equal, there would be no caste systems. Rites involving animal sacrifices would seem *craven* today. Seasons created periods of observances.

Only with human proliferation and mobility could there be *alien* tribes, and could alien tribes become enemies. If women had been freed from familial responsibilities, there would not have been any male-dominated societies—(And if freed from reproductive responsibilities, no societies at all). Birth, death, and rites-of-passage rituals serve to maintain a culture.

Adherence and obedience to anything and everything was shaped and refined by the cultures in which they began.

Secondly, customs bred institutions, and no institution, regardless of its sincerity, forthrightness or forbearance, is free from the law of diminishing returns. There is no perfectly straight road. There is no incorruptible human thought. There is no conclusion exempt from intense self-examination. The more strenuous the doctrine, the more forceful the exertion against any threat or perceived threat—or challenge to any of its principles, regardless how peripheral.

Suppose we substitute the words *spiritually-based person* instead of naming someone a Christian, Jew, Muslim, Buddhist, Hindu, et al., and applied the same rules.

You *can't* truly be a spiritually-based person if you *don't* observe communion, or holy days, or eat pork or drink wine in moderation, or cover your head or face, or believe prophets are equals of God. You *can't* be a spiritually-based person if you haven't been baptized or confirmed or completed a bar mitzvah or any other rite of passage. You *can't* be a spiritually-based person unless you believe in reincarnation or nirvana, or heaven or hell. You *can't* be a spiritually-based person if you don't believe in a proactive God, or a God of action and reaction, of will and judgment.

We quickly understand many tenets of the major faith systems are rejected by nearly everyone outside that specific faith system.

Does this suggest that we establish a generic faith system everyone can participate in? Of course not. Nor do we ever criticize any belief or hold any belief in low regard. But our differences define us, differences repeatedly illustrated and elevated as examples, and we need to ask ourselves, is any path to God supposed to be this way?

> *Many of these differences are at the heart of turmoil in the world, and not the likenesses, or faith in the fundamental goodness of God. Our differences create conflict.*

There is **no** spiritually-based person who could not join with every other spiritually-based person to praise God, to receive grace (by whatever name it's called), to be kinder-in-heart, and to provide service to their fellows without judgment.

Any yet our all-important *rules* prevent this.

So let us ask ourselves, and in the most sober and introspective manner possible, do these things really *matter*?

Not really. These things *matter* to we human beings because of whom we have been, and continue to be, delving into human considerations and attaching them to the divine. They *matter* only to *us*, in large numbers and small.

Even if we believed in the conscious God of other faith systems, do we honestly believe God would care about any day of the week more than any other day, the spiritual validity of any ritual, one gender being more capable than another, one society or culture is better than another, what we eat or drink, how we dress, or one form of worship being more desirable than any other—or a hierarchy of traditions and *rules*?

Do we truly believe God could care about what we as humans believe is blasphemy or heresy, or anything can possibly grant us the right to harm another person?

Do we truly believe God would care about anything but the gift of grace and what we do with it?

So…inevitably and ultimately, those who take these questions to heart and answer from the depths of our spiritual selves, arrive at the same conclusion:

> *Any rule, occasion or occurrence not involving our direct relationship with God, what we are to receive from it and what we are to provide from it, cannot be of God.*

Then let us ask ourselves, why do we care so much about these things?

If we find something or someone else lacking, or have so much faith in any earthly derivative we presume to be of God that we cannot come to God open and available to receive the abundant grace promised to us, what *god* are we then serving?

Are we serving the *god* of cultural prejudices? Are we serving the *god* of self-righteousness. Are we serving the *god* of religion?

Are we truly upon the spiritually-based path or clinging to the means to remain stunted? Are we seeking God or are we seeking to judge others in some sanctimonious way? Are we displaying our souls or our egos?

The divine good we seek to receive is diluted and weakened by whatever portion of our hearts and minds contains such judgments, and is strengthened by whatever portion of our hearts and minds are cleansed of such judgments.

One cannot experience true grace in quiet communion with God and so readily backtrack to any lesser thing. If we truly wish to grow and maintain a spiritual basis at our cores, we must examine every element of *dogma* that rises to the fore.

What we *do* is always going to be far more important than what we *object* to.

***Inclusiveness* is always going to be far more powerful than *exclusivity*.**

TWELVE

Superstition

Superstition can be a very threatening and offensive word, and we must take care. It is a poor choice of words to use in any situation. One person's superstition is another person's faith system. Historically, faith systems have survived or failed simply by how many practice it, or the survival of the cultures that practice it. We are always, **always,** to understand first and question later.

But we must also acknowledge every existing faith system contains elements of superstition.

Superstition is the belief in *things* as opposed to eternal perfection, divine good and the fruits of divine good.

What do we mean by *things*?

> *A thing is any act, beyond simple observance, believed to possess its own power, or possesses any divine power, or requires adoption or obedience in order to maintain a spiritual course, or excludes non-participants from grace.*

Of course, observances of all kinds are important. Birthdays, anniversaries—all recollections and remembrances of both a cultural and spiritual nature are important. We glimpse at our footsteps to see where we have been, and to express our gratitude and delight in the journey, or even the relief we have survived certain aspects of the passage.

But beyond this, there are hazards to ascribing any sort of spiritual authority to any *thing*.

First, what *things* are believed to possess power of their own, especially divine power?

Icons, relics, crystals, alchemy, sacred texts and other objects are believed by some to possess their own *supernatural* power. Some believe certain words, sounds, and phrases contain intrinsic power.

How could this be possible considering God's true nature? Where would such power come from? Do we believe any *thing* can absorb grace other than the human soul? Do we believe any *thing* can hold grace other than the human soul?

It is like Excalibur, or ala kazam. We recognize a good tale. Yet when any*thing* associated with a faith-system, or prophet, or sacred text, is represented, or is believed to have been in proximity to any of these, they are presented as somehow *beatified* by God.

Again, this is contrary to God's nature.

Observances are also important. They represent elements of faith. Easter, Ramadan, Yom Kippur, Wesak, Navaratri, are all observances relating to the prophets of various faith systems.

Yet when these rites transcend the sole endowment of grace, they can become substitutes for grace, and any*thing* substituted for God lessens God.

Secondly, what acts or beliefs require adoption or obedience in order to maintain a spiritual nature, and that failure to do so excludes non-participants from grace?

There are many. Every faith system has many.

The creation story of Genesis in the Hebrew Bible, (and repeated in the creation of Adam in the Quran). The virgin birth and resurrection of Jesus in the Christian Bible. The multi-deism, and *Lords of Heaven* in the Gita. The deification of Buddha.

Is there harm in this?

Unfortunately, there is, if adherence represents a *requirement* for grace.

Every faith system believes in the procedural aspects of their tenets to the extent that *they* are the best able to define God, to reach God, to interpret the will of God, to employ God. It implies a worthiness or unworthiness based upon adherence to a belief.

Obviously, this excludes everyone who does not subscribe.

Consider for a moment how different faith systems view God, as an example.

Jews believe in the Father-God as controller, arbiter and enforcer of behavior. Christians believe in the Father-God and that Jesus is the Son-God, or God made manifest in human form. Jesus becomes the mediator between us and God. Both are inferred to be *perfect*, yet exhibit human traits. Buddhists do not believe in a perfect God at all, in the strictest sense. Hindus believe in both divine and semi-divine beings apart from the ultimate God. Muslims believe in the perfection of God, but also believe in a Day of Judgment, which is shared by both Christians and Jews, and again implies a God of passions and retribution, a strictly human characteristic.

Does it really make a difference?

To strict adherents, it can.

The tenets of most faith systems imply one must believe **all** the tenets of that faith system in order to reach God, or if not, implies a *lesser* relationship with God. And many times, there are dire consequences for failure.

The tenets of most faith systems imply one must believe in the *near-divinity* of their prophets as having been *selected by* God, and their thoughts and directives have been *received from* God, and they have somehow transcended humanity *through* God. We can become more wise, more spiritually-based, more devoted, but we cannot know the *ultimate awareness*, just as God cannot choose us or provide specific information to us.

The goal of *all* spiritually-based people is to extend beyond our own humanity, but it is impossible to *separate* oneself from it.

Thus, several major sects, and many more smaller sects, have embraced the integrity of their own faith systems to the exclusion (or at the very least, the *preference*) of all others, regardless of the presence or absence of wisdom in another.

At the heart of all these is God, though in us, and through the mind, limbs, senses and sensibilities of us, are the inorganic conceptions, formulations and generations of humankind—these having no other course but to *mature* into superstition.

Human ideas espousing perfection cannot progress in any other manner.

The *imperfect* can recognize the *perfect*, but it cannot reproduce the *perfect*. The creation of *things*—of acts and observances—distracts us from the single, solitary purpose of receiving and sharing grace.

We never criticize. Believers can become defensive, or leap into the fray, creating havoc and suspicion of those who challenge any part of what they might believe. Criticism is used to taint the validity of what people believe, and even the gentler, more well-intentioned efforts to enter dialogue can be misconstrued.

The key is only God possesses any real power, and understanding how God functions is where our focus should be.

Every faith system in the world has divine good at its heart. Every faith system desires for us to enter into a relationship with God.

Why isn't that enough?

If what we believe is a distraction from the simple receiving of divine good, sharing divine good, and propagating divine good, then how are we truly served? All faith systems evolve, and as they evolve they become more complicated. As tenets pass down through human hands, each adds his own part.

Superstitions allow people to believe in things contrary to the plainness of God's goodness. Grace is not a board game. There are no secret rules to follow to get from point A to point B. Recitations and rituals do not *save* us.

We need to examine in ourselves (and no others) what we have believed and what we truly do believe.

Then we must examine this in light of how much time we actually spend learning how to receive good, how to exhibit good, how to administer good. If we truly believe good exists, exists as the only source of power for us, is readily available to us, and is the essence of our faith, how can the belief in or ritual practice of anything else provide a real and lasting contribution to our spiritual lives?

If so much effort is placed on preserving any parameters that actually reduce our desire or ability to receive good with great frequency, to cleanse ourselves of the harshest of our human aptitudes such as anger or envy or resentment or judgment, or any desire to do harm, what does that accomplish except to reduce our capacity to be the embodiment of good?

Wouldn't the lesser aspects of our personality continually rise unbidden, and inhibit our sacred duty to administer good in every conceivable way and in every environment we encounter?

Any element of our faith systems that creates fear or lessens the rights of any human being to be viewed as anything but a favored creature of God, or that we evangelize any point of view beyond the rules of good, are *distractions*, and all distractions, by their very complexions, remove us from God.

If we believe **perfection and divine good** exists, as nearly all of us do, and exists whether we accept it or reject it—that it exists of its own volition—speaks, even if we do not listen—shines forth, even as we live in shadow—is an immeasurable source of grace, even if we choose not to receive it—then we must also accept, rationally if not spiritually, that we are distracting ourselves.

That is the true task—to enhance our best spiritual selves. It's all we have. It's all there is.

Superstition is merely sanctioned ignorance.

As mentioned before, all things evolve. Thought evolves. *The world is flat. Earth is the center of the universe.* Science evolves. *Our world was created by God not so very long ago.* Medicine evolves.

Bleeding someone helps cleanse them. Even the great Hippocrates, who is considered the father of modern medicine, believed *one's temperament is determined by the organs, not the brain.*

Our spiritual understanding can evolve. Our spiritual natures can evolve. Our spiritual growth, without the distractions of *superstition* can evolve.

Again, remember the story of the well?

Eventually, either by accident or rationale, someone turned on the faucet. The *secret* was revealed. The faucet was simply a tool, a machine, made by human hands and by human will for human purposes.

Our faith is simple, just as in the truest sense of the word, God is simple.

THIRTEEN

Belief in the Certain

We've all heard many, many times faith is the belief in something that can't be proved. No one can prove the existence of God, so that becomes an element of faith. No one can prove the facts regarding many stories and events contained in sacred texts, so these become elements of faith. No one can prove the occurrences attributed to prophets, so in order to believe, we must have faith.

Faith is the evidence of unseen things, the firm belief in anything and everything that cannot be substantiated. This is what makes faith so compelling—*belief* that defies cold rationality or scientific proof.

There is another kind of faith...

...a potent and purposeful kind of faith that deals with the **certainty** of something, even those things we don't fully understand, because it has been *proven* to us time and time again. This is faith in the natural order of things, in the basic integrity of practice, and as we've suggested, God is a part of that, too.

--- --- --- --- --- --- --- --- --- --- ---

In this, faith is in the reliability of experience.

--- --- --- --- --- --- --- --- --- --- ---

We have faith when we sit in a chair it will hold us, because we understand the nature of a chair, and we've seen it work. Should it collapse, we would not be so certain.

We have faith the sun will rise at dawn, and in the east, and set at dusk, and in the west, because that is the natural order of things—and because we have never known it to fail.

We have witnessed the phases of the moon, the tides, and the seasons, and have no doubt as to their predictability, except we never truly know what the seasons hold. Still, there is reliability.

We believe when we operate a bicycle, a car, or take a walk, we control the movement because of successful past experience.

Whether we understand physical law, we know it exists. We may thwart gravity, but we cannot eliminate it.

We know from *experience* the way many things work (and don't work) through confirmation in our interactions with them.

Even in the uncertainty of events, our lives are filled with faith in the trustworthiness of machines, passageways, environments and, to a certain extent, people.

Our belief in God works exactly the same way. If we truly seek to understand God's nature, then we will also see proof as consistent as the natural workings of our world. When we benefit from our understanding of God's nature, our faith is reaffirmed.

If our faith is such that we believe God hears and sees us, and responds accordingly, we may derive comfort from this, but eventually there will come a time when we doubt, merely because we choose to ignore God's true nature. If our faith is such that we believe there is a reward (or punishment) for us, we may maintain a particular discipline, but such cannot help but be challenged when we feel tested.

If our faith is such that we believe we can stand on a hill in the face of a storm and God will reach down and remove us from danger, or push the storm aside, our faith is actually in something contrary to God's nature. If we believe we can risk harm to ourselves or others, and God will rescue us without repercussions, our faith is also in something else. If we believe God has made a decision resulting in good for some and harm for others, our faith is in a mystical and capricious God.

As we consistently approach God, and receive grace, we will see results in real and tangible ways. If we do not, then the entire concept becomes a purposeless enigma.

The permanence of God, the pure divinity of God, and the approachability of God is where our faith must be.

Once we see the truth in this, and have it work for us, we cannot rationally doubt again. Grace is either real or unreal to us.

Faith's purpose, and ours—is the reliability of our efforts to touch God and receive grace.

It is not God's fault if, in a time of dire distress, we call out in the grips of our emotions and end up feeling God has not heard us, or has abandoned us. It is not God's fault if we pray for a miracle and one does not come. It is not God's fault if we are wracked with grief and receive no comfort.

That is the cruelty of reality. Our faith must be in the constructs of the universe, and the reliability of grace, before it becomes our *reality*.

Again, everything…**everything** works according to its function. An automobile can become something other than a conveyance—a piece of art, a rusty pile of metal, even a shelter. But it cannot function as a conveyance unless we turn the key or push the button, or whatever must be done to operate it properly.

Lightning may appear. It may cause harm or simply be a spectacle, but it is still lightning, functioning according to its essence. It is not an omen or portent. It is not a threat from something on high.

God can become our lord, our master, our savior, our judge, our parent, our punisher.

But God cannot become our God until we adhere to the realities of God's nature.

Whatever we believe is certainty, be it consistent with actuality or not, is what will be *real* to us. If we believe in the power of a stone, whether the stone actually has any intrinsic power, it will still be real to us, even in failure. We will continue to believe in the stone until something changes in us.

The sad thing is that God's reality should be the substance of our greatest joy, yet too often becomes our greatest disappointment because we *want* or *need* our faith to be in something else.

We become so inclined, or so desperate, to have *truth* to be beyond our control, we cannot have it any other way. So we struggle, we falter, we fail.

God *can* save us, if we approach believing we will receive grace. God *can* heal us when we receive. God's grace *will* reign supreme in our world when there are enough of us who seek to share all blessings with all others.

That is to be our faith in the *certain*.

When we seek God in prayer, and open ourselves to grace, and receive it in whatever abundance we can hold, that is the *proof* of our faith. The *certainty* we can do this again and again and again.

When we dispense goodness in our actions, that is the *certainty* our faith has purpose.

We all share areas of certainty from practice. We can find our way in our own environments. Yet beyond these environments, we are not so comfortable. Our belief in our abilities or tools enables us to succeed. Our *faith* in reliability allows us to prevail and survive.

It is the same with God. Our practice allows us to return, always—to approach, always.

Suppose we find ourselves in some unfamiliar area lost and blind, and there is no one to give us directions. We can circle aimlessly. We can hide in fear. We can await more light. But sooner or later, if we don't surrender, we will find some form of recognition that will eventually lead us back.

So it is with God. The *certainty* of God's presence and God's gifts anchors us to the faith.

Many times we believe in the certainty of things that fail us. Strong, consistent relationships can decay. Careers and positions at work and in our communities can alter, diminish and evaporate.

Belief in the Certain

Governments, economies, and entire states of being can transform in ways that can be confounding and disturbing. The entire sociology of a region or culture can become more hostile to outsiders.

There is much we *trust* and believe in as certainties, to the point where this trust is a kind of faith. We do not doubt because we have never been given reason to doubt. We believe in permanence because we have never imagined impermanence.

If we live on a mountain, we would never believe it could flood. If we live on an arid plain, we would never believe fire could reach us. If we live near the sea, we would never believe it could recede beyond our vision. If we live in a quiet neighborhood, we would never believe a violent crime could occur. If we are *good* no *evil* could ever befall us.

Yet any violation of this trust crushes our faith and sends us reeling, often to the point of despair and *faithlessness.*

We lose faith because the certainty is no longer there.

Our pain is real. Our doubts are real. Our disappointments are real. Sadly, this is a repercussion of faith in the corporeal and the material. Does this mean we should not have faith in such things again? Of course not.

We have relationships, and trust in relationships, despite the fact that there can never be complete certainty. We pursue our work, our pleasures, even though we realize the potential impermanence of such these. Our homes, our communities, our culture, our nations, are all subject to upheaval.

Yet even then, our **only** recourse, our **only** certainty, is our belief in the God of grace, the God who is always there for us.

That is the way it has always been, the way it is now, the way it always will be.

The nature of God is all there is, but ceaselessly sufficient.

FOURTEEN

Sacred Texts

First, we began to think. Then, we began to speak. Then, we began to write.

As we sought to know our spiritual selves, we developed faith systems to practice our relationships to the divine. Each of these has produced **sacred texts**. These are testaments to our desires to name *good*, describe the qualities of *good*, show examples of those who have grappled with what they have believed to be qualities of *good*, and what the outcomes might be should we succeed or fail.

Each contains *truth*. All are valid. Each contains the earnest beliefs of men and women who have devoted themselves to seeking God.

There is now and always has been more than one way to discover and build a relationship with divine good.

We must **never** deride or seek to diminish the efforts of those who have gone before us.

Yet neither can we ever allow ourselves to believe absolute perfection exists in anything divulged by human thought.

Our human capacity is enormous. But we will never know it *all.* Our human constraints will not allow it. As it is a spiritual impossibility for any human behavior to contain ultimate perfection, so it is impossible for any human author to tell the ultimate truth, save the goodness of God.

There is incredible inspiration to be drawn from communication with the divine. But beyond the authenticity of the communication, there can be no *perfect* inspiration.

If we open our minds long enough to understand this, we will know. It's true that faith is not always about common sense. But common sense cannot be ignored, either—or at least the common sense of God's nature and function.

By common sense, we do not mean suspicion, skepticism, or judgment. It means we can view everything by what we believe and still find the *heart* of it.

Let us consider the story of Noah in the Hebrew Bible, for example.

Scientific common sense tells us there was not sufficient genetic material to create all the life we now share, human, plant, and animal, from such a fairly small sample.

Spiritual common sense tells us in order to believe the story as fact, we must choose to believe in a proactive, disappointed, and emotional God who decided to destroy the world and begin anew.

Yet the heart of the story—that the human race is capable of such decadence as to destroy our entire world—should serve as a warning, and that we are capable of redemption should serve as hope.

Even so, we will be at odds with those who believe in the authenticity of such parables as historic fact.

Sacred texts are vital to every faith system. How the truisms of each are interpreted is crucial to that particular faith system. And the level of *perfection* ascribed to each determines the nature of their faith: in what each believes God's nature and function to be, what our responsibilities are, and what happens to both who adopt and fail to adopt these principles.

So how are we, as seekers of the spiritually-based life, to view any sacred text?

First, we understand the difference between the *divine* and *divinely inspired*.

The divine is what God is, what God does (and doesn't do), and how we are to relate to God and each other.

Divine *inspiration* is what an author *believes* what God is, what God does (and doesn't do), and how we are to relate to God and each other.

Many sacred texts have been inspired, many have eloquently illuminated paths to God, many advance principles of service, yet none are *complete*. They simply cannot be.

We must understand any and all inspiration is limited by the human condition.

It's difficult to cite examples without treading on feelings or provoking passions. The whole of any sacred text is to advance a philosophy of what God is, how God works, how we are to relate to God and what we are to do, and we will understand appreciating the beauty of any philosophy is far different than subscribing to the principles of *inerrancy* and *perfection*.

Again, we return to our own sensibilities. To believe in God as a mysterious, enigmatic figure is not common sense, but to name God as the source of divine good—and only good—is. To believe we can have such a relationship so we might receive good is common sense. To then believe we must prove that this is real by our growth and action is common sense. To believe God functions in some other way is not *sensible*.

If we truly believe in God's nature as perfectly impassive, then we cannot believe God can *literally* whisper in one's ear or guide one's hand.

We understand placing our faith in the strict adherence to any philosophy, creed or doctrine instead of the true, perfect goodness of God, is to *distract* ourselves *from* ourselves, our best selves, the selves that go to God in faith, and, essentially, distract ourselves from God.

Our primary function is to attain the spiritually-based life so we are continually in tune with the power of good.

Secondly, we find the *truth* in all.

Every sacred text contains things that simply will not ring true for us, simply because the writers were human and because we are human.

Yet each contains profound truths. The Fatihah in the Quran. The causes of suffering in Buddhism. The proverbs in the Hebrew Bible. The Apostle Paul's first letter to the Corinthians in the Christian Bible.

What touches us as spiritually-based people is not confined to any particular faith system, nor are we required to accept any in its totality.

We may be uplifted by the lives and teachings of those who diligently, and even fiercely, sought God and wrote about it.

We will *know* good instinctively.

The fact is, the more good we receive, the more good we recognize.

And this will also enable us to understand how certain things we have heard or have been led to believe, or have believed until this moment, may not ring true.

We understand, without reproach, there are going to be parts of all doctrines that do not serve us well, just as we understand all these contain truths without being the *whole* truth.

This frees us from dogma, or the necessity of believing all in order to glean the good.

We can do this without being critical of anything else it may contain.

It will not change how we are relate to God and those around us, though absolute, if such a thing truly exists, believers in the perfection of such manmade articles may bring their scorn to us.

We still know what we are to do.

Despite ourselves, our humanity contains so many wonderful things. How grand it feels to love someone. How satisfying to have when yearning rewarded. How deep is our joy when a sense of pride we have is fulfilled.

We also comprehend how faith in the *ultimate* truth of any sacred text gives rise to destructive or *distractive* thinking.

Consider how such thinking has affected our world and continues to do so.

What is the spiritual basis for naming one *friend* and another *enemy*?

What is the spiritual basis for naming one *clean* and another *unclean*?

What is the spiritual basis for naming one *redeemed* and another *damned*?

What is the spiritual basis for naming one *holy* and another a *sinner*?

What do we truly gain by claiming any spiritual inheritance for ourselves at the expense of others?

We feel a sense of purpose when we seek to receive divine good and succeed. We feel a sense of accomplishment when we are compelled to help others by the divine good we have received. But we must also acknowledge these qualities contain dangers. How it hurts to have a broken heart. How we struggle when hardship befalls us. How often jealousy or envy or disappointment or anger can overtake us.

We should appreciate our humanity because that is what we are. We should learn to use every resource in this journey to practice a spiritually-based life.

We must not be afraid to question the purpose of any teaching or suggested action that elevates the imperfection of human thought to perfection. We do this within ourselves, of course, but we do it.

Some part of us *knows* the difference between good and harm. The more we embrace the concept and practice of divine good, the more it penetrates us and alters us. Good is good, and it is our function, challenge and delight to find it, tap into its nature, express it and share its qualities.

No matter how callous, or un-*god*-like it may sound, divine good does not alert us to its presence. It exists for us to seek it and claim it.

> **And let us be alert, though always with patience, understanding, and no harsh judgment, to any teaching of the spiritually-based life that contains intolerance, wills to do harm, or justifies suffering as divine retribution.**

The perfect nature of divine good simply does not allow for it.

FIFTEEN

Prophets

Every faith system was either founded by a prophet or a prophet's teachings. God has never founded a religion except through inspiration.

As in sacred texts, the relative authenticity of prophets has always been and will always be a sensitive issue, and often defensively so. Why? Because each labored to bring people closer to a spiritually-based path?

Because each labored to bring the individual closer to God? No.

It is because we, as human beings, followers, students, and interpreters, have, with the very best of intentions, distorted nearly every original premise and principle in our search for understanding.

Ironically, the prophets themselves would probably cringe at the exploitation of their fundamental principles.

How did this happen?

First, the followers of prophets have always separated themselves from other existing groups, ideologically and even physically, some more pervasively than others. With separation comes suspicion of others.

What should bring about open dialogue and goodwill tends instead to focus upon the *rightness and wrongness* of differences. This tends to grow and become more demonstrable over time, often to the point where such differences outweigh all other considerations.

Certainly, there have been times when groups were persecuted by outsiders, which created a desire to be apart, but eventually and ultimately, there evolved an *us against the world* mentality. This cannot help but translate to a *leave us alone and we will leave you alone* disposition.

Many have found strength in grouping together. It is part of our evolution. But if we group together to avoid being influenced by another, we create an environment of fear and mistrust. It is inevitable.

What is the spiritual basis for this? There can be none.

Secondly, prophets tend to become god-figures to their followers, especially as generations pass, and in many instances against the teachings and wishes of the prophet himself. Prophets are elevated by subsequent followers in order to attract converts more readily. This is how faith systems grow.

The more *human* a prophet seems, the more likely those aspects are *deified* instead of the prophet *humanized*. A prophet who was righteously indignant, angry or judgmental means the cause of such a reaction is to be demonized, and the outburst acceptable, instead of considering the prophet may have been submitting to some strictly human, and yes, *ungodly*, throe. Most prophets did not consider themselves to be *perfect* nor comparable to God. Evolution has led to the deification of the mortal as opposed to the elevation of the concept against all mortality.

Whatever a *divine* prophet has said or done must be appropriate because that prophet cannot err in spiritual matters.

What is the spiritual basis for this? There can be none.

Thirdly, the teachings of many prophets were not set to rule during their lifetimes, and even those that were are subject to interpretation.

Prophets written about by others shortly after their lifetimes was done in retrospection. This process continues from hand-to-hand, mouth-to-ear, to this very day. This does not apply only to prophets. See how history is revised by subsequent leaders until the facts are awash with legend. See how the attributes and acts of prior rulers, statesmen, philosophers, scientists, etc., have diminished or removed lapses in character or behavioral inconsistencies.

The teachings set to rule during a prophet's lifetime were **always** encumbered by prevailing political, societal and cultural issues. Slavery, polygamy, righteous war, retribution, the accumulation of wealth as *divine* reward, classes, castes and lineage were seldom addressed as having no spiritual basis, except in the grand scope of things. There has always been the *concept* of all are equal in God's eyes, yet somehow some *deserve* less by tenet, decree, or failure to decree.

Whenever we have the concept of *all are equal in the eyes of God*, without its practical execution, we cannot help but find lack in this.

Some interpreters who followed are considered to be prophets or sub-prophets themselves, because they are believed to have knowledge exclusive to them. The most basic elements of a faith system are often lost to dogma. The simplest *truths* have fallen by the wayside. And any issue with the whole is considered heretical.

What is the spiritual basis for this? There can be none.

It may seem subversive to some, and we **never** take the beliefs of others lightly, or criticize them, but we must acknowledge, to whatever degree we are able, that our objectivity holds the following true:

Enlightened imperfection is still imperfection. Thus, we are able to accept or reject any aspect of a prophet's teachings as they reflect on God's divine nature and greater good for all if they seem contrary to what we believe God's nature and the role of humanity to be.

No one born of human flesh can *be* God. The mortal mind prevents it. Certainly, there have been prodigies who have come closer to God's perfection than the rest of us, but there can be no real perfection as long as the human mind exists, capable of thought and emotion that cannot be controlled to the uttermost extent.

The mere fact that we must eat, sleep, and do whatever it takes to maintain our human form establishes a direct difference between ourselves and God.

There are none who represent the one, true path to God.

Anyone who contends, past or present, or any representative of the one, that he alone contains the means through which God is found, and goodness encountered and reaped, has effectively removed himself from the spiritually-based path by this very contention. The assertion he is the one avenue to God is rooted in vanity.

Where is the truth in the ideas that those who do not *believe* are somehow eliminated from the divine process? And those who believe, but do not act, are still beneficiaries of the divine process?

This defies the basic equality, and then responsibility, of all who seek grace and respond to its impetus.

It harkens back all the *things* we place between ourselves and God.

So, what do we do?

First, as in sacred texts and all spiritually-minded things, **we seek and find the good.**

Every faith system contains much good. And as we grow in grace we will recognize it. It occurs when we find truth that enables us to go to God in prayer as much as we can, receiving grace in increasing abundance, leaving us in the *peace that defies understanding*, growing this in ourselves and elevating our outreach.

Much good lies in the teachings of Moses and the Judaic prophets. Much good is found in the teachings of Jesus, Paul and

Prophets

other Christian disciples. Much good exists in the teachings of Buddha and Mohammed, and much good in Hinduism. Seek it. Find it. Ingest it. It will speak to you.

Secondly, and again as we are *always* sensitive and completely non-judgmental in these things, we understand many variations in the teachings of all prophets stem from the cultures and societies in which they lived—and the cultures, societies and *passions* of those who taught and wrote about them.

The Hebrew Bible is filled with accounts of how the people of God struggled with *enemies* and violence as acts-of-God to overcome them. The *Crusades* were ostensibly to return *holy ground* to the control of *Christians*. Mohammed's entire earthly life was spent in a time of enormous conflict. Siddhartha Gautama believed in monastic rules which separated him from many in fundamental need. The list is voluminous.

Politics has always played a crucial part in this. The trial and execution of Jesus was political. The strife in Northern Ireland between two *Christian* factions is political. The struggle for Tibet is political. Various interpretations of certain passages of the Quran are political. The Hebrew Bible's dealing with the enslavement and struggle of an entire people, and with a bent toward recompense is political

---

> **We accept that any teaching which does not espouse the direct communication with God, universal grace, and service to the causes of grace, first and foremost, are diluted forms of purer teachings.**

No prophet of God ever placed himself or herself above God. *We* did that, human beings filled with false certainty and prejudices.

Just as importantly, never criticize or demean anyone else's faith system, even when the purposes and causes of grace enable us to see beyond the distractions that hold others to these callings. We should seek to befriend them and enrich them, and they us, and provide for them and console them without judgment, and regardless of what they believe. Our desire for spiritual bases must create this.

We lead by example, and teach by success.

Lastly, we are to be wary, and again without judgment or criticism, of current-day prophets of the unkind (those whose beliefs are so entrenched in the harsher elements of their doctrines—justification for doing harm to any human being—that nothing good has value unless done under the banner of certain concepts and rules—that God punishes because of our failure to adhere to certain tenets—and the self-justification of intolerance from the lack in their own perspective of God's true nature) because they themselves have strayed from the essential foundation of God, the inexhaustibility of grace, and its impersonal nature.

The spiritually-based path requires of us our willingness to believe, our willingness to accept and our willingness to provide.

That is also what we seek first and foremost in any prophet.

SIXTEEN

Supernatural Evil

To believe in the cosmic construct as we believe, leads to an inescapable conclusion; there is only God, and then there are creatures, such as we are, developed through biological evolution.

Many of us believe in a supernatural evil—an intelligent, organized and powerful force about us that exists to deceive us, to entice us into wrongdoing, to wreak havoc upon our spiritual lives, even directing its minions to oppose us, to distract us from the will of God, to damn our souls to an eternity of torment.

These *subgods* and their realms are alive and well, and ready to reel us in.

Some believe in a *master of evil* who once shared space with God but chose power instead.

Satan, demons and hell are all parts of most conventional faith systems.

If we believe in God's true nature, and not as the *wizard of heaven*, there are only two ways this would be possible.

First, perfection would have to somehow be corrupted.

Whatever iota of divine energy first became matter, these building blocks of the universe came from a perfect God. Of course we are a part of this, and we are imperfect. While the substrata of matter can indeed be corrupted, *corruption* is more likely to come from sentient beings acting upon it.

We may one day find the means for interstellar or even interdimensional travel. Beings capable of this may already exist somewhere. We have unlocked many secrets of the human genome, just as we are delving deeper into the creation of the universe itself. Still, these are products of sentient development and not supernatural forces.

Mythical evil would have to be part of an evolutionary process, and not created intact, sentient, nearly all-powerful, capable of creation itself—of its own environs, legions, and dark forces. No kind of matter, especially divine matter, exists from which this could be created except as acted upon by scientific evolution.

It is more likely, however absurd, that any preternaturally corrupt being(s) would have been created by some far-superior race eons ago before humans evolved.

Then, of course, *where* would they exist? Not upon the earth. Not in any environs we are yet aware of. Perhaps they could travel back-and-forth from their source to the plane we inhabit, but could not maintain such a presence here.

Secondly, for such creature(s) to otherwise exist, there would have been some kind of secondary evolution apart from ours.

Somehow, a super-entity would have to evolve at a pace different from ours, and into a different being than us. Again, it would have to have the capacity to invade our existences, influence our consciousnesses, and control our experiences after death.

This would also mean that such a creature, determined to inject us with all manner of evil, would exist in this plane, and simply wait until we came to be and influence us in our world. Thus, it would still be here somewhere. But where could it possibly be?

Such could not be created by God, nor evolve from any part *of* God, nor exist at all except as counterpoint to a proactive God. And, obviously, the God of Perfection could neither need nor want such a foil.

Supernatural Evil

So, we come to a simple conclusion we already and instinctively know. All sinister thoughts and actions come in human form, and the choices we make contain whatever evil exists.

There is only God and the world beneath, and our world is part of long-term evolution.

Why are such beliefs so prevalent?

One reason is this belief is a distraction from the way things truly work—when we stumble, some evil force is responsible; when terror erupts in our world, some superhuman, demonic power is behind it all. An entity is out there contrary to God whom we cannot defeat.

Because of these beliefs, we are free to ignore the cause-and-effect of strictly *human* influences, no matter how malevolent, the perfectly predictable results from physical laws, no matter how cruel, and the results of human decisions, which are calculated with no greater influence than a conscious break from the spiritual path, no matter how devastating.

Another reason is to provide a cautionary tale for those in this world who do evil—that damnation awaits in another sphere of existence.

There are opposites; hot and cold, high and low, east and west, good and evil.

But no *one* or no *thing* can take energy from God and subvert it into something less that divine good except *us*.

Human beings create weapons and do violence, not from some exterior force, but because of unchecked passions, limited thinking and their own decisions. Human beings are responsible for suffering in this world. Human beings create the temptations to do ill, the predilection toward harm.

Evil, in whatever form it takes, is a solely human attribute. Ill feelings lead to ill thoughts. Ill thoughts lead to ill actions. Ill actions lead to ill consequences.

The whole purpose of a belief in supernatural evil is to create fear—to prod us into a devotion to fear. It also gives us excuses to shirk responsibility for our own poor choices and decisions, or the false liberty to cast blame onto something beyond ourselves.

When we begin to consider that all injury has its *cause*, its source in **this** world, we can better understand it. When we have a better understanding of it, even without naming it, we can negate it. When we learn to immerse ourselves in God's divine good, we can overcome it.

Think back to the last time you were a witness to what you believed was some supernatural, evil force at work. Was it a terrorist attack, created from misguided passions? Was it a weather disaster, created by the forces of nature? Was it a horrific crime or conflict where the perpetrator(s) seemed to be possessed by some demonic force? Was it famine and starvation in some remote bend in the world? Was it a group of people who claim to worship the *devil* and committed heinous acts?

Every day we hear, see and read about atrocities, from domestic and child abuse,to murders, to troops squared off in some remote place, to suicide bombers who use their own bodies as weapons.

Is there a laughing Satan in an underworld delighting in our misfortune?

All temptation is ours as human beings. Every submission to temptation is a human decision. Every poor effect results from humanity.

Whether a person is predisposed to addiction or simple carelessness, or strikes out in anger at any level, or commits a crime, these are still the results of purely internal forces. Giving into them is an internal decision. The fallout is a result of cause-and-effect.

We cannot diminish the seriousness of these situations. But we are to understand and respond with understanding. We are to respond in the way intended for us, no matter how difficult or how our own passions are inflamed—to respond the way necessary for us, having received good, and as beneficiaries of good, to now exhibit abundant good in real, tangible ways to aid those in conflict with internal forces, and to care for these affected by the actions of others.

Supernatural evil is a remnant of the old god. Some natural disasters are even referred to as *acts of God*. Some believe God compels them to acts of terrorism or wars, or using one evil to combat another.

Natural disasters cause horrific damage to lives and property, yet follow a predictable pattern. Acts of terrorism are conscious decisions of those desiring to do harm. Violence upon others is the horrific loss of control and the absence of grace. Crimes occur when people make decisions to commit them. These are equally predictable, again if only in hindsight, when we look at how people are influenced by their environments and their own predispositions.

God cannot punish, cannot reel us in or teach us a lesson.

And the sad fact is, we, as humans, do not need a devil. The devil is within us.

Two specific lessons are here for us to learn.

First, as before, and as always, the rules of cause-and-effect can only be changed when the *causes* are sufficient to alter the decisions made.

Believing in the power of divine good, taking it to heart and practicing it until it becomes a natural part of us as it should be, is what truly matters. Providing compassion and tangible effort is what changes the heart, and the causes that create harm. The same applies to natural disasters, when people are struggling with the awful powers of nature. Nature, not evil, and certainly not God, creates the storm.

Knowing the *cause* of *all* human conflict is internal, every single decision made, from the most fleeting to the profound, will have an effect, and if the desired effect is destruction, that is the way it will be. Only when the internal is connected to divine good will the external be productive.

Secondly, our responses to such events, large or small, make the difference in the lives of those affected by *evil*.

If we are not truly enablers of divine good, then nothing will ever be whole. We do what must be done to restore those affected by events, to help alter the causes of these events, to prevent and offset the potential damage of such events, whether the original cause is human or natural.

Even more difficult is to make every effort to understand those who have made conscious decisions which harm us, to treat them in such a way they know the true depth and substance of our faith until they no longer wish to do harm.

To grow in faith is to understand evil exists only within us, and can be rendered impotent only when we practice divine good. We must understand some part of ignorance perpetuates concepts of organized evil, and we cannot adequately practice our faith as long as we believe some exterior force is there to thwart us.

Once we accept no powerful, conscious destructive force is *out there* whose purpose is to make us stray, then we can draw nearer to the truth without distraction or fear.

The only real power is divine good. Evil can be explained and dealt with and overcome by our willingness to practice divine good in all ways, so it becomes increasingly difficult for us, by our renewed natures, to succumb to any evil's hold over us, or think we are powerless against it.

SEVENTEEN

Prayer

No matter what we name it—be it meditation, higher consciousness or invocation,—prayer is the only means we have to communicate with God. It is the way we receive good. It is the manner in which the channel to grace is opened.

Most of us have been taught ways to pray. Most of us have learned prayer as confession and petition—where we apologize to God for our shortcomings and then ask for whatever is on our minds at the time. Some believe in intercessory prayer, where someone gone before approaches God on our behalf.

At its best, we praise God for all the blessings in our lives and seek help for ourselves and those we know are in need.

As has been presented, this still operates on the presumption God controls our world and intervenes in our world, and is predisposed to affect events in our world. It presupposes God *hears* and *responds*. Most of us have come to believe **the way to get things done** is to ask God. We do this earnestly, believing the more earnest we are, the better our odds. Then we wait. If the outcome is not what we had hoped for we believe God said *no*.

If something we have prayed for comes to pass, we thank God for endowing us. If something we have prayed for does not come to pass, then, obviously, something is wrong with us, or God knows our needs better than we do and has his own ideas what is best for us.

Again, this fosters the belief God has favored us while disfavoring someone else, and for reasons known only to God. It advances the belief of purposes and plans beyond our reckoning.

This bears repeating. The true God cannot possibly work in this manner.

As disappointing and disheartening as this can be at times, we must understand what we are actually doing is *diminishing* the power of God by failing to take to heart what *perfection* truly is. To communicate with a god who is dispassionate and impersonal is difficult for many of us. Perhaps our preference would be otherwise.

But the benefits far outweigh all perceived disadvantages. The grace we may receive is limitless. The spiritual energy we may osmose is also limitless.

Far better for us to take responsibility for *reception* than to hope for some *dispensation* that will never come of its own volition.

Many of us actually pray *at* God, or what we believe God to be, and, unfortunately, we are always going to find this lacking simply because we choose to misinterpret how this is supposed to work. We hurl intellectual and emotional darts toward the heavens in the hopes of being heard and responded to in the manner we desire or need.

We beg for things and plead for mercy out of our sorrow.

We pray for guidance and deliverance.

We beseech God for knowledge in a confused state.

If we truly believe God's nature is as it is, we already *know* there can be no response save the assimilation of grace.

Grace is the only recompense we receive from God.

However, the farther we move on the spiritually-based path, the more we realize grace is all we really need, more than we have ever previously hoped for, greater than we have ever before imagined.

In any other way, we fall prey to the belief God will respond if we are *good enough,* or does not respond because we are *not good enough.* This not only removes us from the possibility of grace, but from the tangibility of grace.

Only the most cruel and *unspiritual* of us could believe that any hardship or disaster is a response from God.

Yet often we are so quick to believe God will intervene if we just pray hard enough, or the *right* way, or if enough of us make the same request. We *hope and pray* some condition or circumstance will be resolved by a divine hand.

Many of us have been taught to *surrender* ourselves to the will of God. What we are really doing is surrendering ourselves to chance and circumstance and forfeiting our belief in the authenticity of grace.

Again, all good or ill in this world is either created by us or remedied by us.

We are conservators of the balance of nature, and should we fail, our prayers will not change things. We are to receive in prayer all we ever need to grow our spiritual natures, our better selves. Through prayer we better understand our emerging capacities to be the *more* and give the *more.*

So as we reach a kind of coherence in our dealings with God, one thing becomes increasingly clear.

Prayer changes us.

Prayer does not change conditions, environments or events, except through us desiring to do good.

Prayer certainly does not change God, the great *Unchangeable.*

Through prayer we receive God's bounty.

Through prayer that we grow our divinity.

Through prayer we are healed and given the capacity to help heal others.

Through prayer we gain the greater understanding of what our lives should be.

This is what prayer means to those who grasp the cause-and-effect of the genuine God.

We should be thankful for our God, for the grace available to us without limits. Gratitude enables us to better understand the potential of our households, our neighborhoods, our towns, our cities, our countries, our world. Appreciation helps free us from the bonds of self and enriches our movement toward others.

When we are fully in tune with the power of grace, we want nothing more than for all within our reach to be healthy and whole. We want every environment to less fractious. That's the only way it could be.

When we pray, our natural desire is to be closer to God. When we pray, we allow ourselves the worthiness of receiving, even though we are bound to feel less than worthy at times—God is there to give, not to judge us. When we pray, we access the divine. When we pray we drink in *good* until we can drink no more. God never stops the process. We do. When we pray, we *know* the good we consume is not really digested. It permeates into every conscious and subconscious thought of our being, cleansing doubts and concerns, frustrations and anxieties, harsh feelings and disappointments. When we pray, what remains is the peace-of-soul that enables us to move forward. When we pray, we are powered by grace to reach beyond our flesh into the world about us and disseminate good with our every thought, word and deed. When we pray, we move toward a wholeness we cannot gain otherwise.

Essentially, when we pray we are to become spiritual artists, awakening to the canvas that is our world.

Of course, and as always, we have to recognize the influx of good and accept. We must *want* in the best possible sense.

If we can play the notes, does that make us true musicians? If we can do the steps, does that make us dancers?

The difference is being in tune with God's nature. This has to do with spiritual awareness, or for lack of a better description, *spiritual feeling*. It is like the difference between when we observe our children in the hubbub of the day and the way we see them when we peek into their rooms and see them fast asleep in bed. It is like the difference between a cold, blustery gray winter's day and a bright, sunny one. It is like the difference between receiving an expected gift and an unexpected one. It is like the difference between loving someone and loving someone uniquely.

Our commitment to faith and practice and our love of God makes it possible. The more we pray, the easier it becomes, and our prayers become more frequent. The easier it becomes, the longer these fruits of our prayers last. The longer these last, the healthier we are between the times of prayer. The healthier we are when we come to God in prayer, the fuller we become. The fuller we become, the more we are able to come to God. And coming to God is the hallmark of our faith.

The Christian Apostle Paul said *pray without ceasing.*

It *is* possible for us to live in a constant state of prayer—to open wide the gate God has already opened. Obviously, it is not always practical. We know how easy it is to be distracted. Our lives require us to focus in so many directions and so many tasks, often at the same time. The demands placed upon us can seize our attention and hold it. In time, we may find some part of us is always ajar.

We are not alone. The entire purpose of the spiritually-based life is to first grow in grace and practice, to become more whole. That makes it easier to cope, if nothing else. Then, as more of us do likewise, especially as we lead by example, our environments improve. Our households are more peaceful. Our work environment can become less fractious. Our communities can see more possibilities. There are fewer areas of contention, and even in disagreements we are able to *be* more.

Our world becomes more whole.

All this comes through prayer, through direct interaction with the power of God. It can come from no other source, and we are to be exasperated by our *humanness* without it.

EIGHTEEN

Divine Love

We've all heard the phrase, **God is love**. But isn't love an emotion? Wouldn't a God of love be *emotional* in that sense? To humankind, love *is* an emotion, perhaps the most powerful emotion of all, or at least the proffered source of emotional upheaval.

Perhaps it would be more prudent to substitute the word *perfection* for the word *love* when we refer to God's love.

Still, that does not answer the question.

When we examine the prospect of *divine love*, our entire definition must change, just as when we began to examine God's nature, our entire concept of God was altered. So what exactly would divine love be?

Wouldn't perfect love be the absence of all emotions? Wouldn't perfect love be unrestrained good, with no imbalance? Wouldn't our love of others in relationship to God be the best and highest fulfillment of grace?

Wouldn't what we have termed *unconditional love* be a love with no desire save good for all?

Every spiritual treatise designed by humankind deals with *love*. Love has been described with every superlative created by language. And every description of God includes the quality of *loving*—and perfectly so.

All our emotions are subject to weaknesses, and *love* seems to create the most chaos. Love of a child can become fear if something is wrong. Love of a spouse or partner or friend can become anger if we are hurt, or jealousy if we feel threatened. Love of our country or culture can become aggressiveness if we overreact. Love of self can become arrogant, conceited, restless, and even adversarial.

Even love of God—which may defy the definition entirely—can become judgment, self-righteousness or even disdain if we believe someone else is operating beyond the boundaries of what we believe God is.

Love is capable, at times, of near-divinity.

Through our communication with God, receiving grace and divine good, we are able to move forward in the spirit of love, because that is how grace would best translate itself in the human consciousness and corporeal world.

Love is the way divinity is felt in us and translated by us.
Love, through kindness, is the way good is dispensed by us.

In this way, love can only be defined by its characteristics, and, just as describing God's nature, must be continually bent toward perfection.

In its purest form, love is the only emotion which can be refined. None of the more tumultuous emotions can be purified. They can only be removed.

Love must be moved beyond want, need or desire. It must not be yielded to any harshness whatsoever. Divine love is eternal, just as God's grace is eternal. Only our use of it makes it transient or temporary, and then, in reality, this is not love at all.

Divine Love

The ancient Greeks had multiple definitions of love: sexual (or intimate) love, friendship, familial, and unconditional love, which was used to describe everything from the divine love of God to the best of kinship. The last was not related to God until the early Christians.

Even then, the lines were blurred. Unconditional love could be used to define marital relationships beyond the sexual. This could also be used to describe a good meal, and a sense of overall contentment. Sexual love could lead to spiritual transcendence, though it could be argued this usage was self-serving in that it said nothing of monogamy or fidelity.

Beneath the bough of love are many shades of love. In order to relate this in any real sense of the divine, we must begin anew.

All goodness born of grace can be called love.

Though fraught with burs and barbs, love could not exist without the divine. Everything would be reduced to instinct, or at the very least, the drive to act without consideration. We would take what we need or want, and never give it a second thought. We would resort to carelessness in the guise of caring.

Caring is part of our human evolution. To care for friends and family, to assemble into tribes, is part of our human heritage without any consideration for the spiritual. But the spiritual enabled us to move beyond the *self*. Predators may hunt in packs. Yet they will fight over the kill. Apes may tend to the offspring of another, yet they will abandon them if put at risk, and will even cannibalize their young.

Though some cultures have subjected their members to horrible atrocities, the evolution *beyond*, toward sympathy, devotion, and self-sacrifice, was born of the spiritual, even before it was recognized as such. The tug toward *grace* came with the growth of intellect, but more importantly, branched away from mere intellect and emotion into the yearning for the *better*, the *greater*, the *more*.

When we truly care without expectation of mutuality, that is love.

When we are generous, the same part of the brain that responds to food and sex is stimulated. Though this is strictly a physical occurrence, it does support a spiritual principle. It would be nearly impossible for anyone to consistently *do* good without *feeling* good. It may be possible for us to do serial acts of kindness by rote without feeling love, but it is impossible for us to do this without a sense of good coming to us unbidden—a sense of good that can be called *love,* that exists far beyond the rational.

For the spiritually-based person, the belief in ultimate good, and the receipt of grace is an inspiration. That inspiration can be described as *love*.

In human relationships, the deep empathy we feel when someone struggles with a situation or condition we ourselves have endured, or when we feel the joy of their successes, can be called *love.*

Genuine compassion for anyone can be called love.

When we act with compassion, this is love.

The fewer the restrictions, expectations or desires we place upon it, the greater this *feeling* becomes *love.*

We love without touching. We love without asking. We love without cooperation.

Perhaps the most complicated form of what we have learned to call love is *romantic* love. The first stages produce elation. Then, and invariably, yearning follows. Physical attraction is also called love. Consummation is called making love.

Is it possible to have any kind of spiritually-based, physical *love* with another person?

Some individuals on their spiritually-based paths forego this altogether, believing romantic love is a distraction. It certainly can be. One cannot enter into a human relationship of this intensity without the more destructive elements of emotion coming into play. Poets have waxed philosophically about the bitter-sweet hungers of this love since the beginning of language. Yet nearly all of us are called to it. We desire...or even *need* the emotional and physical partnership of another.

So what then is its purpose? It certainly isn't a rational process. If it was, none of us would ever make mistakes. If it was a rational process, there would be no pain, no divorce, no anxious moments of doubt and fear. We cannot control who attracts us. We cannot control or even choose whom to love. Procreation is a physical drive deeply imbedded in our genes. All creatures are compelled to reproduce. There are scientific studies to explain why we are the way we are in these areas, but we are oblivious to them when it occurs. We are captivated and engaged and desire contact and companionship for far more reasons than the next opportunity for the physical.

Is that all there is to it?

Of course not.

At its highest and best, romantic love is designed for sharing the spiritually-based path. It is to find common ground to seek grace. It is to acknowledge and understand in its likeness what another is trying to accomplish. It is to appreciate the abundant life together, and to pursue grace together, to receive, to dwell in, and dispense the fruits of grace together—and to do this in all things.

It is to explore the affections and intimacies of such a partnership with the sole and higher purpose of identifying and securing all avenues to grace. It is to assist and to share in the goodness we are able to claim. It is to live in the single and communal awareness of the grand cause—to acknowledge, absorb, act.

It is to realize and accept, with *love*, that we will stumble—to forgive, to seek forgiveness, to resume.

It is to transform longing into devotion, reverie, and all the sublime aspects of giving, receiving and becoming complete in every fashion.

God may not be able to *love* in the literal sense. But love through the divine is another and vital part of the path toward perfection.

Divine, or perfect, love is the barometer by which all actions are numbered.

Love is that part of our humanness descended from countless generations, that can evolve and be honed into something greater than anything else we are capable of *feeling*—the emotional byproduct of eternal grace.

Those who are most capable of love, who allow themselves to swell the soul beyond what has been thought possible—to enhance themselves for the sole purpose of enhancing the world about them, are the most able to grow in grace, the most able to demonstrate *divine love*.

Divine love is the process of refining ourselves.

NINETEEN

The Soul

All things are contained within the mind. Even our *hearts*, those imperfect seats of feeling, which can propel us into a near-constant state of grace or send us plummeting to the depths of despair, are contained within the mind. Our mind is what we use to seek God, to acknowledge God, to drink from God's cup, to savor God's grace. Our mind is the tool for every human experience.

So what then is the soul? Is it a separate part of us that somehow lingers after our earthly life expires? Is it a quaint description of that part of the mind that seeks good? Is it some ethereal quality we all possess?

It is both and neither.

> **The soul is the God-part within us—that seed of divinity, that part of divine substance which enables us to venture beyond the physical workings of our mind.**

Consider our brains. Our brains do grow, of course, but not beyond the boundaries of our bodies. Yet within we learn. From infancy to adulthood, and throughout all life's experiences, we can continue to learn. We are still learning when we depart this life. We are limited only by time and experience, not capacity.

Consider anything in our experience with great elasticity. Imagine anything in our experience that demonstrates expansion. Consider the universe itself. Is there a finite end? Not within our reach, and certainly not within our grasp. Consider what we have learned about grace—that we are able to procure an increasing amount of God's goodness as we become more spiritually inclined.

That is the soul. The soul can never be filled to finite completion; the soul has no edge or end. The difference between the mind and soul is the difference between intelligence and spirituality.

Where does it come from?

God.

Just as we understand God's non-intercessory nature, we know God is not truly capable of what we would call *creation* in any active sense.

Likewise, we understand God is the only purely divine substance in existence.

Yet we are drawn to quantify as much as we possibly can so our faith is forever *real* to us. And so we arrive at another intersection of mind and spirit, another unavoidable conclusion. God did not create the universe—

–the universe was created from God.

All things were created from God. Eons ago, all the elements to build this world, produce, and sustain life, came together in perfect synchronicity, including those elements that would eventually become *us*.

God is the **only** original substance. Nothing existed before God. There were no parts or particles, no building blocks or adhesives, except God.

We do not know how the original and merest mote of matter was derived from the ethereal, non-substance of God. Scientists and theologians may argue such is not even possible. Yet we also

The Soul

know the genesis of *everything* had a beginning. And we may posit and disagree how the beginning became, but we cannot escape the fact there indeed was a beginning. So, it becomes increasingly difficult to deny, save those who do not believe in God at all, that the generation of evolution from a single atom came from God—that the very first atom sprang from the one and only source…God.

This means fragments of *perfection*, however slight, however invisible or untraceable, still permeate *everything*.

Every element contains God, however unacknowledged or unrecognized. Only humankind can recognize this and benefit from it, appreciate and use it, at least to this point in our understanding.

After all, we are not made from clay. We are made from stardust.

This requires faith, of course, just as the belief in God requires faith.

But *any* belief in the eternal perfection of God requires the belief God is the universal substance—the DNA of all things.

Perhaps this fleck was an active force in our evolution. Perhaps it lay dormant in our early ancestors whose lives were occupied by mere survival, and remained asleep until *we* became self-aware enough to acknowledge it. Even now, it can remain covered and unused.

This substance is surrounded by and encased within mortality, frailty and humanity.

Yet we also know each of us has the same capacity for good. Each of us shares in the promise of grace. Each of us is capable of participating in the ever-expanding delight of enhancement that goes far beyond our mental capabilities into something unmistakably *spiritual*.

That exists only because of the soul.

We also know God's nature is not to simply be an idle source of energy. Though grace is not to be imparted arbitrarily, and must be sought and received, its function as grace is to nurture all in limitless, ever-increasing abundance.

This can only be received through the soul.

Again, the sun shines whether we seek its warmth and remain in the shade.

So what does this have to do with the so-called soul?

Where is the proof?

The proof is in the inherent goodness we see exhibited every day, and in every day since the first human thought. The proof is in those, who like ourselves, embrace the spiritually-based life and expand far beyond their original natures.

The proof is we are not *innately* good. We are not born pure and perfect, ready to seek perfection. We are not pre-disposed to analogous charity. We are not instinctively kind and benevolent creatures—except through the soul.

Consider what we once were. We were creatures like any other, fighting for food, shelter, and only biologically disposed to procreation.

How did we grow into spiritual beings? How did love come to be? How did kindness and reverence come to be? Our minds, yes, but there were creatures here before us and creatures who have occupied this world far longer than we have who do not possess these traits.

Did sentience create the soul, or was sentience created *for* the soul?

Is a *conscience* a normal part of intellectual evolution, or was evolution a process for us to catch up to our true capacities?

Seeking God and gradually understanding divine beneficence is simply a byproduct of intellectual evolution does not make much sense. Created spirituality just so we could *feel* better does not make much sense either.

We are truly incapable of sublimity without *Godliness*.

The soul is like every hidden thing. The soul is like the hidden God. We must evolve to a point where we understand and acknowledge the urge to seek. The soul is what prompts us to seek, to find, to embrace.

It exists, as always, waiting for us to perceive. Once we perceive, we extend. Once we extend, we grow.

The soul is the understanding there is always going to be *more* than we are capable of on our own.

Faith is not a matter of physical survival. Faith may not even be a necessary part of relative contentment in this world environment, if that is all we desire.

Our souls enable us to seek its likeness, and in its most undiluted form.

Our souls reach beyond the confines of our emotions, our physical limitations, our intellectual reasoning. Our souls move us again and again to the spring of the divine, drinking all we can hold, and then beyond that—to seek and find and hold the *more*—and then to live in accordance with its purposes.

Our souls enable us to develop beyond our physical, psychical and emotional needs.

Our souls enable us to reach beyond ourselves to those about us.

Our souls enable us to empathize with the plights of the less fortunate—and to seek solutions.

Our souls enable us to love truer to the divine source.

Our souls enable us to evolve far beyond what we were in the beginning.

Our souls enable us to feel the tug toward our best selves when events and circumstances draw us away.

We see this around us every day. We see those who are happy within themselves, kind to all, who seek every opportunity to serve others, and who do this again and again.

The soul makes us children of God. The soul prods us to be more than we are now and brings us so much unhappiness when ignored.

To think is to be, as human beings. To feed our souls is the divine compulsion that begins and ends with God.

TWENTY

Sin

The concept of sin has existed since the first of us realized a mistake, and regretted it.
Sin simply means anything that separates us from God.
These are conscious things, decisions that clog the conduit between ourselves and the divine. We create areas of interference that dilute the flow already encumbered by our humanity.

God did not and does not create sin. We do.

And unless we have some serious psychological condition which relieves us of conscience, we know when we have faltered.

Most of these short-comings are in the form of self-service, an effort to bolster our standing in some arena far removed from our relationship with the divine. When we lie believing we will gain by it, we sin. When we cheat in any fashion to gain by it, whether it's something as serious as adultery, or something as simple as taking a sick day when we aren't really sick, we sin. When we steal from another, we sin. When we covet, we sin. When we are jealous or envious, we sin.

We also seek to protect ourselves from the consequences through alibis, more lies, more machinations that take us farther and farther away from our better selves.

Regardless of our motives, and realizing our relationship to the divine is already cluttered by our subconscious, sin makes receiving our good even more difficult. Therefore, our effort to maintain an open communication to the divine must be continuous and as free from any distraction as possible.

When we do this, the good we receive helps us in the decision-making process that causes us to the stray in the first place, and as our relationship with God grows, and good becomes a more consistent part of our consciousness, the desire to sin, to separate ourselves from God, becomes less acceptable.

After all, **it is also human nature, and in our best interests, to desire the continuation of anything that helps us to remain whole—that creates a sense of well-being in us.**

There is also the concept of **Universal sin**, in whatever form we call it—things that may permanently or irretrievably separate us from the divine. Some believe in *original sin,* set down from the very beginning. Again, we delve into areas of dogma and *superstition* that stem from a belief in a judgmental god.

True, we humans are prone to error, but it will always, *always* be of our own making.

― ― ― ― ― ― ― ― ― ― ― ― ― ― ― ― ―

Nothing can permanently or irretrievably separate us from the divine.

― ― ― ― ― ― ― ― ― ― ― ― ― ― ― ― ―

Good is ours to claim, in whatever portion we can accept and maintain, at any time and as long as we draw breath.

Additionally, a part of the entire concept of sin is the *act of deliberation,* of purpose in the act. Swearing at or accosting someone in a surge of emotion is far different from striking them, or spending countless hours plotting our revenge. Once we have an opportunity to reconnect with the divine, whether it takes seconds or minutes or hours, and seek to do precisely that, we can soon recover.

Our intentions *do* matter.

And with our intentions, our subsequent actions, whether we call it *repentance* or *atonement* also matter. The negative results of all intended acts require reparations.

There are only three fundamental or universal sins—things that must be corrected in order to resume an active and vital relationship with the divine.

The first is obvious.

Deliberately ignoring or avoiding any communication with God is a sin.

We cannot receive divine good without communication. We cannot avail ourselves of grace unless we do it. We can die of hunger on in the middle of an orchard if we do not realize the fruit is edible.

To cut ourselves off from God, to deny divine nurture, defies common sense. Yet we do this from time-to-time, sometimes permanently, because as human beings we can be incredibly stubborn and willful. Afterward we can even blame God for abandoning us, or punish ourselves for imagined transgressions.

Sometimes this is *spiritual inertia*. For whatever reason, we procrastinate or reduce our times of contact until we've completely fallen out of touch.

The only true spiritual balance comes from the consistent practice of receiving divine good. And, unfortunately, God will not reach down and tap us on the head if we choose to separate ourselves from it.

When we cut ourselves off from good, we also hurt others. We cannot be the person, mate, friend, or emissary of good when we have chosen not to be our best spiritual selves. A rippling effect spreads out from everything we feel, say or do, and only when we have consistent intercourse with God does this wave of influence reflect the divine.

The second is deliberately harming anyone.

We always hurt people. We can't avoid it. Most of us have initiated separations from partners, punished our children, deceived others, held grudges, and been cruel. Sometimes it is something fairly innocuous. We ignore someone or something we could positively impact. We realize someone is in pain and do not reach out. We relish any difficulty experienced by someone we are not overly fond of, or disagree with.

The two keys, of course, are *a) doing such things consciously,* and *b) inflicting pain for its own sake, knowing the damage it will do.*

If someone seems alien to us, or different from us, or is in some way unpleasant, we can ignore them. We have *chosen not to understand.*

If someone hurts us, our first thought is to retaliate, instead of seeking the quiet to reflect. If we are in a position of authority or influence, and someone does something to rile us, we can return misery to them.

We do this because we have allowed ourselves to feed the most base aspects of our humanity instead of receiving grace. It's easier. It's almost instinctive. If we are not comfortable enough in the practice of receiving divine good, or not consistent enough, or are still fettered by our beliefs in *things* instead the simplicity of grace, it is far easier for us to be our lesser selves and *let God sort the rest out.*

This makes us spiritually lazy, and laziness can be comforting and addictive. Rationalization and self-righteousness are hard habits to break.

Think of all the harm done in our history by spiritual sloth—denying the effort, for whatever reason or self-justification—to move ourselves to a higher way of feeling, a more divine viewpoint.

We have all inflicted pain for its own sake. Someone has upset us in some way and we want to reciprocate. We can't seem to help ourselves. We always regret it afterward, but we do it anyway. The spiritually-based person possesses and seeks to maintain the constitution to resist.

We have all deliberately hurt someone just to make them hurt. Sometimes it's just easier to do. Sometimes when we are emotionally twisted, finding and receiving grace is just too much work.

There are even those among us who seek to harm others believing God has assented to their actions.

Yet we know such is an impediment to God.

Whether it is an act of omission, of ignorance or laziness, or an act of commission, harming someone before regaining our equilibrium, both are equally damaging to our own greater potential as well as those we hurt.

The third is the deliberate failure to distribute good to others.

We know if goodness is not dispensed, it will evaporate. If shared, it will open us to greater abundance.

We also know if we are not compelled to do this, we have not truly received divine good at all. It's some other, more intellectual form of lucidity we wrongly claim to be of God.

This is not dogma. This is the hands-on work, if you will, of outreach.

We are to provide aid whenever, wherever and to whomever we encounter, and without judgment as to whether one deserves it. To elevate ourselves in grace is to do so without such judgments, to love all believing each has a right to the same abundant portion of grace as anyone else.

This is not easy. To comfort the struggling who may have a significant hand in their own downfalls is not easy. To seek to provide basic sustenance to someone who may have no inclination toward productivity is not easy. To help someone who may having difficulty in any area we find repugnant, or where we ourselves may also be faltering, is not easy.

Yet that is what is required of us. More, what is required of us is to nurture the true *spirit* of grace where we are able to do so without a second thought, where it becomes almost instinctive for us to do—naturally uplifting to do.

If we believe we are receiving divine good, absorbing divine good, filling ourselves with such divine good that we can feel it in joy like the first breath of spring, and are not genuinely and naturally motivated outwardly in love, we are kidding ourselves. Whatever it is we may feel, it is not divine good.

Only when we are urged outward in the true spirit of kinship and love is our relationship with God *real*.

To not seek this, believing in the outcome of joyful service, is to not know the true God.

The wonder of grace is we can always return, always reach out, always absorb, always dispense.

God is perfect, unchangeable, available, and will always be so.

God is the means and the method through which we do not sin.

TWENTY-ONE

Salvation

What is salvation and what does it mean to be *saved?*

There are many practices and rites involved in welcoming someone into a community of believers. Some baptize, some come of age, some believe in a conversion process, some believe in *special* words.

The Apaches had a four-day ritual called The Sunrise Ceremony, a physically demanding rite in which young women were painted and not allowed to wash throughout the entire process. Hindu boys have a sacred thread ceremony called Upanayana. Hindu girls have a ceremony called Ritushuddhi. These are all similar to Christian confirmations.

For each there is a process through which one is deemed to be a more spiritually-based person than before. For each, there is to be a greater communion with God and with that particular fellowship.

For some, salvation is a series of steps that move them from the carnal life to the spiritual life.

For each, there is to be a moment (or period) of transcendence from the guilty to the free.

Yet should we look too deeply, and as always, without criticism or judgment, we will find such steps are more about doctrine than genuine growth. It is a purely representative rite, a substitution for beginning the spiritually-based path. And, sadly, we may find any long-term expectations of transformation are disappointed.

This is not just for those looking in, but also for those looking out. Whatever was *supposed* to alter is not altered. Whatever condition was hoped to evince is absent. All *feelings* of renewal are transient and unsatisfying.

Something simply didn't stick.

Only when the outcome results in true affection and implementation of the spiritually-based life is there *conversion*.

We do not say who is on the spiritually-based path and who is not. We do not debate or find fault in differences. Yet neither do we stray from our convictions, or flinch beneath the assertions of those who believe *theirs* is the *one true way*. All evolution, physical, mental, emotional, spiritual, is a process.

All evidence is in the *living* of life, and the proof found in our footprints. Wherever one has been, even unnoticed, the condition of the land and the people in it are the only testaments necessary to the validity of our faith.

Our faith is that **all** may access divine good. **All** may receive grace. **All** are required to serve.

It is not merely putting aside old ways. It is not to cleanse ourselves of past wrongdoings. It is not even to behave more *devoutly*, so others may see that we are no longer the person we once were. It is not to evangelize, or offer testimony, or claim liberation from past behaviors others have associated with us.

It is not to merely change our words, but our tone. It is not to change our mien, except to befriend. It is not to change our habits, but our lives. It is not to change our gods, but to find the one, true God.

Most of us need to be redeemed from bad habits and faulty practices. But if we believe God is what God is, that we all have access to the same grace and spiritual nourishment as anyone else--that we all may receive as much divine good as we can imbibe at any given time—**then we must also accept each of us has already**

achieved whatever salvation there is, and from there we continue to grow.

Either we seek divine good or we don't. Either we absorb divine good, or we don't. Either we dispense divine good, or we don't.

Some are farther along the path than others. Some are so weighted by culture and convention they will not allow themselves to believe any other way. Some are so heavy with turmoil they cannot see clearly enough to reach for and accept their divine good, but there is no other course involved.

There are many evidences of faith. There are many diversions, necessary or not. There are times when we wander from the path. There are even times when we find ourselves in near-darkness and cannot seem to find our ways clear.

But the God of eternal perfection and divine good is all there is, and all anyone needs to begin.

Our lives reveal what we truly believe. How we conduct ourselves reveals what we truly believe. How we treat others reveals what we truly believe. Our relationship to God is evident in these things. We all know *actions speak louder than words.* Yet there is far more to this. Our actions are *prompted* by spiritual tenor. Our actions are *induced* by spiritual tenor. Our actions are *executed* according to our spiritual tenor at the time, and always. Our actions are *demonstrated* by our spiritual tenor.

To reach out to God in frequent prayers is to be *saved*.
To let divine good flow into us is to be *saved*.
To function as bearers of divine good is to be *saved*.

Many of us have been taught to believe salvation determines where we are to be in the next world. For the moment, however, let us look to what it means in *this* world.

Our lives are composed of many factors. Our stations in life are determined by the environments we are born into, at least in the beginning. We've already examined in part how the confluence of billions upon billions of decisions and events affects us. We know we all do not necessarily start on an even playing field as far as the world is concerned. We know fortune and luck are duplicitous things. We know genetics and biology can make things easier or more difficult for us. We know we cannot avoid struggle and hardship. We realize some of us will simply fare better in the agronomy of this world.

Yet our spiritual lives are where all things become equal. In our spiritual lives, each of us begins at the same place.

Obviously, a life of strife makes it so much more difficult to seek and find our spiritual inheritance. If mere survival is our main focal point, the spiritual may not seem to have much value to us.

But let us never forget once we are mentally and emotionally sound, which occurs at a fairly early age, we are able to open the channel to God and nourish our souls.

No matter how difficult our lives, no matter how unfair, no matter how distracted we are or rampant our thoughts and emotions, or how clamorous our environments, a quiet place is always within reach where we can learn to open ourselves and receive the divine good that is ours to claim.

We can learn how to do this. On the scale of all the things we are expected to learn in this life, reaching isn't that difficult. We can learn and improve and grow and receive more each time we do this. We can claim our grace and build our internal selves into potent spiritual beings. One step forward—two, a hundred, a thousand steps backward—it still exists for us and we can reinstate it and rejuvenate it.

That is its purpose and ours.

To be saved is to recognize and enhance our spiritual natures.

To be saved is to seek and acknowledge in good in others.

To be saved is to comprehend instinctively where we are along the path at any given time, and to make corrections.

To be saved is to become increasingly introspective, and yet not dwell upon ourselves, but rather *know* what has a spiritual-basis and what does not in all we think and do.

Also, we must never forget seeking equanamity for those who are experiencing difficulty, unfairness, overwhelming thoughts and emotions, unsuitable environments, and the like are a part of our spiritual responsibility, and a direct and desirable result.

This is where we deeply and sincerely comprehend the plights of those whose search for the *more* is stunted by the ambitions of simple existence: to feed themselves, to find shelter, to overcome illness and disease, to exist in harsher confines they cannot seem to escape…to wonder if each day will be their last.

To be saved is to be in every way a wholesome and vital part of *this* world. To be saved is to be in love with this world and all its inhabitants, to nurture and protect all for the sake of love, and to bear it in all aspects of our lives. To be saved is to believe in the *more* of God and the more of others.

We claim our grace, we build ourselves into potent spiritual beings, we help others do likewise through service. We help others feed and clothe themselves. We help others with emotional disabilities find treatments. We help others endure. We find new environments for the displaced and downtrodden. We create hope through tangibility. We help them find a sense of purpose, a sense of value.

We teach them how to claim their divine good by example.

And so it goes.

That is its purpose and ours.

That is what salvation means.

That is all it means, and there is no salvation without it.

TWENTY-TWO

The Next World

Nearly every faith system believes in a world to come, an existence after death. Though there are many variations, most share one property—in the next world all will become clear, all will be made perfect.

Introspection, ours alone among all creatures, gives us the path to divinity. This helps us realize what we, in all our base humanity, would be otherwise. Without grace, we would know a profound emptiness. Without a true sense of who we are in relationship to God, as well as our environments, we founder. Even then we find life harrowing at times, and witness the distress of others. So it is no wonder we may await a time when there is only *perfection*.

> **But are our imaginings of a world beyond this one a part of our divinity or a part of our humanity?**

Our human-ness dreams of a perfect place where we are finally relieved of the human condition. We find friends and family there and dwell in peace.

Yet as we have come to understand what *perfection* really is as in the nature of God, we must then consider in perfection we would become *like* God, absent of any self-awareness at all.

A conscious life of extra-humanity is still a part the belief in a conscious God of extra-humanity. Is it truly likely we would remain in familiar, recognizable territory when such has been rife with all our mortal experiences? If we somehow removed everything we have believed to be *negative*, would we even recognize ourselves or others? What kind of consciousness could possibly accommodate such beliefs?

Of course, no one truly knows what the next world will be. It is a matter of faith and to a point, guesswork. Perhaps, like the belief in reincarnation or Purgatory, there will be a more evolutionary process that will enable us to grow beyond what we held true in this world. Yet if we remember nothing of the past life, what would be the purpose? We cannot overcome what we do not recall.

Perhaps we will undergo a series of changes that will elevate us farther and farther along the divine path—the next world is not the final world and we must wait, or even *earn* the last steps to God. Some believe we can even be earthbound as ghosts.

But again, all this presupposes in the next world we will retain at least some part of our human cognizance, which is the same as saying we will retain some part of our humanity.

So we should consider the *soul*, the part of us that carries with it the perfection of God—the part that enables us to develop a relationship with God in the first place—cannot, by its very nature, retain human consciousness. This same part of God inhabiting us is contra-alert to our humanity. It is our function in life to bathe our mortal selves in divine good in order for our existence to be more complete, and our journey through it more satisfying. Without our earthly character, only the soul—the Godseed—could survive.

To truly be a part of God would be to have no earthly likenesses at all.

The Next World

In spite of our humanity we are enabled to find God. *In spite of* our humanity the soul grows beyond the tiny seed of the beginning.

Our thoughts, our memories, our longings, our every emotion, are parts of our humanity, and thus a part of our mortality. None of these things are a part of the soul.

Any passage to God would remove all earthly likenesses.

If, in the next world, we return to God, the divine source, we would become a part of the perfection that enables us as human beings to communicate with it, draw spiritual energy from it, and dispense it. We would have no recollection at all of being anything else. We would have no identity at all, just as in the same sense, God has no identity. We would simply become a part of the divine whole.

So what does this tell us?

There is no point to being a good and decent person, to practice a spiritually-based life, to bear witness and action to the *truths* of God?

After all, if we remember nothing, experience nothing, what does it matter?

It should tell us—

First, this life is our *reward*. This life, with all its faults and foibles, struggles and disappointments, traumas and tragedies, is for us to draw nearer the template which we know to be God.

We live and breathe and love. Our spiritual lives are not trials to be survived. Our spiritual lives are to be reconciled to the divine.

Our earthbound life is the proof of God-on-earth. All enrichment, all joy, all are parts of our growth as spiritually-based people.

Consciousness itself provides any and all wisdom, any and all happiness, any and all redemption.

Only in these counted years will we have such awareness.

Secondly, this life is all we have as a reference point to the divine. To be aware of the capacity for divinity is to have *life* as it should be.

Think about it. Nearly all of us possess an interior barometer that tells us when we are out-of-sync with our better selves. Does greed, lust, self-indulgence, debauchery, mean-spiritedness, indifference, etc., create any sense of well-being within us? Do we not yet *realize* the pitfalls we experience when we deviate?

How is well-being established? What is our touchstone for all goodness in our earthly experience?

God, the divine.

The spiritually-based life is all about growing the *divine* in this plane of existence. There is no true contentment otherwise. There is no opportunity for wholeness without it. There can be no real joy, no genuine love without it.

The soul simply cannot function without nurture. If not for the opportunity to grow into more spiritually-based creatures, we are already dead.

How we may wish at times the *evil* among us suffer in the next world; that those who have harmed us, either as individuals or as a part of our societies, are punished.

Deep-down, however, we know. These feelings are not of God. These feelings are the worst of ourselves. Certainly we will feel them. Certainly they will occupy us the same way too much food or drink or weariness or impatience occupies us. But sooner or later, we know we must open the channel to God again and absorb the goodness or we will wither. If we wither, we effect our own demise in one fashion or another.

It is not always fair. Perhaps it is not even just. But it is the truth. Poisoned feelings remain poisoned. Disappointment remains disappointment. Hate remains hate.

Only grace, and our willingness and effort to bring it in can purify us. Only God can provide adequate enrichment to have peace in our earthly lives, and all the senses contained therein.

Of all the doubts about the next world, one thing is certain. Our role in this world is clear—to find, to consume, to share. And our motives must be absolute. If we believe by our attention to

The Next World

the rites and details of dogma, we are *storing up treasures in heaven*, we are deceiving ourselves, and inviting misunderstanding and misery into our lives; and to the lives of others by our ignorance.

If we are burdened, we have been shown a way to lessen that in this world. If another is burdened, we know what we must do.

To deny the purposes of this world simply in the hopes of a better world to come is to deny God. To deny God is a universal sin.

There are times when we all long for perfect rest. There are even times when the prospect for eternal peace beckons. Even as we grow in grace and realize the greatness of the power we absorb, knowing as human beings we always have a filter through which grace must pass, we may long for the *perfection* yet to come, when the gauze of humanity is completely removed. Our passages through this world can make us weary.

Yet some part of us is always aware of the *other*.

There is only this world and the next world, and this world was not made for torment or dissatisfaction. This world was made to reach toward its greater potential. This world is for our growth in realization, of becoming. And in the next world, there is only God. Our sole spiritual function is to bring God into this world. Afterward, is eternal rest.

This life is what holds us. It is this world into which we were born and in which we became sentient, and capable of spiritual causes. The lessons of the soul are made here.

This world is not designed to be merely a proving ground, to see how much hardship we can endure or how many riches we can accumulate.

Let us look at it a different way. What if there was no life beyond? What if this worldly life was all we had?

How would we live then?

We must find all the delights of this world through divine grace. There is nothing more simple or more profound than that.

We know how to live. We know what to do.

TWENTY-THREE

The riches of God?

One of the more prolific sets of teachings in recent history deals with the premise God is ready and able to provide us with our hearts desires if we follow certain processes to obtain them. Generically, this is called **prosperity theology**, or the law of attraction. It purports, in whatever language, if we follow certain steps we will have the perfect job, the perfect car, the perfect mate, the perfect home—the perfect *life*.

It is a seductive concept. All we have to do is right our minds and formulate the *perfect* invocation, the *perfect* attitude, and these things will come.

It claims to use elements of faith to accomplish these ends. Faith is very real and very powerful, of course. Faith can help us believe in the rightness of anything. Faith can also be a self-fulfilling prophecy—even if it is not truly *of God*.

We have said this before…whatever we believe in, *that* is our faith.

This has been discussed previously as an example of what many believe to be the *mystery* of God.

Remember the stone? If we have faith in the stone, then in some way, the stone will serve us.

This is the lure of false faith—a faith of some imaginary God who has somehow agreed to serve us in this manner, and should we fail, our faith is lacking and not the power of God.

It is neat and tidy. The stone decides if our petition is worthy. Our sincerity, our language, our deservedness, or our belief in our deservedness, determines if the stone honors our request.

Yet we have come to know that only when we believe in God's true nature do we understand the true cultivation of grace.

Why are these teachings so popular?

Because they provide hope for and relief from our perceived inadequacies by sheer mental exercise—without really *doing* anything. All that is required of us is to convince ourselves these things *should* happen to us and for us and they *will* happen. If we *envision* success long enough and hard enough, it will come. Standing before a mirror and telling ourselves we are beautiful, wonderful and will become prosperous may help our self-esteem, but it isn't God. Undergoing some kind of self-hypnosis that supernaturally removes all other behaviors we do not wish to modify is not God.

Truly, we can have the faith to move mountains. But the certainty of the spiritually-based *mindset* reveals to us there is no point in moving a mountain—instead we should be adequately immersed in grace, to enrich ourselves in grace, and then the lives of every human soul between ourselves and the mountain.

The faith to *move mountains* is a metaphor, of course, but one corrupted by those who seek the *power* to accomplish such an otherworldly act, rather than contend with the necessities of a living faith.

We all have heard of the *placebo effect*. Many patients with real ailments improve merely by believing what they are taking will make them better. Our minds are extremely potent instruments, capable of affecting great positive changes in our lives.

That is far different, however, from believing in a god who grants our every desire, or any *material* desire. Statistically, the vast majority of symptoms in any person whose condition improves with a placebo—the same majority as those with no treatment whatsoever—will return, and usually sooner than later.

Eventually, and not always gently, we realize the stone is just a stone.

Even if our minds were somehow focused to the point where we truly believed the divine is somehow going to reward us, we are forgetting a few things.

First, that is not why God exists.

Divine good has never and will never mean we are to be prosperous in worldly standards or immune from life's casualties. God provides grace, and in whatever abundance we can hold. This is for us to have whole spiritual lives, to succeed in this world from the perspective of love and goodness.

We do not always find *equity* in our cultures and societies. We also know the role of all spiritually-based people is to work for and *provide such equity*.

Obviously, it is easier for us to give God responsibility for what we are supposed to do. It is also a primary reason many reject any consideration God's nature is different from conventional wisdom. Without joy in the spiritually-based life, we will shun such responsibilities.

Secondly, the world in which we live is extremely complex.

It has so many interwoven and interlocking cause-and-effect forces in play we cannot possibly expect to roll sevens on every pass. We have the grand reality of God to provide divine good, the greatest of all possibilities, yet we may fail on this earthly plane on any occasion save the equanimity of grace.

The discouraging fact is we will all face *unfairness* in this life. We will all be subject to inequality and arbitrariness. What should motivate us toward a spiritually-based sense of *rightness* can instead break us down.

This is one of the great spiritual ironies. We will encounter difficulties not of our own doing. And our awareness of God's true nature will not always make the difficulty less painful. In fact, it may exacerbate the situation because we will be prone to feel we are *on our own*—or no one really cares about us.

Of course we have the promise of grace. Of course we have a greater understanding of God's nature and function. Hopefully we will have the support of other spiritually-based people. But it remains a part of *our* function to serve the causes of grace at all times.

We cannot escape the irrefutable premises of the spiritually-based life:

If all our fellow inhabitants of this world believed in divine good, the true nature of God, and the causes of grace, the opportunity for true equity and less struggle—certainly less contention—could come to pass on this earth.

As grand and glorious as the faith systems of our world are, without such basic beliefs, the world will remain a careless and temperamental place.

And there is no mystification to alter this. There is no short cut to *our fair share*, save grace.

Thirdly, merely believing we are *worthy* does not make us worthy, especially in the corporeal world.

Believing good will come to us simply because we believe it will does not make it happen. We cannot *believe* anything into existence. What exists is God, God's nature, God's function, and our function.

If we believe our own worthiness extends from a *unique* and *rare* relationship with God, we have surrendered to our egos, and nothing of grace.

Of course, we *can* envision our lives in grace, but why envision it when we could simply *do* it?

In buying a lottery ticket we already dream of what we will do with the money. The dream that deceives us. With the dream of some exterior manifestation of good we mislead ourselves. We simply cannot *imagine* it into existence.

The only part of the divine existent in this world is in our souls, and the only function of our souls is to seek grace and goodness through a personal relationship with God.

Also, we must come to terms with the reality that the cosmic construct simply will not allow it. The checks-and-balances that hold the universe together do not accommodate any human control of the arbitrary. We may become wealthy by hard work, perseverance, talent, skill and luck, but not everyone who possesses identical qualities or makes the same effort will achieve the same results.

We may do all the *right* things by societal standards and still fail to receive the proportionate benefits.

Grace is the only equalizer, and its fruits may not be measured in earthly benefits, but in the fullness of bliss.

Of course, even this can seem as trite as the familiar explanation *God has a reason* for our setbacks, struggles, and even outright disasters.

Again, the difference is there is no grace without God and no evenhandedness without grace in us.

Then, let us ask ourselves honestly, why would we crave such a thing?

It is good and proper that we are grateful for all the many benefits we receive from grace, but do we truly want the ability to *wish* something into existence and then believe it's because of our unique relationship with the divine?

Is that not more of narcissism than grace?

Do we really want to believe we are more worthy of good than others? Or—believe others are more worthy of good than us? Do we really want to believe God prefers for us to have the *perfect* job, mate or home more than someone else? Or—believe God prefers for others to be more worthy of good than us?

Do we actually want to believe God operates like the leader of some coven where the *right* words determine who is invited for membership and who isn't? Do we want to believe all it takes is a special button to push?

What a bleak prospect that is.

To develop a dynamic, prayerful relationship with God is to receive a divine good that manifests itself in spiritual enrichment that gives peace of mind and soul, strength of mind and soul, and the desire to reach out in love.

After all, isn't that what true prosperity is?

TWENTY-FOUR

Worship

The vast majority of spiritually-based people participate in worship as members of a congregation.

Worship is a vital part of our lives. We cannot acknowledge the presence of divine good without it. We cannot absorb divine good without it. We cannot conduct ourselves as spiritually-based people without it.

In fact, every thought, every action is a form of worship, just as it is a part of prayer.

If we believe as described, how then should we worship, beyond the obvious? Is there a place for *communal* worship, and is it even necessary?

Our primary contact with divine good is personal and solitary. No two people, let alone a group, can open themselves at exactly the same moment, receive at exactly the same moment or in the same quantity. It is extremely unlikely that such could even work if this was the focus of our faith, which, of course, it should not be.

It's the same as dreaming. None of us can dream the same dream at the same time. Our individual architectures are too complicated to ever be identical.

Through certain mediation skills we may very well be able to teach others how to calm themselves and find the perimeters of God, but we cannot coach them into the next, and most vital step. That step *must* be made by the individual.

However, gathering together to praise, rejoice, acknowledge and share outreach is also a desirable thing.

Consider a marathon.

Thousands of people on a course at the same time, each with the same purpose—to reach the end. Some are professionals, there to win or better a time. Some want to push their physical limits. Some merely want the camaraderie of so many people attempting to accomplish the same end. Some may even be content to walk, enjoying their surroundings.

At the end people gather to discuss their *individual* experiences over the course.

That's what worship is.

God doesn't *need* to be worshipped in the conventional sense. God has no ego, no desire to be worshipped.

Worship is for us, the people of a faith, the people whose lives are defined by their personal relationships with God and each other.

There can be music, drama, lessons, recollections.

The purpose of communal worship is to share the validity of our experiences, to reach out to others, and to continue on the path.

There is strength in numbers. It has always been so. It will always be so. All gatherings of believers, no matter the elements of faith, may

Worship

draw strength in the combined recognition and adoration of God. Our expressed gratitude to one another for the sheer existence of the God of eternal perfection and divine good should reinforce our potential in this world. This is all worship should be.

We must be wary of vanities. We may believe our way is a better way. With personal successes may even come the desire to extend lessons to others, or to evangelize. But is this really worship?

Our objective in worship is the same as *acknowledgement*, the first of the steps to receiving grace. Our objective is to live with our faith every day in every circumstance, and to do what is ours to do.

As our faith progresses, we will rejoice in mutual successes, offer compassion and tangible assistance to those who may be struggling, re-energize ourselves to go about our business. We will find the kinship of souls, regardless of our differences, seeing nothing of our human experience rises to the prospects of spiritual nourishment.

No hierarchy exists in these things. There is no good, better or best, nor should there be any enterprise beyond what is described in our faith. We do not clamor to be seen or heard. We do not preach the faults of others. We do not uphold our beliefs above any other.

And when we come together as *doers*, we elevate the efforts of all others, love one another, comfort one another, and affirm all may draw near to the ultimate benevolence of the universe should they be so inclined.

The paradox of any faith system, including this one, is the more it is ingrained in tradition, the more resolute its practitioners are in its teachings, the more it strays from its own original heart, the greater the temptation and ease with which it can become the *only* way or the *right* way in our hearts and minds… and what we believed in the beginning becomes diluted and stagnant.

Certainly we understand many have created impediments to the wonder of God through their beliefs in how God works, what their relationship to God consists of and how they are to respond. We know there are practices which have always been and will always be ineffective because they are contrary to God's function, misspent time and energy, just as we know and acknowledge the sensitivities others have to their own practices.

We also know we are apt to be misunderstood and even criticized because what we believe is contrary to what others believe, and time and energy defending ourselves is just as misspent as any other discipline in any other form. Nor should we seek to be in any environment where we are not welcome, though the bulk of history clearly shows service under any banner or none at all is nearly always accepted.

But we are to engage with others of different faith systems in worship. It is not our intention to build churches of our own. We may meet in groups to discuss practices and possibilities, or unite in service, but there are sufficient avenues of worship already at hand. We need nothing new to *acknowledge*. We need nothing new to share. We need nothing new to *believe* what we believe.

We do not even have to speak our beliefs. We know what we know and what we are to do. We join in praise and reverence.

We do this for several reasons

First, the creation of groups inevitably leads to business beyond what we need to function.

We need no organized structure or order. We need no leadership or chain-of-command. Every enterprise requires management, of course. Every enterprise requires finances, facilities, and people to carry out its work. Inevitably, every faith system becomes a *business* in some fashion.

But we will create no such order because it is not required. We contribute to groups that include us. We serve in whatever capacity we choose, or are asked to serve. We are grateful for these environments. We support them financially.

Yet we should not seek to occupy ourselves beyond the worship experience, even to propagate our own teachings—or especially to propagate our own teachings.

The simplicity of our faith is due solely to the simplicity of God, and that is where our whole worship attention should be.

Secondly, such things are distractions from our purposes.

Worship

The business of God is simple. It is virtually impossible for any two people, never mind hundreds or thousands, even like-minded people, to create an entity without it becoming a distraction—even a hindrance. Time is always better spent than building a structure, literally and figuratively, for our faith.

No matter how noble, how benevolent, how rational and sane such purposes seem at the time, we cannot allow ourselves to be caught up in plots and plans, no matter how inspired, that distract us from what we are to do as individuals for the causes of grace. Certainly, we may pool our efforts for service beyond what we can achieve as individuals. Yet we must also acknowledge our natures often act contrary to the prescribed end.

As children some of us had clubs for camaraderie and entertainment. How long was it before differences of opinion led to bickering, and bickering to the end of our objective? Are we as adults so different?

Thirdly, we share this homage with others for genuine kinship, and so we will remain non-judgmental and earnest in our love of all.

Our faith is simple: acknowledge, absorb, act. The first and the last can be done in any reverent environment, and that is where we should be.

All spiritually-based people share a kinship that should (and could) surpass all misunderstanding. We have allowed lesser elements of every faith system—and, in fact, in many cases these elements have *become* the faith system—to elevate our differences to the point of compliance and noncompliance as *truth* and *heresy*.

This should not be. Of course, we are not naïve. Two candidates for any position or office strive to delineate the differences between them. Any two people of disagreement seek to declare their positions in contrast to the other. In nature, two males compete for the acceptance of the female by everything from song, dance and mortal combat. Humankind cannot seem to help but wave the flag of self when each has a different perspective.

Yet the rational in us will always direct us to *commonalities* should we thwart the tenor of our emotions, and all parts of

our lesser selves, by our spiritually-based practices, and allow it to be so.

For in the beginning of all things, in the creation of all religions and spiritual processes, all who believe in God, worship God. Name, gender, personality and provinces notwithstanding, God is still God.

TWENTY-FIVE

Evangelism

We hear the word *evangelism* used frequently, more often than not in relationship to certain faith systems. Evangelism is the means through which certain principles are taught. All believe demonstration by example is better.

At its best, evangelism is teaching, reaching out, helping.

Evangelism, like all forms of information, is essentially selling a point-of-view.

This assertion is not to denigrate evangelism, but simply to point out a difference between espousing a set of beliefs and merchandizing it.

What is the difference?

First, as in worship, evangelism inevitably leads to bureaucracy. There is no fundamental harm in this. All of us have organization in our lives; our day-in, day-out routines, our work, our worship, even our play. The means in which we go to God involves structure. We cannot exist without it.

Our outreach is self-contained. Our outreach is fueled by the causes of grace. Once we divert our attention from outreach to fueling our outreach from ecumenical sources, we also divert ourselves from the grace that has *saved* us. To divert ourselves from grace for any purpose is still a diversion from grace, and is profitless.

Others joining in the causes of grace is wonderful, and it is also logical a single teacher may inspire many others. But the *one* must first and foremost execute and maintain all spiritual bases in order to be a creature of grace.

Life is not a solitary pursuit. Grace is. We do not remove ourselves from kith and kin because of it. But we must in order to be enriched by it. Our *aloneness* with God is what allows us to be better friends, partners, neighbors.

Secondly, evangelism inevitably leads to *conditional service*.

We are here because of what we believe, and we want you to believe as we do.

Make no mistake. Service is service. Any good done is good done. It doesn't matter who does it or what the underlying motivation may be.

However, it is nearly impossible to believe in evangelism as an active part of any faith system without ultimately dealing in rightness, wrongness, and the necessity of *adoption* or *conversion*.

All faith systems are based upon ideas. All faith systems espouse the relationship between ourselves and God. All who believe seek to share their beliefs. But in sharing a particular belief, we so often fail to acknowledge there are *conditions*, even if unspoken. And that always extrapolates to the unpleasant results of nonbelief.

These *conditions* define the crux of these beliefs, and cannot help but create a mindset that encompasses a structure through which these beliefs are advanced, and a conditional response to those who do not share those beliefs. Certainly, those who may not believe are still served. But those who *do* believe are served more readily. Human nature allows us to respond more favorably to someone who is engaged than someone who is resistant. God's nature does not.

This invariably moderates the purity of God's grace.

Our belief has conditions, too.

Evangelism

In order to receive grace one must go to God and claim it. Grace isn't going to rain down on you or strike you from afar. Grace isn't going to magically materialize in time of need or rescue you from misfortune. But once sought, it will be received. And once received, it is the most powerful force in the universe.

Another *condition* is in order to grow in grace it must be dispensed, or what has been held will evaporate, and what is able to be held will not grow. Just as food is converted into energy, grace must be converted into spiritual energy or else the results of our intake will become as sedentary as unused muscles until the intake itself barely sustains us.

There is no prerequisite to claim grace. Obviously, our practices will define us. If a thief seeks grace and continues to be a thief, then he has not found genuine grace, or else he would no longer steal.

But the *conditions* as described are simple, and require no fashion or form beyond the acts themselves.

We seek to display the spiritually-based life in our behavior and our deeds. Nothing else is as powerful.

So how we are to interpret the evangelism we encounter, and how are we to evangelize, if we evangelize at all?

First, (and again), we must understand the way we believe God works is contrary to many other faith systems. This is illustrated, perhaps even more so, in many of those faiths that practice evangelism.

In prescribing the conditions through which God is reached, little room is left for open thought. A step-by-step process allows for little variation. The concepts are more important than the way of life that should result from such understanding. The methodology has become more important than the end result—or the end result cannot possibly be achieved without this methodology. Of course we believe our methodology is crucial to fruition, but we also *believe* in the originality of every individual.

We realize this without judgment and level no criticism, but we do acknowledge the simple measurement of it—if the common good is served to a greater extent than the sum of the conditions set forth.

If more energy is spent on the process than is delivered to the common good, the *process is actually being evangelized and not divine good.*

Secondly, we cannot teach or preach anything that does not work for all, and the primary manifestation of its viability is through *our* lives and *our* service.

If our faith does not work for us, then we cannot adequately convey how it might work for others. If we are not embarked on the long, gentle flow toward *perfection*, even in the knowledge we can never achieve it in this world, we certainly cannot presume to teach its benefits.

Nothing is more important than the one-on-one relationship with God. We can help others in the process we advocate, but we cannot do it for them, nor can we do it *with* them in the customary sense. Opening oneself to grace is an individual process with individual results.

None is excluded. None is denied. There are no rites to be performed to gain access.

Certainly, there are steps. Of course there cannot be a positive result without these steps. But the steps are merely steps, and not the end. One does not plant the flag halfway up the hill and say *see what I have accomplished!*

Each step is between one and *the one*, and every success is between one and *the one*.

Those who try until they succeed, and receive grace, then know their own way.

Sometimes it is to ski and fall, to try again and move farther and fall. Eventually one will ski and not fall. This does not mean one will never fall again. It means simply one contains the knowledge to succeed, and will ultimately succeed.

To many, receiving good is an abstract concept. It is far simpler to pray to the great void, hoping something internal will change, or God will somehow reach down—or when this doesn't happen, we are at fault.

Though obvious, and true of every faith system, **our lives reflect the potency of our *God*.** Only through grace can we find the spiritual wherewithal to alter the lives about us, and this will come by example.

If anyone should ask us how we are able to find the joy we have, the sense of well-being, the desire to aid, the effectiveness of service, *then* we tell them. We tell them of our belief and our practice in the simplest of terms.

We tell them of acknowledgement. We tell them of absorption. We tell them of contribution. That is all. And if not asked, we say nothing. We *do* everything.

It is fruitless to sermonize about anything not readily apparent in true, pure *goodness.*

God is the endless fountain. We are the cups and the water bearers.

God is the source. We are the rills through which it flows.

God is God. We are the fortunate sojourners and *receivers* of divine good.

Like children, we learn to drink.

We cannot teach others *how* to drink in any specific sense. We merely display how we became more whole.

This requires no preaching from the mountain, no soapbox, no promise, save what we believe to be true, and certainly no threat of condemnation.

This requires nothing but ourselves for dispensing what we believe.

Though we may certainly believe what is right for us is right for all, we do not expect anyone else to *change* in order to receive the benefits of what we have learned, and what has worked for us.

To accomplish this, we need not say anything at all.

The key to the spiritually-based life is how *grace* manifests in us.
We *must* be changed, or else what we have imported is not grace.
What we believe is a reflection of ourselves…the face we wear.
What we believe *plus* what we do is who we truly are.

TWENTY-SIX

A More Perfect World

How often have we heard someone say, or said ourselves…
in a perfect world…It has become a platitude, empty and threadbare.

Sometimes it is said wistfully, longing for something we feel cannot happen, or regretting something we could not or did not mitigate or stop at the time. The world is not a perfect place, and there is very little we can do about it.

More often than not, dismissal of the world as imperfect, is a kind of conceit, an excuse to accept a status quo that does not serve all equally.

We use it to explain (and accept) why something is the way it is.

In a perfect world, I would see another's point-of-view and have less room for disagreements.

In a perfect world, I would have more energy, would not be so stressed, would have more time for my family, would not struggle so, would have a stronger faith, would be able to help others more.

In a perfect world, there would be no war, no hunger, no disease.

What we are really saying is, In a perfect world, I would live a more spiritually-based life.

The world will never be a perfect place, just as we will never be perfect people. Yet as spiritually-based people we need to alter our perspective and change our thinking. For in our acceptance we are admitting our environments cannot improve, or *we* cannot create any improvement.

Even as we realize *the perfect world* will never come, we can never use it as justification for spiritual inertia. We cannot limit ourselves just as we cannot limit God. We should have already come to understand *we* are the only limitations of God. The limit of our capacity to receive grace. The limit of our capacity to be good and do good. The limit of our capacity to seek God, find God, and reflect God.

We do not seek the *perfect* in our world. We seek the perfect in our God.

We need to revise this phrase to in a more perfect world, and transform it from an empty wish to a conviction, and more, to a complete way of being.

We must learn to consider our every thought and action in relationship to its relevance to the spiritually-based life. We must become so in tune with ourselves and with God that this becomes a natural process, an almost instinctive process.

Why should we do this? Why should we *work* at having a greater spiritual foundation in our lives? Why is the present not good enough?

What's in it for us?

Enduring peace. Consider everyone you know or have ever known. Name those you honestly and wholly believe are at true peace with themselves, the world, those around them, and their environments. Name those who did not fret, who did not struggle with their interior selves (which always translates to a struggle with the *exterior* world). Name those who labor against circumstances far more than they should. Were they truly at peace?

Now consider those who at times are visibly imperfect, but who are quick to befriend, quick to serve, quick to come to the aid of others, quick to be a pacifying presence in the midst of potential chaos.

If we truly believe in a perfect God, we must also believe in the betterment of all.

> **Why do we seek to move toward perfection, knowing we cannot achieve it? For the same reason we live, knowing some day we will die.**

All we have are counted years. Time itself, like eternal perfection, does not care how we spend it. Time will pass regardless of what we do. It will not wait for us. Only our spiritual lives make a difference.

We need to move toward **idealism**, and do so constructively. We need to view everything in us and about us in terms of what **could** and **should** be. If we do not allow ourselves to see the possibilities—in ourselves, in others and in our world—then we've already eliminated them as prospects.

Seeds are not planted with the certainty of fruit, but because of the potential for fruit. As we learn what it takes for the fruit to come forth, our faith that fruit will indeed come forth becomes more tangible.

Any *reality* changes when it is impacted by those with a spiritually-based purpose. Want and need are diminished by those who provide. Anxiety, in all its forms, is eased by those who salve. Peace blossoms when none seek enemies. Communities, great or small, are made amicable by the gentle hearts of its inhabitants.

When we believe whole-heartedly in the potential of our spiritually-based efforts, our efforts cannot help but bear spiritually-based fruit. Perhaps not always. Perhaps not on every single occasion. But tangibly and noticeably. The effort may be small and confined to an anonymous area of our encounter, but it matters. It will always matter.

What we are missing in this world is that divine sense of awe and wonder. What we are missing in this world is the potential for the furtherance of all from a truly spiritual basis. What we are missing in the world is the divine intention of grace.

We must develop a sense of divine expectation. We must remove the barriers we impose upon ourselves to help make our world a more perfect place. We must remove the walls we have erected between ourselves and others of different faiths, different cultures, different perspectives, different ideologies, different *truths*.

We begin where we began, a vital relationship with God. We know how to reach God, we know how to receive good, and we know what this does for us in terms of our internal constitution. This prompts outward changes in how we see and treat all we encounter. And this leads to a more perfect world at whatever level we are capable of.

We translate the divine goodness we receive from God to the world we encounter. We do this because it is our function, not God's. Every single area of need or neglect, every absence of goodness, every want or lack upon this planet is something we can change for the better. For the most part, the world is as it is because we made it that way. Every bit of optimism, every ounce of love, every soothing word, every positive deed, is ours to have and share, through God. And yes, this would be enough.

These tenets and their like have been preached since the beginning of free thought and language. Yet for the most part, they remain unfulfilled. They are like the phrase *in a perfect world* itself...a surrender to some discouraging realism we, too, have created. We have to know differently, and by now, we should know.

There are several reasons why they remain unfulfilled: lack of time, lack of energy, lack of practice, lack of true purpose, lack of wherewithal, lack of commitment…so many other focal points around us.

What we have now learned is the sheer necessity of such actions in order to maintain and enrich the spiritually based life. We simply cannot grow in goodness unless we do so.

We are aware many of the world's faith systems *let us off the hook.* We are told service is a vital part of each. But often we listen, *hearing* what needs to be done without ever having to perform. No one is the wiser.

In our belief, we already comprehend (and hopefully have taken to heart), we will never receive the whole abundance available to us unless it is dispensed along the way. Our *salvation* is the world's *salvation.*

The cup of our soul is filled with grace in whatever measure we can hold. As our practice becomes more effective, our cup becomes fuller. But only when we allow (even strive) to have others drink from our cup does the cup itself expand.

Whatever the future of our beloved Earth, it will be of our creation. Whatever happens to those who inhabit it, we will have a hand in it, however small or large. Whatever good may come, we will provide it. Every misdeed is ours to correct. Every unpleasant aftermath is ours to moderate and allay.

We broaden our vision but narrow our focus. We do not see an ilk, but a need. We do not see a cause, but a remedy, or at the very least, a comfort. We do not see a person at all, but the grace of our God.

It begins with us and moves beyond us, and whether there will be good or ill will depends upon us. No one or no thing determines what emanates from us except us.

Rare and thin is the remedy that comes without some action by spiritually-based people. Because of this, we should be encouraged.

To seek the ideal is to see the conceivable good in all things.

This process gives us peace. The loving willingness to heal ourselves and move forward leads us toward the divine.

As with all practices, the effort becomes easier, and we will be able to accept greater challenges, or at the very least to deliver more of what we receive to those around us, and a purer form of what we have received in the past.

There is nothing we cannot affect positively. There is nothing beyond our reach. There is no one anywhere who cannot be uplifted by some action of ours. More, we see things in a new light and for its potential, not how it can affect us negatively.

We will find innumerable ways to raise the standard close at hand. It will be a part of our spiritual practices.

As we become *more* **perfect people**, we create a *more* **perfect world.**

TWENTY-SEVEN

Sincerity

Often times it seems we have replaced **sincerity** with **civility**. We are **nice** to people instead of being **kind** to people. We have trained ourselves by rote and habit to be pleasant without any real feeling or action behind it.

Does it really matter?

Nearly every environment in which we are a part—our work, our schools, our churches, our neighborhoods, even our homes—allows us to go through the motions of sincerity without ever having to *be* sincere. We can exchange pleasantries and compliments with nearly everyone we encounter and still remain uninvolved.

This is understandable. We encounter many people we do not know, and a smile and a nod of the head may be sufficient. But even the more casual interactions with strangers can and should contain a spiritual basis. When we open a door for someone it is a positive act regardless of whether we know them or how we might feel at the time. We often act based upon good manners.

Even with those we call *friends* our exchanges are very close to the surface. We are content with the superficial. We do not want to delve deeper, even if they obviously desire it, because that implies a certain responsibility to respond. We want to keep things nice and easy. We do not want to complicate matters.

We choose to remain ignorant because in ignorance we are shielded from reaching out, stepping in, or even asking *how can I help?*

There is spiritual danger in this.

Sincerity is the tenor of all actions in the spiritually-based life. Grace is the thrust of goodness, and sincerity is the note upon which all goodness is carried.

How we truly feel does impact our actions. The feeling behind any action must be sincere goodwill or else we risk a part of our spiritual selves.

Why?

First, all genuine goodwill comes from grace.

Grace is our prompt, our authenticity. We must have grace in order to provide.

The less grace we receive, the more difficult it is for us to generate goodwill. When we receive, we are invigorated and fresh. When we receive, we are more sincere.

We may still respond. But when we respond without first receiving, we lose spiritual energy, and so our sincerity suffers. Without sincerity, our action becomes half-hearted. As our spiritual energy fades, we may stop responding at all until we can revive ourselves through God. If we do not seek grace frequently enough, the process stagnates.

Goodness for goodness' sake is wonderful. But when we respond by simple habit we lose spiritual *satisfaction*. Is the act more important than how we may feel? Of course. But without love from grace, our purpose is diminished until our interest wanes. Without sincerity, we ultimately lose. Without sincerity, we ultimately fail.

Secondly, we risk falling into the habit of *faking* it.

Sincerity

We can do good works without any real feeling at all. We can be civil and non-confrontational and few would know the difference. But this can stifle and impede spiritual growth, because we have essentially opted to leave God out of it. What we do is bereft of any true spiritual energy. It becomes something self-generated. Eventually any impetus toward goodness runs out of steam.

We may even believe ourselves to be upon the spiritually-based path, and adhere to all the principles we have learned. But if we continue to *do*, even under the best intentions, without the prescription of sincerity through grace, we will have no joy. Even if we are able to perform as frequently as necessary, our spiritual selves suffer from the absence of interior goodness. If there is no or limited feeling *in* there is no or limited feeling *out*. Again, our efforts will decline.

This also has repercussions to our outlook.

At times we may find we are only truly sincere when we believe someone is sincerely wrong. We find the ease of embracing honest feelings only when we find lack in someone else. It is so much easier than finding the good in another, to have genuinely positive feelings about them, to understand differences.

Without sincerity, we begin to doubt the reasons for our actions. Why feed, when the hunger will continue? Why embrace, when the addiction is still there as powerful as ever? Why assist, when the other should have sufficient resources to fend for himself? Why build, when adequate care to preserve will not be taken? Why cover, when the other will uncover as soon as the rain or cold passes?

The cycle of blessing is corrupted into something else entirely.

We do what we do because grace impels us to act, and if sincerity is absent, then we have not truly received grace.

Above all, we must consider the feelings of others.

Our sincerity helps keep others positive. It validates their roles in our lives and in the world. It reinforces the goodness we wish for them. It helps alleviate their doubts and fears. It lifts them up.

Our sincerity demonstrates the value of grace, the value of outreach, the value of such efforts, the value of all. Without sincerity, motives can be doubted. Without sincerity, efforts may be dulled.

Consider the orator, and from any arena. The words spoken may inspire us. The words spoken may move us. Yet we also see in many of these promises in exchange for consideration. *If* you do this (for me), *this* will happen for you. It is a shallow promise, devoid of real altruism because the speaker's desire for gain supersedes all else.

We do not have to question the sincerity, because in genuine sincerity the words would never be spoken. The action would have already taken place, in some fashion and at some level. There is no quid pro quo in grace. There is no condition that need occur before help is given, except within each receiver of grace. There is no *if you, then I...*

The simple fact is many need, and first and foremost is to be viewed as worthy of goodness—and sincerity is the means through which we affirm this in others. To treat all need as worthy is sincere.

Many people crave sincerity so much they are satisfied with civility and are hurt when they realize the difference.

Each of us has realized some disappointment in this. It may not mean long-term debilitation, but each of us has been dealt a dose of insincerity. Remember ourselves as young and having affection for someone who made us believe the affection was mutual. Insincerity showed us differently. Have we ever received praise from someone only to later discover they derided us behind our backs? Have we ever been betrayed by someone we cared deeply about, and discovered how hollow their regard for us was?

Just as all grace comes from God, true sincerity comes from grace, and the fruits of grace cannot be demonstrated without it.

When we treat someone as special and unique, then we must believe they are special and unique, to help *them* believe they are special and unique.

Sincerity

We must be sincere in all things and with all people, and in a positive, constructive way. We must display our spiritual structure in all our relationships, however transient or ingrained, and no matter how much we may disagree with them. We must elevate them in our hearts and minds to the place where we long to be, and where they are entitled to be. We must have faith in all sincere effort, even if poorly or suspiciously received.

We must **sincerely** provide **all** with dignity and understanding. We must **sincerely** want the **best** for them, and be prepared and give them only our best.

All good things must be sincerely done.

Insincerity is a form of apathy, of uncaring, and there is no spiritual basis for this mindset.

Of course we all realize we could labor from dawn into the night in service. We also realize the impracticality of this. Our lives, our families, our work, our play, all have great value in our constitutions.

The key is no matter what we do, how much or how little we do, and whenever we do, we must be sincere.

More, we must be sincere in **all** actions and dealings, from the merest smile to the most mundane tasks. We must be sincere with everyone always.

The spiritually-based person must have a mindset, a heartset, at all times that reveals our relationship to God. We are reflections of grace and divine good. And anyone who crosses our paths is to be a beneficiary of this.

To be sincere in all things is the greatest testament we can provide to our foundation. God has provided us free access to abundant good. We learn to receive it in ever-increasing supply. This **has** to alter us. If it doesn't, then we are kidding ourselves. If we cannot be sincere, then something in our method is lacking.

We must break the habit of civility for its own sake, not toward anger, of course, but away from indifference. We must **sincerely**

care in all we do, and do this without fear of loss or expectation of reciprocity.

We must love for love's sake, and let its fruit—sincerity—nourish those who pass our way just as it nourishes us.

TWENTY-EIGHT

The Opposite of Love

Hate is not truly the opposite of love. Often the most powerful emotions are not what hinder us. The opposite of love is the quiet subterfuge of **apathy**.

In nearly every case, indifference is the enemy of love. Indifference is the counterpart to caring, and the must cruel response of all.

Indifference is also the primary indicator between actually receiving *grace* and any other attitude that gives us a temporary sense of well-being. One simply cannot receive the grace of God and remain indifferent.

We are all indifferent at times. We have become inoculated against the trauma of the *real world*. Bodies on a battlefield or after any attack, natural or unnatural, no longer bother us for more than a few moments.

Images of people starving to death in some faraway place no longer bring us to tears.

The aftermath of some horrific natural disaster no longer affects us except for a brief shaking of the head or silent prayer.

Perhaps it has always been this way for some. Is it worse now? Are most of us so *numb* to these things we can see a corpse without flinching?

At other times our apathy is not for those enduring extreme suffering. It is for those we see daily, those who may simply rub us the wrong way. We have failed to remember people evolve only from external stimuli, and some are not yet ready to unlearn fear—of change, of not being heard, of losing their positions in whatever venue—and some wear negativism like a cloak.

No, we are not going to point an accusing finger at anyone. We are not going to hold others accountable for our inactivity. We are not going to blame someone else for propagating our disregard. Nor are we going to blame our cultures, our communities, the stringent pace and stress of *life* for our ability to look into the faces of suffering without blinking, just as we are not going to make excuses.

We are going to acknowledge, without accusation, our spiritual selves have not been adequately fed.

Our *faiths* have not engendered our own incumbency in a strong relationship with God—we are singly and individually responsible for healing ourselves and then those about us.

Our *cultures* have not underscored the beauty of ultimate cooperation—as a whole we are better than our component parts.

Our *societies* have not espoused the blessings of service, at least partly because its leadership, for whatever reason, does not truly serve—we are only as *good* as those we choose to guide us.

Our *communities* seem content to run the business of the community without regard for all its citizenry, and in fact, probably lack the resources to do so—it has never been the *business* of a community to first serve the least, and then move upward.

And our *friends, associates and families* all seem to operate by routine, without the deep and profound heart of love as its engine—where *life* is often a gauntlet instead of a repose, and we don't seem to know how to change it.

It **all** emanates and flows from the grace of God, and the profound results of such grace—to love deeply—to lead by example—to contribute without complaint—to serve unconditionally, and without notice.

Those who claim to be at peace, yet show little in the way of compassion and caring, or lack any genuine altruism, or any contribution to the common good, are misleading themselves and others as to the reality of God and their relationship to it.

This does not mean they are to be judged. This simply means we understand grace is the catalyst for all good and others may not. This also means we are to respond regardless.

One simply cannot be a creature of grace and continue to remain indifferent without realizing it and making adjustments.

As always, we first look to ourselves.

We will always struggle with our thinking and our emotions. Yet if we do not feel a fundamental, though evolving, internal change as we learn to go to God and receive abundant good, then we must also realize our efforts are unsuccessful. It is not the end of the world. If we are on a diet or exercising and we step on a scale to find we have lost no weight, then we realize something is off. Obviously there are physical reasons why the results aren't as desired, but it is a physical impossibility to decrease caloric intake and increase metabolism and not lose weight, if we are overweight to begin with.

Any true spiritual character will make us aware of our place on the spiritually-based path.

We will either try again or we will not. Grace cannot help but create good. In whatever doses we are able to manage, and the continued practice of reaching toward the divine, progress cannot help but be made. Any forward momentum at all moves us beyond where we were.

It is the same with grace. We will either continue or we will stop. There is no spiritual basis for indifference, and we cannot practice indifference in anything and claim a spiritually-based life.

Secondly, we will recognize these absences in others.

We do this without self-righteousness or opinions of lack, but we will see it. It will manifest itself in our world, our communities our families, our neighbors and friends, and even in other religious practices, and we will know it.

Faith does not make us ignorant. Faith makes us more perceptive.

It may seem like a contradiction that as we are able to see more, we must somehow view what we see without judgment or mortification, but perception and assessment are not the same as judgment. It may strain our senses that we instinctively *know* the lack of true caring, and may even cause spiritual crises within ourselves as we seek the divine without naming fault in another, but there is a reason for this.

We must do what others fail to do.

Whether someone claims a spiritual basis for these attitudes and acts does not matter, though it is perhaps more disheartening when those exhibiting such traits advance themselves as having a specific relationship with God. There are many and will always be many who claim to serve God or the greater good, yet *whose actions and inactions always seem to carry some indifference toward those who disagree or do not comply or seek to sway others toward a less-than-spiritual perspective in the guise of spirituality.*

There is no spiritual basis for indifference, and we cannot practice indifference in anything and claim a spiritually-based life.

By now we know what is *of* God and what isn't. It is not our place or right to name anything as a fault or flaw, but we will be aware of anything contrary to the fundamental goodness available to us all.

So how should we respond?

First, we do what is ours to do.

We receive and we give. We do so because it is our place to do so, because we can and because we are compelled by grace to do so, and do so lovingly. We do this because we *want* and *need* to do so in order to feed our souls.

We do this regardless of the *who* or *why*. We do this simply because it is *our way*.

The spiritually-based path makes us *desire* to do these things.

Secondly, we are never to become sources of conflict to those who are indifferent.

We are never going to change the indifferent by confrontation, especially those who have become empowered by it. We do not name them. We do not point them out. We merely go about our business *without* them.

There may be times when we are asked by some *why* we do what we do. We may be challenged by the indifferent because they do not want to be cast in a poor light. They would rather provide *reasons* for their indifference than claim it.

Because in reality, indifference is a form of disdain.

We must also acknowledge there are innumerable organizations and individuals whose sole function is to serve the common good. They exist to aid the needy, the helpless. Would that each of us be so inclined.

As in all spiritually-based practices, we *do*, not merely because we are spiritually compelled to do, but because it is the transmogrification of the divine.

Indifference is an entrenched byproduct of the absence of grace. It is the uneaten bread, the unsipped water, the unfelt warmth, the unacknowledged liberation, the unclaimed love.

And when indifference is opposed by an outside source, it will become combative in its bearer, and will be defended and clung to like any other impediment. A thief will cling to his gains just as a tyrant will cling to power, because that is what holds them body and soul.

Indifference is the narcotic that binds those who believe but do not serve.

We will sometimes find dismay in caring when there are others in closer proximity, with greater resources and even a function to do what we will do. They may not lift a finger, and may even seek to thwart us.

But this is only a reminder of what we are to do, and that they have not yet learned or believed, and perhaps never will.

And because we *know* and they do not, we do what we are bent to do because we can no longer ignore what we know, and because only by our actions can others know.

It is ours to seek and do, no matter what anyone else does.

We cannot claim to love divinely, in whatever portion we have received, and remain indifferent to anyone within our grasp.

It would be better for us to say we simply do not love.

TWENTY-NINE

Spiritual Introspection

Despite its difficulty at times, one of the greatest values in what we believe is we **must** turn within in order to find God. We find God through consciousness and awareness, and must be attuned to God's potency in order to receive.

This process also helps us with our internal evaluations and refinements. It can be painful, and a part of our humanity would wish to avoid it, but through these internal assessments we find our potential. A disorganized closet only gets worse. A hard-to-reach corner does not become cleaner with time.

The reality that we must learn to view every aspect of our thinking and our conduct in terms of its spiritual basis creates the need (and desire) for spiritual introspection.

This is not to punish ourselves, or to find fault with so much of what we do or fail to do, but rather to reduce the impact the psychic detritus we harbor has upon our souls.

Haven't we all rationalized something we know is not good for us into something more palatable to our egos? Haven't we all shrugged off our errant thoughts and actions toward others as something tolerable or *only human* or *just the way things are?*

Haven't we all taken the concept of *everything is okay* to the inevitable conclusion that certain actions or inactions are excusable in the context of general acceptance?

As we grow with God, our spiritual sensibilities also grow and we cannot help but wish to cleanse ourselves of contamination. How successful we are in this also determines how successful we are in our relationship with God.

We already know many things. We know in order to commune with God we must open a pathway ourselves. We know in order to receive good we must focus our attention on God and not ourselves. We know in order to receive in greater abundance we must tender good to others.

So, then, we must also know we need to do some mental and emotional housekeeping on a frequent basis.

Again, and despite its difficulties, this is growth. How often have we moved from day-to-day, place-to-place, in some kind of dull routine without so much as a single thought except to focus on the task at hand? How often do we fail to view the passage of time except in hindsight? How often does it seem we've put our lives on some kind of automatic pilot, that we spend most of our time as automatons—that our jobs, our families, even the way we pray and worship is simply maintained by habit and not true experience?

Perhaps even the concept of introspection is alien to us. We have never viewed our thoughts and feelings in any deeper sense. Maybe we have been taught stoicism and acceptance is the way we should behave, or we do not *feel* much at all when it comes to certain environments, and we certainly do not express our feelings except when we can no longer subdue them.

Spiritual Introspection

Many of us have simply never practiced contemplation as it relates to our internal well-being. We move on to the next moment, the next *thing*.

The fact is, however, all humans store what is not expressed, and most of the time this storage is not healthy.

This does not mean that we spew our feelings in any impulsive fashion, or seek to *get things out of our systems* at the expense of others. This simply means every thorny thing within us must be dealt with. **Everything.**

As we seek to take any kind of inner inventory, we might try the following steps:

First, and most simply, we ask *how do I really feel?*

Most of us would declare, *I feel fine.* Are we happy and content? Do we feel we're operating at high efficiency? Is our energy level where it should be? Do we need more rest, more recreation, even more work? Are we in touch and in tune with our families and friends? Is there any tension in our environments (or in us) that needs attention?

Are there obstacles we have been ignoring?

Is there anything keeping us from growing as a spiritually-based person?

If there is nothing, we are on the right course. If there is something, we need to identify it.

Secondly, if we find a thorn, we ask ourselves *what is really bothering me?*

We have already learned we release our anxieties to God during the times we go to God, but we must identify them.

So ask yourself. Do not be afraid to name it. Do not be afraid of what might arise.

What is it in myself that is unresolved? What keeps coming back time and time again?

We all harbor doubts and insecurities. Perhaps we are struggling in our educations or professions. Perhaps our relationships are doused with tensions and other issues. We must go within using everything we've learned to identify any ill feelings toward others or ourselves. We must reconcile these things to the spiritually-based life. Sometimes we must make difficult decisions to move in a completely new direction.

Whatever else we do, we pinpoint it. If we say it aloud, does it ring true? If it doesn't, then it must be something else.

Once we identify a situation or condition, then we can no longer ignore it. We are forced to rectify it.

Thirdly, we resolve.

Are we at odds with someone? We seek to resolve it. We resolve it by understanding and acceptance. Perhaps we have never bothered to understand someone who manages to *get to us*. Once we understand this is a hurdle to our better spiritual selves, the need becomes obvious.

Are we depressed? We seek to resolve it. We resolve it by understanding our own feelings and reaching out for assistance if necessary. Has some event shaken us, or do we have an unrecognized ailment? This also applies to many forms of anxiety. Is it rare of frequent? Do we find ourselves constantly tense or unhappy? We may need the help of a professional.

Are we unhappy about something? Unhappiness with a situation or condition is not the same as depression. Something awry is bringing us down. A great deal of the time this is something repetitive. *I don't know how to deal with my child. I hate my job. My partner and I don't see eye-to-eye about anything any longer. I'm lonely. I'm afraid.*

Are we angry? Is there something stuck there like a pill we cannot swallow? Has someone done something we cannot abide? Has something we thought was consigned to the past risen again to agitate us? Is there a source of needling that appears time-and-time again we have not adequately dealt with? Does something in us continue to fester?

If we are to have a spiritually-based life we must be willing to understand our own inner workings, understand the ways of others, deal with conditions effectively without ignoring them, and have a sense of peace that we are doing all that is necessary.

But if external situations inhibit our spiritual growth, and our spiritual growth is insufficient to resolve them, because the grace we receive is not sufficient remedy, (or because they may involve others who are a continual part of our lives), we must make every effort to alter them.

If our spiritually-based introspection does not change the situation, the situation must change.

If we are abusive, our spiritual growth changes us. If we are being abused, the situation or condition must change.

We must clear the pathway to God. We must be clean in our thoughts and feelings. We must address burdensome feelings we have regarding others. We change environments if it becomes necessary, but we are proactive in every effort to reach God.

It is difficult to move on a crowded sidewalk. Likewise, it is difficult to concentrate on our spirituality with a head full of noise and a heart full of conflict.

Finally, we name *goodness*.

Feelings are not always rational. Sometimes a relatively minor irritation can cloud and overwhelm any sense of good. So we *do the math*. This does not mean we blindly accept awful circumstances that need attention. This does not mean we accept a situation harming us or others. This does not even mean that we try to find a *silver lining* in everything.

It means simply we need to evaluate our growth.

What is good in our lives? What is good in ourselves? What is our fundamental state-of-mind.?As our practices become more frequent, and we are more efficient in them, what has grace done for us? How have our spiritual lives improved?

What do we revere? What do we love? Are we able to love more fully and more completely?

Are we better able to distinguish between the petty or trivial and the things that absolutely require our attention and energies?

Are we becoming better people? Are we more grateful for the things we may have taken for granted in the past? Have the people closest to us seen a change in us?

Are we moving toward an inner life where we can see the good in ourselves and others, where we are able to go about our business with greater understanding, where we are able to serve with genuine caring?

Have we learned to seek answers within that enable us to live, work and act freely? Have we learned what it means to be *a whole person?*

Introspection provides the means through which we are first aware of the productive and the counterproductive elements within us, the perspective through which we assess these things, and the processes we use to either enhance or eliminate them.

It can be no other way. Without the desire and need to do this, we cannot evolve in the spiritually-based life.

THIRTY

Spiritual Rationalizations?

Spiritual growth is a phenomenal thing. We find it easier to be at peace, our focus becomes sharper, we see solutions instead of problems, our contributions to our environments are more potent, our health improves.

Our relationships with those closest to us are bound to change. We all evolve at a different pace and in different ways. Often we will go through a period where we don't seem to communicate well at all, especially if those closest to us do not join us on the same path to the spiritually-based life.

There are times when we need a change of scenery. But we must always *stop* and examine when we feel compelled to change the players.

> We must be aware of, and also be wary of, any thought patterns that allow us to justify doing harm to anyone because of our so-called spiritual growth.

These are **spiritual rationalizations**—not spiritually-based—but excuses to injure under the guise of progress, and are just as poisonous and harmful as those used by some to condone every manner of conflict, demonizing others, self-righteousness, and all other forms of self-justification.

If we choose to stop self-destructive habits because of a *new path*, great. If we do not frequent the same places, or revel in the ways-of-life that have not served us well, wonderful. If it becomes necessary to remove ourselves from groups that fostered unproductive or damaging ways, we will do this. If we find ourselves in need to like-minded companionship, we should do this.

But make no mistake. We *outgrow things*. We do not *outgrow people*.

Rationalization is the internal method we use to validate something our best selves would not allow us to do.

If we lie, we rationalize there is benefit to it. Our better selves would not allow us to get away with that. If we cheat, small or great, we tell ourselves there is a higher reason for it. If we demean others because we believe we are somehow *better* now, we are actually moving away from the spiritually-based path. The spiritually-based path requires us to be more loving, more understanding, more tolerant.

The same applies to so-called spiritual rationalizations. *I cannot have the same friends. I cannot attend the same church. I cannot work at the same place. I cannot stay in this marriage. I must remove myself from what I have known before.*

It may be easier for us to do this. It may make sense. It may even seem like an epiphany: now that I am on a new, spiritually-based path, the old must be swept away.

Granted this entire concept may seem absolutely contradictory. Wouldn't our spiritual evolution require extracting ourselves from past blights? Suppose our relationship with a significant other was founded in drinking, or drugs, or some other lifestyle we can no longer participate in, or even a particular faith system we no longer adhere to in a literal sense?

Suppose our friendships are based upon similar circumstances or bad habits?

Suppose we have been in a work environment where discord is the norm?

What if we have been a thief, an adulterer, a back-biter or gossip, an idler, a radical, seemingly heartless or mean-spirited, a denier, or one who sits in judgment and criticizes almost everything?

Why wouldn't it be better to make a clean sweep? Internally, yes, but that also leads us to a conclusion:

What grace has provided to our evolution is what now grants us the ability to better understand and relate to others without harsh appraisal, and to love without reservation.

Others will make judgments about us. We will not make judgments about them.

Obviously, we must seek to eliminate any toxicity in our lives.

We change our behavior. But we do not abandon the people who have been important to us unless they so choose.

Let us also remember what the spiritually-based life requires of us: a kinder attention to all we encounter.

Relationships will end. Paths will diverge. But the concept we will *outgrow* others is a vanity, and not a part of the spiritually-based life. If people shun us or fail to understand us, or deny us because we seek a more formidable relationship with God that is different from theirs, it will be *their* decision to separate themselves from us, not ours.

Of course, there will be changes. But we cannot use *growth* as a weapon.

In many instances, spiritual rationalizations are also used to keep us from doing spiritual work our growth requires of us.

Though this appears unbalanced, the *knower* must always reach farther than the *unknower*. It is the responsibility of the seeker to be more understanding than those comfortable in their current states of being. At times this does require more effort on our parts, but the effort is a residual of grace and is not to be shunned. In fact, grace should ease the effort to a greater degree than our prior bad habits.

As seekers, making such efforts may seem fruitless, certainly tiring, and tipping the *meet-in-the-middle* scales away from those who may even be spiritually lazy.

But that is the price of the spiritually-based life. More, our faith should actually create a yearning to be the more.

Why? Because the spiritually-based life is not a stepping-off place.

Certainly we will make new friends, have new opportunities. But we do not use our presumed *growth* to remove ourselves from our spouses, families and friends for the sake of a new life. Grace does not create new lives wholesale. We do not overcome malnutrition with one meal. It is an expanding process.
The longing to begin anew is valid. The longing to shed the weightiness of our former lives is understandable. Change is inevitable for us.

Yet to shrug off our commitments to partners, children, friends and others because we believe we have somehow surpassed them is ego, not evolution.

We may not always be in love. We may not always have the type of relationship we crave. But we cannot use our faith as a justification to break bonds simply because there now may be others who are closer to our ideals.

Nothing in our desire to find God, receive grace and dispense goodness allows for self-indulgence in the guise of growth.

Also, merely spiritual sloth would allow for us to move from one partner or environment to the next without justification. Our faith allows us to create solutions, not submit to whims.

We should never sacrifice loyalty to anyone or anything that has been kind to us or enriched us in any way.

Who has loved us, even if not always nurturing? Who has provided for us, even if not always benevolent? Who has given us the means to earn wages, even if not always satisfying or complementary? Who has been a friend to us, even in ways not spiritually-based?

We do not appraise the tree that gives us fruit. We do not appraise the worth of what gives us shelter. And we do not appraise the quality or quantity of what has given us sustenance.

Lastly, to submit to such judgments, however expeditious, represents a never-ending cycle. Superficial connections are transient. There will *always* be someone new who seems to be exactly where we are at any given time. There will *always* be a better mate or a better fit. There will *always* be something better out there.

And this will *always* be transitory.

We will *always* grow at a different pace as others. We will never be in emotional, physical or spiritual lockstep with anyone over the whole course of time. There will always be issues and there will always be the *business* of Life. There will always be matters of the routine and generic to conduct.

Promises are born of affection when that affection is the most intense. When that affection ebbs and flows do our promises disappear?

What if our relationship with God was structured in the same manner?

What if we were denied grace because we had fallen short at any given time?

There are many legitimate reasons for ending relationships, whether with a spouse, a friend, a profession, group or activity.

But at the heart of all these decisions are our reasons for doing this. And beyond all else, we can never use our spiritual growth, or our *presumed* spiritual growth, as such a reason.

If our friends have destructive habits and we no longer want to be a part of this, should we move on? Of course. But we should always reach out. If we have an opportunity to change career directions, should we? Of course. But we do so because it will make things better for ourselves and those in our household. If our partner or spouse wants to sever our relationship because of changes they cannot reconcile themselves to, and we cannot resolve it, we may be forced to let them go.

But if we trivialize our faith to the point where we break connections on the basis that it is *necessary* in order for us to *grow*, then *we* have lost God.

What a tragedy that would be.

THIRTY-ONE

Spiritual Confidence

Confidence is one of the great ambiguities we confront as mortal beings. Confidence can be the worst of vanities, in that we believe we are right or strong or to be upheld because of some lesser, human fortitude. Our confidence can be rooted in the basest of human arrogance because this is how we have lived.

Confidence can be ego and narcissism and sanctimony.

Confidence can be the result of anti-spiritual actions that have provided some gain we relish and want to repeat. Confidence can be a by-product of conquest, domination, deception and coercion.

Confidence can also be one of the greater components of the spiritually-based life.

Anyone, even a new practitioner of the spiritually-based life, will know one from the other.

But how to build and use a more spiritually-based confidence without the intrusion of an ego-based confidence is the key.

There are two primary elements to the more ego-based confidence we all share.

The confidence of success.
We have become more confident in what we are able to do because we have already done many like things with success. If we are successful in our professions, we tend to believe we can continue to be successful. If we have been successful in any arena, we believe this will continue. No matter what form it takes, accomplishment breeds confidence, and the greater our successes, the more confident we are.

This comes from processes, as well as the implication that success breeds success. Someone in business stumbles upon a new product or method and is more successful. A runner finds a different training method and becomes faster. Even a burglar gains confidence when he is not discovered.

However, in nearly all instances, this success is relative. Using our past performance as a guideline, we *are* better. But if the environment changes, or elements within the same environment change, we may not find the same success.

A runner who wins a local 5K may not do as well on a larger stage. A salesperson who hypes a product that does not live up to expectations may find future efforts hindered.

The risk is also two-fold. If the environment changes beyond our control, then we may have an ego-based crisis-of-faith rooted in nothing. Also, if there is a limited spiritual basis to *what got us there originally*, then there can be no underlying goodness. We not only *lose*, we gain nothing in the experience. Like a rainmaker, our success may be sporadic and short-lived. Like a seer, our predictions will not materialize, or be so vague as to defy common sense.

And should we falter or fail, we will lose this confidence.

The confidence others have in us.
This is not always a vanity. The confidence others place in us can help us to grow and better others as we better ourselves. There are always valid reasons for others to have confidence in us.

But at times the confidence of others is a self-fulfilling prophecy. If there are those who believe we can succeed, and enable us to succeed, then our odds are better. They may even look the other way as we stumble until we become what they believe

Spiritual Confidence

we are to be. There is something at stake for them. They need our success to validate their opinions, so in some cases, we will not be allowed to fail.

The support of others is always important. But there must be tangible reasons we inspire such confidence. We are dependable. We are diligent. We incorporate the knowledge of others. We endeavor.

Yet again, there are a couple of risks. The confidence placed in us may based upon completely arbitrary criteria. Some may simply have *the look,* or appear to have *the right stuff.* There is often no step-by-step process in this. Someone simply empowers us through confidence. And our egos allow us to believe in our own efficacy. There may not even be any internal guidelines through which we subscribe to a particular ethic.

The danger is not only to us, but to them, and anyone influenced by these decisions. This is the way of the world, of course, but we are speaking of confidence perhaps not earned, but bestowed.

Also, relying on the validation of others for confidence means there can be a quandary and descent into doubt should that support be withdrawn. We cannot always control if someone has confidence in us, but confidence earned and reaffirmed in good times and bad, is more durable. Confidence granted for superficial reasons can be yanked at a moment's notice, and just as capriciously as it was originally given.

The confidence of others is also gained through dishonesty, subterfuge, guile and deception. We present ourselves as someone who can change an environment for the better while seeking only to serve ourselves.

Ultimately, this will combust, and most will be worse for it.

Spiritually-based confidence is the belief in certainty amid uncertainty.

It contains no ego or vanity, and grace will show us the difference.

Setbacks and doubts hold no long-term effects for us because we believe in substance and the potential for better purposes. We know there will be uncertainty in our lives and in our environments. We know uncertainty will grip us and everyone else throughout the world.

But we will not collapse, and those within our spheres will be strengthened by us.

We will not always know the answers, but we will not relinquish ourselves to doubt. We will be circumspect and introspective, of course, weighing all our efforts in full reckoning of spiritually-based conduct, but we will not *crash and burn*.

Spiritual confidence is akin to faith. We believe a thing to be true simply because we have seen it work.

We have confidence we can go to God and receive grace, because once we have accomplished this, we know it is real. We know we can always return to the *source*, and again see it work. We have confidence through grace we can impact the lives of those around us in a positive way, again because once we have witnessed its viability, we know it is real. We have confidence anything that works for us will work for others, because that is God's true nature, and because grace exists for all.

We are what we are, and do what we do, because we know what we know.

We know the key: we can rely on the aspects of spiritually-based certainties to right ourselves.

The spiritually-based person develops an internal compass that nudges us back to the path. God is always there. Our equilibrium is always there. We should always know, even if it is afterward, when our egos have gotten in the way.

Whether we have the confidence of our peers or our superiors, we will continue to do the better for all concerned.

We are to be confident only as any action corresponds to the rules of the spiritually-based life.

We know everything we think, say or do must be examined in that light. Our confidence can only be in the purity of the prospect, and not anything of our own design.

We are to be successful only as any action corresponds to the rules of the spiritually-based life.

Even if we find *success* in things contrary to the spiritually-based life, a part of us will recognize this and change course.

Any confidence we have must possess these three elements: the reality of God, the reality of grace, and the reality of service.

Anything that meets these criteria will ultimately be found worthy. Anything that does not, regardless of any outward appearance of success, will be found lacking.

Finally, any spiritually-based confidence must be absent of the wish or want for any external validation. We do not need the validation of others to seek and receive grace. We do not need the validation of others to believe what we believe. So then we do not need validation for any act or deed that has the spiritually-based life at its core.

We can have confidence in our actions and our acts simply because they serve a greater purpose. If we help feed a person who is hungry, clothe a person who lacks, house a person who is homeless, or provide the means to help accomplish these things—and even the seemingly trivial, anonymous occurrences such as letting someone more feeble ahead of us in line, offering a gentle hand, a smile, an acknowledgement, a warm greeting—we can be *confident* we are serving the causes of grace.

We can do so without hubris, and with no desire for acknowledgement or recognition because all these things contain the reality of God, the reality of grace, and the reality of service.

The reality of God is eternal perfection and divine good.

The reality of grace is an endless abundance for all who seek it.
The reality of service is that grace is multiplied.

Our belief, adherence, and execution provides us spiritual confidence. Nothing is more powerful and we need nothing more.

THIRTY-TWO

Regret

We all have regrets. We've all done things or failed to do things that return to remind us of our impotence or ineffectiveness or immaturity. It could be something simple, like forgetting an appointment, or something that haunts us, like hurting someone is some particularly cruel way, or personal losses we have incurred along the way.

For the spiritually-based person, rare is the circumstance where all has worked for the best possible outcome, except in retrospect. We make decisions throughout our lives that have far-reaching effects, and as we grow, we realize we could have handled certain situations better. This is not merely a spiritually-based process. This occurs to anyone who grows as a human being.

What is important is how we deal with these recollections. The spiritually-based path cannot help but heighten our sensitivities. It is the same with memories. As we remember, we take note of our former selves and wonder what motivated us at any particular time. We realize our childishness, our lack of discipline, our lack of maturity, even our meanness, without seeking alibis.

The fact that we recall can illustrate spiritual growth. And what we recall is not to be ignored.

Regrets are our teachers. They illuminate the path behind.

We cannot alter the past. We should not dwell on the past or *in* the past, and doing so robs us of the present time. These paths have led us to where we are, step-by-step, and will call to us as we move forward. By changing a step we would have altered our present, but in our present we heal. Our present brings grace to us. Yet this does not mean we should ignore our past poor behavior and the unpleasant results it produced, nor be exempt from its consequences.

There are people who say they have no regrets. Perhaps that's true. Regrets arise unbidden and often unwanted, because our subconscious has unfinished business. And unfinished business must be attended to.

This is especially true of people new to the spiritually-based path or who are enhancing their journey on the spiritually-based path. It is a residue of what we were before and needs to be *cleaned* or else it cannot be resolved. A sooty chimney can only be used so long before it chokes us.

So how can regrets become a more positive influence?

How are we to heed the call of regret without ignoring it, justifying past actions, or worse, chastising ourselves to the point of torment?

How are we to respond to the haunting of our past selves, however innocuous or severe without excoriating ourselves?

There are three crucial factors in effectively dealing with regret.

The first is that regret has value.

Regret illustrates what we have been and makes us look within. It requires us to ponder things we would not ponder otherwise. It urges us to resolve matters we should resolve to be in a better frame of mind, a better *spirit*. It provides the means through which we can view previous lack from a stronger perspective.

As we progress in the spiritually-based life, we will also understand one of the values of regret is to show us by changing the past we would also eliminate the lesson to be learned. This does not mean earlier carelessness or callousness can be justified, but it does help us reconcile ourselves to past behaviors. We, as individuals, need some frames of reference of our growth. Our growth should never be at the expense of others, but feeling regret for past actions is an indicator we are growing.

We must acknowledge it. We must understand it. And we must make some effort to resolve it.

Secondly, we must seek to make reparations and restitution to anyone we have harmed in the course of our lives.

Even spiritually-based people continue to make mistakes, hurt others and have regrets. Dealing with mistakes quickly and effectively is a part of our ongoing *redemption*. The more heavy-hearted and incomplete we are when we go to God, the less we are capable of receiving. For our own good we right former wrongs and make peace. As we seek to clear the air, we also seek to unclog the ingress.

Rarely is there a perfect outcome for past action. Yet it is equally important that any effort to *atone* includes embracing and reaching out to the person(s) we hurt. This is for several reasons.

We cannot escape responsibility. Ignorance is not a by-product of spiritual growth. Neither can we forego this part of the process because we are afraid, or simply want to *let it go*. If we are not compelled to take action, then we must question our spiritual growth. We cannot let ourselves *off the hook* without making some effort. Also, we should desire to know, for better or worse, what, if any, were the repercussions to others of our past actions. And we do this regardless of the circumstances at the time, or the circumstances now.

We must make the effort.

We must also understand many others have a *math of harm*. No spiritually-based person can maintain such an account, and we may find others on the spiritually-based path have long forgiven us. But others damaged by our actions may still carry bitterness and resentment with them.

We must accept that reparations and restitution must be made equal to their perceived harm.

Why? Should we submit to the bitter retaliation of another? Should we allow someone else to determine the level of *punishment* we suffer?

Of course not. It is for us to grant them the full measure of redress for themselves, so we may continue with or without their blessing. It is also to grant them an opportunity to search themselves for the capacity to forgive.

The key is for us to erase the footprints of past errors.

We must apologize without self-justification.

We must ask what we may do to set things right.

We must listen even if it becomes painful.

We must offer to do whatever is necessary to part on new footing, even if we are to never to have contact again.

Atonement is such a cleansing process. We do not metaphorically whip ourselves, but rather we allow love to encompass us and those we may have damaged, even if they do not believe us.

We may even discover they, too, have undergone spiritual evolution, and are grateful for the encounter.

Our sincere efforts mean everything.

Finally, we must live with the unchangeable.

There are past actions that cannot be reconciled, either because we cannot reach others who may have been involved, or because they will not hear us, or because they do not believe us, or because their pain is too great.

Suppose we injured someone in an accident where we were at fault. Suppose we actually committed a crime in the process. Suppose our behavior was so cruel there were long-term, catastrophic consequences. These are extremes, of course, but others may hit closer to home.

Suppose we emotionally injured someone in a relationship because of our own self-centeredness. Suppose we intruded into someone else's relationship and damaged or destroyed it, and our own. Suppose we damaged or ended someone's career by artifice. Suppose we betrayed a sacred trust, or lashed out in anger to the point where all contact was severed. Suppose we misled someone so far down the wrong road they have yet to make it back.

We still try. If our efforts are rejected, we seek to understand, we cope, and we forgive ourselves so our scars do not inhibit us. But *only* after we make an honest attempt. We send an email or write a letter if that is the only thing left for us.

We leave the door open. We offer restitution—most times not in actual currency, unless the harm we did had financial repercussions for them—but in spiritual currency, as well. We are willing to hear them, to consider anything they ask of us (even if it proves untenable), and ask for forgiveness.

And we must not make the same mistakes.

Regret serves no worthwhile purpose unless there is a positive outcome. Regret without spiritually-based employment serves as a conscious or subconscious barrier to God, when we go in prayer to receive our good. Regret is a reminder we have internal work yet to be done, followed by external action. Regret means we have an opportunity to help clean up past messes, even if incompletely.

Our perceived failings can and should be used to illuminate our spiritual growth, where we have been, where we are, and where we want to be.

It is our purpose to draw as near to perfection as humanly possible, and the more we achieve, the more we realize we've just scratched the surface.

We must not leave residue to molder. We must not leave refuse in an untouched pile. We must not leave our words of regret unspoken.

We must use all things to bolster our nearness to the divine.

THIRTY-THREE

Forgiveness.

Most of us have always looked at forgiveness as a tool to bring others closer to us, or keep others close to us. Forgiveness is a rich part of the spiritually-based life. We forgive because it is necessary to do so in order to maintain relationships. We forgive because this makes it easier to keep the channels of communication open.

We do not want to *lose* something, so we forgive.

In forgiveness we can bridge the gap between someone we've separated ourselves from, either physically or emotionally. Forgiving someone can help both parties heal and pave the way for new, more holistic encounters. All sojourners on the spiritually-based path forgive.

Yet the primary function of forgiveness, as with all constituent features of spirituality in human relationships, is to cleanse ourselves of every malignancy, great or small, that hinders our approach, and the depth of our approach, and thereby the success of our approach, to God—with or without the cooperation of any other party.

So make no mistake. **Forgiveness is for the forgiver.**

Disfavor toward anyone is a burden. Our thinking is cluttered with angst and bitterness. The hurt we feel permeates everything. Our perspective is jaundiced, and this influences every positive thought we can muster. It's like the detritus in a pond. The water can never be pure until what clouds it is washed away.

This is a yoke of acidity that does not improve with time, does not fade without effort, does not pass into invisibility. Until we forgive, we cannot maintain a spiritual bearing. Until we forgive, we cannot regain our better selves. Until we forgive, we will find ourselves astray no matter what else we do.

Many times we wait, hoping the person who injured us will make some overture. This does happen, of course. How liberated we feel when someone takes this step on our behalf! Perhaps we continue to wait, and in the interim we find our feelings deteriorating to a point actually disproportionate to the act itself. We despair in the vain hope the conditions will right themselves.

At other times we may actually embrace the wound, however irrational, clinging to it as if a treasure, holding fast as if a token, or the only connection we have to someone. We know how unhealthy this is, yet we do it. We become more comfortable with it, even as it blocks our pathway to God. We do this knowing we can never improve until we let it go. We do this as we hope it will somehow miraculously change. We may even torment ourselves because the feelings of shame and guilt somehow make us feel alive.

The solution is we do not have to wait. We forgive. We do not even have to understand why someone did what they did. We do not even have to have the cooperation of another. We forgive.

It is helpful to understand the actions of others, but isn't necessary. It isn't necessary because in such exercises it is often our first instinct to find fault with another, especially in light of the feelings we carry at the time. As we list the *reasons* someone has done something that affected us, these things can cycle and we are again filled with anxiety and bitterness. That accomplishes nothing.

We forgive because we cannot be whole otherwise.

Forgiveness.

We need to disinfect ourselves. We forgive with no expectation of reciprocity. We forgive in silence, without any concurrence with the *offender* if need be. We release the hurt and hard feelings that would otherwise restrain us from grace. We forgive until we can hold this person in our hearts and minds with no ill will whatsoever.

Many times this is easy. As we grow in the spiritually-based life it becomes so much more important to us to maintain an unobstructed channel to God, that we do not want any form of congestion to hamper us. It becomes self-serving, in the noblest sense of the word, to eliminate all barriers between ourselves and the Almighty. This is not for self-gratification, but for a genuine regeneration of the good we wish to nurture. This is not for self-satisfaction, but to begin anew with a clean slate.

We forgive those we love who have hurt us, not as an invitation to be hurt again, but so we may continue to love. If there is ever a cause which requires us to assert ourselves, we know we can do this lovingly, and not from the anger of pain.

If we wish to continue the same relationship, we must forgive so we can again relate to whoever has hurt us. In many cases we are hurt because of the *who* as much as the *what*. We are always more sensitive to the actions of those we care about. These seem to create the deepest wounds.

If we do not forgive, the nature of that relationship will change. If we do not forgive, we cannot help but move farther apart.

Once we have been successful in our unity with God, we will not want anything to alter it. In many ways, forgiveness is a necessity.

Sometimes this is extremely difficult. Sometimes the results are dire. Sometimes there is a very real sense of betrayal. Sometimes there is such a serious breach we cannot immediately fathom or process it. Sometimes we find we must remove ourselves from an environment for a time in order to forgive.

Some of us have been through family court, and know first-hand how the love we once felt for someone has dissolved into acrimony.

And yet eventually we do move on, and then we wonder why we couldn't have moved on sooner because we were so miserable in the interim. Of course, there are steps in this process. It is equally damaging to swallow our pain whole without engagement. Otherwise it will rise again and again. But we often ignore it, do not make a conscious effort to deal with it, to release it, to dispense with it once and for all.

We make ourselves vulnerable to those we have loved the most, and this causes us the most pain. We will still find the way to forgive and allow our love for them to evolve into our greatest desire for their safety, their peace-of-mind, and their happiness. We do not have to be vulnerable to them again in order to share a peace, even if they still harbor ill feelings about us.

There are also times when our hurt is not specifically personal, and due to something that seems to violate our values, our environments, our culture, our sense-of-self. If someone attacks our country, we hurt. If there is a crime in our community, we hurt. If a company closes or moves and our neighbors are put out of work, we hurt. If someone we care about is in the midst of controversy, we hurt. Ironically, the spiritually-based life causes us to suffer vicariously for those who also suffer, though we must be ever mindful of the difference between empathy and experience.

We may even feel our forgiveness would be tantamount to absolution—the parties involved should not escape *justice*—our resolve for certain actions to be taken keeps the fires burning.

Yet who truly suffers for this?

We've all seen court cases where the families of victims are allowed to give impact statements directed toward the accused. All are marked with anguish and an incredible sense of loss. Who could blame anyone for wishing the worst upon the offender?

And yet years later we invariably find the absence of healing, of the closure they so desperately sought to find. We hear statements of forgiving but not forgetting. Is there really a difference?

Does our internal virulence truly punish another? Do our feelings toward another even reach them? And even so, were we able to determine the sentence, or repercussion, or mode of retribution, would this gain us an iota of peace? Or if we feel helpless, and voiceless except in communal pain, would we not merely grow louder, our hostility grow deeper, our desire to castigate swallow us whole? Would this not lead to revenge, the worst of all human depravity—the greatest chasm between the mortal world and the light of God?

What has been gained? Honestly. What part of God has been served?

Should we do this knowing *someday* we will return to God? Should we let these passions run their course until we are left dire wounded and sore?

The absence of forgiveness is a plague upon the soul of the spiritually-based person. It clogs the arteries of the metaphysical heart, and will only grow worse with each passing day—and will not stop until we stop it.

We are compelled to forgive, practically—so we do not suffer, and spiritually—so we may continue on our journey.

This does not mean those about us are immune from the consequences of their actions, or are free to perpetuate behavior that is damaging to themselves or others—even in what would be considered to be relatively minor slights. This does not mean we relinquish our desire for true justice. Nor does it mean we are suitable to determine what the repercussions should be.

This does not mean in forgiveness there is capitulation on our part, or approval of any behavior.

This does not mean we will not guard ourselves more in the future, though this, too, can be a roadblock. This is especially true when the perceived hurt comes at the hand of someone who continues to be a presence in our lives. This does not mean we are to be oblivious to traits and conditions potentially damaging to us. This does not mean we ignore them. This does not mean we must submit to the continued ill tempers or indifferences of others. This does not mean we are to endure an unkind or damaging status quo without complaint…provided we can do so gracefully.

This means that in genuine forgiveness we develop a deeper understanding and are able first to cope with certain actions in the true spirit of love, and then respond in a way that displays our love without judgments. This means we are capable of genuine communication of sensitivities without accusations or reprisal.

― ― ― ― ― ― ― ― ― ― ― ― ―
All perceived harm toward us is just a pause in our persistent path to God. These pauses will endure as long as we allow.
― ― ― ― ― ― ― ― ― ― ― ― ―

For our own sakes, may these pauses be brief

THIRTY-FOUR

Values?

Values is another of those standardized words that has come to mean something other than what it is designed to mean, often actually contrary to its intent.

Literally, *value* is relative worth. A dollar is more valuable than a quarter, gold is more value than silver in the same quantity, good health is more valuable than illness, truth is more valuable than a lie.

Of course, *value* can be subjective. A quarter is more valuable than a dollar for a parking meter when we are in a hurry. An illness is more valuable than outward health if it indicates an underlying condition that needs treatment. A lie can serve a higher purpose if a genuine quality is behind it: *Did you like my gift?*

But this capacity to interpret also allows definitions to be convoluted to achieve certain ends or excuses that are inconsistent with the spiritually-based life.

We hear about *family values,* even as we can become obsessed with everything beyond our homes, participate in activities by choice that keep us away from our families, or adopt roles in which one parent participates more than another, or remain untouched by the many families in distress under our very noses. We see entire families homeless, or in crisis, or one of our own in conflict, and choose not to *see* it—even as we provide every outward picture of unity and wholeness. We do not even attribute the title *family* to a single mother who is totally unprepared to care for her child. At times our families are in such disarray we prefer to create a front rather than deal with reality.

We hear about *moral values,* even as we excuse ourselves and others for the sake of business or pleasure or politics, from behaviors such as greed, lust, bias and bigotry, and the pursuit of influence. We claim to have moral values even if they or we are not overtly unkind and belong to a faith-based fellowship, and have all other outward signs of *goodness,* yet at heart seek the denigration of others, or the upper hand, or some elevated status. We pretend to function by some *moral* code we preach, but do nothing to exhibit the code beyond words. We are so able to overlook avarice among the stalwarts of our societies, great or small, as long as it serves us.

We hear about *religious values* (or *Christian values*), even when the material effects of our lives, our jobs, our positions in the community, or the absence of basic beneficence is more visible than the better elements of our faith. We meet and gather and praise each other for such *belief,* when we are just as eager to fault those who do not share our *belief,* and place more value upon our *rightness* and their *wrongness* than either mutual recognition or mutual service—or our own independent service regardless of *belief.* We are not required to serve the *sinner* beyond our evangelism, nor the wounds that are self-inflicted, nor the potential goodness of our political *enemies.*

It's really pretty basic. Our values are a list, either formally or informally, of our priorities. And we cannot hide our true priorities.

Values?

We *are* what we *value*. Whatever is most important to us, *that is what we truly are*. This can fluctuate during various periods of our lives. It can also fluctuate from moment-to-moment, day-to-day.

If we have a little red car we spend more time maintaining than our families, the little red car is higher priority, no matter what we say otherwise.

If we are more devoted to aspects of our work than we are to any others, especially if we control our workload and our time doing it, our work is a higher priority, no matter what we say otherwise.

If we do not want any intrusion into our leisure time, even from those who might need us, (especially knowingly), our leisure time is a higher priority, not matter what we say otherwise.

Money, material possessions, positions in the church and community, the outward appearances of happiness and success and service, is often a greater priority that our own spiritual health and the health of those about us.

When our children are young, they require our full attention. As they grow, we sacrifice our activities for theirs. As they grow in independence, do they still remain a priority? They may need us more in those years when they believe they don't need us at all.

The demands of our work often take precedence over all other demands, because that is how we provide for all. But are we actually seeking satisfaction and recognition for ourselves and our personal *well-being*, or using these demands as a means to ignore other areas.

Most of us seek to have a vital relationship with a partner in love and affection in the hope of building a life together. Sometimes this too, suffers because of other aspects. But do we settle into roles that separate us from each other, or fail to remember this relationship is the first *child* we have created and needs nurturing to flourish?

Sometimes even our recreation takes precedence if we are willing to abandon all for it.

In these situations, our core values can remain intact if our *priorities* are born out over the long run.

We need forays away from responsibilities. But our true *values* are *at a moment's notice*, so we are ready, able and eager to *live* our faith.

We must also acknowledge these are still *choices*, and every time we choose any thing over any other thing, *that* displays our values. Good reason or not, the choices we make display our priorities.

This is not cause to castigate ourselves, and especially others. This is simply to come to terms, through introspection, of what is truly and genuinely more important to us—evaluate and adjust as such requires.

Of course we make sacrifices for our families. Our course there are times when we need stimulations this world provides. Of course we want to rise in status and appreciation for the work we do. Of course there are times when we simply need a short-term escape.

What is most important, what truly feeds us or harms us, is what many call *core values*—those options we take and decisions we make that are almost second nature to us, or should be second nature to us as spiritually-based people.

There are certain paths culturally outlined for us: the path to adulthood, the career path, the parent path. There are also core values most of us share: the right to make these decisions, for good or ill, the right to seek happiness, the right to freely move about, the right to express ourselves—and that all others have the same rights.

But do we also have core values, acknowledged or not, that do not truly serve us well, have not served us well, and will never serve us well?

We have seen people who strive for self-aggrandizement. We have seen people immersed in greed. We have seen people react with rage and violence simply because others disagree with them. We have seen those whose partners and children are merely extensions of their own personalities, or displayed like ornaments. We have felt our own reactions to people who are poor, or uncouth, or dirty, or from a different culture. We have seen what addictions do to people who do not seek help.

We have also seen what unchecked zeal has produced in those who espouse any form of superiority: nationalism, culturalism, elitism, political partyism or sectarianism.

If our core values do not truly reflect the spiritually-based life, then we are failing.

Values?

In the spiritually-based life, certain things are to become clearer, and as they do, we will wonder why so many other things were so important to us. This is the true sign of growth, and we must be aware when these lesser things rise up in us.

We are to do what's right, being led by the knowledge of its rightness because of the greater good it will produce, and doing so simply because it needs to be done.

There are many complicated matters in the web of this world. There are many important decisions we will make.

Yet *right* will come to the spiritually-based person like an unconscious breath. If someone hungers, feed them, if someone needs shelter, house them, if someone is in pain, help them find healing, if someone is struggling in any situation, do all you can to find a solution; and at the very least, comfort all.

The utter transparency of *right* is the great paradox of our times. The simpler the solution, the harder it is to come by. Someone who is hungry should be fed. Everyone knows this, especially the spiritually-based person. Yet it doesn't happen. A part of this is because the most *human* in our natures lets us avoid reminders of it, even to physically remove ourselves from its path.

It is also resisted because of judgments as to who is deserving and who isn't, judgments as to why someone would produce children they can't adequately care for, judgments against idleness or self-infliction…

We have already discussed one of the primary reasons it isn't done—and this applies to all fundamental *right*—what some believe to be their relationship to God does not compel them to do so.

We can never accept as *right* the concept *what I believe does not actually require me to act*—that the conditions in place have requirements of others before we do anything.

The spiritually-based person has a very short list of fundamental *right*. It isn't complicated.

God is the source of ultimate goodness through grace. Grace is readily available to all in equal portion. We are the eyes, ears, hands and feet of God.

There are no conditions. It does not matter who someone is. It does not even matter if they believe what we believe. It does not matter if they have a relationship with God, or seek to receive divine perfection the way we do.

As we seek to discover, enhance and rearrange our core values, we recognize seven fundamental rights we all share, and in accepting those rights, we are required to act.

First, once any person becomes a sentient creature, that person has a right to exist.

Second, all people have the same right to food, water and clothing.

Third, all people have the same right to shelter and protection from the elements.

Fourth, all people have the right to choose an avenue of productivity.

Fifth, all people have the same right to physical, emotional and spiritual care.

Sixth, all people have the same right to peace without threat.

Seventh, the planet we all share must be preserved.

For the spiritually-based person, to do what is *right* is to initiate, take part, and to serve in the purposes of these things.

In all ways the fruits of grace both enable us and move us toward action in these areas. That is the function of wholeness. Wholeness comes to us from God through grace, and through our efforts this wholeness is enacted.

Service is not a qualification of grace. Service is the one and only meter of the good we have received. Without it, we will always bear some uncertainty as to the truth of our relationship with God.

To do what is *right* is the fruit we bear.

These are the *values* of our faith.

THIRTY-FIVE

Opportunity

We all crave opportunities for ourselves. This is understandable, even if these desires do not strictly conform to the spiritually-based life. We all want to improve our station in this world, improve our accessibility to what we desire, create stability in our lives and enhance our status. We want to flourish and take pleasure in our experiences. Opportunity breeds opportunity, and when we are successful, opportunities increase.

> **Opportunity is also a great conundrum to a spiritually-based person, because in it lies the greatest opportunity for separation from God.**

Opportunity is seductive. We never truly know how we will respond to it until it presents itself.

In essence, the peaks and valleys of our lives are determined by how we respond to opportunities.

What stimulation we derive from any opportunity tends to arbitrate its effects upon us whether the result is short- or long-term.

Opportunities come to us in two main ways.

An opportunity is either *sought after*, or an opportunity *comes unbidden*.

What opportunities do we seek?

We already know we have the same opportunity for good as anyone else. We already know grace is ours to take and grow. We already know operating on an even keel spiritually can give us peace.

When we dedicate ourselves to these pursuits, the humanity of our lives improves. When the worst in us is ameliorated, the worst in us is elevated to a higher level.

We understand others more. We take no untoward advantage. We see opportunities taken by some do not serve them well or really make them happy. We see them eager to have more when they cannot digest what they already have

When dealing with these elements, as in all matters of the spiritually-based life, especially in being a true implement of God, we know of abundant opportunities available to us. We have opportunities to help others, advance justice and equity, provide staples and raise the standard of living for those about us. We **know** this. We recognize its value and necessity, and we understand its importance to the entire concept of **divine good.**

Yet sometimes it is not enough. Sometimes our humanity makes us crave something—anything—more than what we have. We *want*, and at times the test of our desires is not in the object we seek, but in the desire itself. Our *want* may become an unhealthy *need* if we focus only on lack.

We may even be resentful of those we see who appear to be less *deserving* than we are. We see others who appear to have greater opportunities. There are those with greater resources, those of some stature whose opportunities flow from something other than their own creation. We may be envious. We may rue that the opportunities given to some seem to be *unearned*. We may become jealous.

Opportunity

This is a drawback, of course. We know it even as we feel it. Even then, we may crave more. So let us remember—

Those with the greatest opportunities have to make the most difficult choices.

No matter how great the opportunity, there are inherent properties which cannot be shirked even if desired. There is a machine to be fed.

At times opportunities come to us unbidden. Some of these are wonderful. Others are not.

We may get unexpected praise or a promotion at work. We may experience a financial boon. We may stumble upon someone with whom we share mutual attraction, and build a relationship. We may discover others along a path such as ours who wish to share service and experiences.

The great irony of opportunity is when any opportunity comes to us unbidden, how we respond to it determines the spiritual bases of our lives at that particular time.

No one has an affair unless presented with the opportunity. No one lies, cheats or steals unless presented with the opportunity. No one demeans another unless presented with the opportunity. No one even acts upon an idea until the opportunity arises, even if we believe we have created such an opportunity ourselves.

The greater the wealth of opportunity, the greater the temptation for dishonesty, exploitation, intrusiveness, absences of conscience, self-gratification and ultimately, self-destruction. The rarer the opportunity, the more corruptive it can become. The more ascendant the opportunity, the higher the risk of perversion.

The seduction of greater opportunity is what one is able to do, one is always tempted to do.

And once one tastes this kind of success, it is almost inevitable that boundaries expand until the equally inevitable ruin occurs. The corporeal is as capable of burgeoning as the spirit. Limits blur as do rules of conduct.

We've seen this in politics and governments from the beginning of time. We've seen it in our entertainment, where influence is granted to celebrity merely because of celebrity. We've seen it in business leaders, sports stars, people of wealth and status, religious leaders and every ilk and capacity of prominence.

We've seen harm replace the potential for goodness because other temptations are too great, and the unique accessibility granted by such opportunity is too beguiling to ignore.

Are we to shun opportunities, or limit our opportunities to the services of grace?

Of course not. But the spiritually-based life requires to *know* the upshot of everything we seek and everything that comes our way, and to cast the light of spirituality upon all choices and experiences. We do not disregard such things, especially out of fear, but are better able to regard them as to potential benefit.

We should take to heart three simple guidelines:

First, we should never seek opportunity that appeals primarily to our vanity.

When does attention or recognition become ego? When it is desired or necessary.

Anything sought, be it a position, a relationship, or financial gain, for the sake of notoriety or to appeal to one's ego contains no spiritual basis.

Positive things do happen that elevate our status. We may apply for a better position and win it. We may make an investment that pays great dividends for us. We may ingratiate ourselves to someone of importance who eventually rewards us.

But if we do any of these things to be seen by more of our peers in a better light, to elevate our status in any environment in order to make ourselves feel more *special* or *apart*, then it becomes something more self-serving and less altruistic.

Secondly, we should never seek opportunity with the foreknowledge of deliberately harming another.

There will always be occasions when opportunities come our way that have been sought by others, and their feelings will be hurt when they do not receive it.

This is not the same as *seeking* an opportunity, through subversion, backbiting or deception that deliberately harms another.

Nor is this the same as *getting even* with anyone who has harmed us before the tables turned.

Also, as in nearly all business, our opportunities come at the expense of others operating in the same market, seeking the same customers, providing the same products and services. This is a *natural* part of commerce.

However, if we use greater resources to willingly put someone out of business, or make it more difficult for them to do business, and we *know* this going in, we cannot claim any spiritual basis for our actions.

It is the same if we are attracted to someone who is involved with someone else, regardless of the circumstances, and even if the attraction is mutual. If the existing relationship has not been resolved, we cannot claim any spiritual basis for continuing.

There is simply no spiritual basis for enhancing any parts of our lives at the expense of others.

Thirdly, we should never seek opportunity where the ultimate outcome creates more harm than good.

Are we to be seers with knowledge of the future? No.

But if we enter into any endeavor we *know* from our spiritual bearing will ultimately add more toxicity to any environment than the good it creates, even within ourselves, we cannot claim a spiritual basis for it.

We know when this happens. We are not ignorant.

Are byproducts more potentially poisonous than the benefit of the product? Is the entertainment value (or profit) in alcohol or drugs greater than the capacity for damage on a large scale? Would we seek to gain by any enterprise that relies upon temptation of any sort, knowing without the temptation the likelihood of participation would dwindle to nothing?

If the opportunity provides us with little more than avarice, or the lure of the same, we know better. Even if there is seemingly nothing more virulent than mere pride, we know better.

To rationalize, to ignore, to accept no responsibility or blame, and yet continue along any path of *self service* is to falter on the path of the spiritually based life.

Sought or unsought, opportunities are always to be measured by the good that can be generated by them, and ultimately, the good that *is* generated by them.

THIRTY-SIX

Power & Influence

How many narratives have been written about the corrupting influence of power? We're all familiar with Lord Acton's premise *power tends to corrupt, and absolute power corrupts absolutely*. How true this is. Only perfection can have absolute power, and only perfection cannot be corrupted by it. And, of course, the God of perfection does not care about power.

Many would argue this is not so, perhaps those who seek power. From a spiritually-based perspective, why is it so?

We of the human race are concerned with power. Gratefully, none of us can attain absolute power, but we all know the horrendous effects of those who were corrupted by formidable power and influence…and continue to be so.

> **From the spiritually-based perspective, all power is corrupt. It cannot help but be. Power is influence over others. One simply cannot be in control or have influence over others and be free of corruption. It is an impossibility of humanity the same as it is an impossibility for God to be anything other than God.**

Power and influence do not have to be evil. But they are absolutely tantalizing.

The corrupting influences of power are evident in nearly every aspect of our daily lives: the parent who pushes a child into a sport or other activity for his/her own satisfaction, or publicly punishes a child for embarrassing them in public; the boss who lords over subordinates to the point of mistreatment; the political leader who uses access to enrich him/herself beyond what might otherwise be available or acceptable; the spouse or partner who manipulates the other because he/she can do so with seeming impunity; the swindler who preys upon the elderly or the naïve—the bully, the glib, the *fakir*.

Most of us find ourselves in positions of control that comes from authority. As parents, we seek to control the activities of our children of a certain age. As leaders in our jobs or within other groups, we seek to control the flow of information and activity. Even as servants there must be leadership to organize, within and without.

At times we may even find ourselves lobbying for some position of influence.

Power comes from both the authority to influence or control and/or the ability to influence or control.

Every influence contains the possibility to be damaging, but not all influence *is* damaging. We educate the younger to grow, to thrive, even to protect themselves. We educate others in areas where we have more knowledge or experience than they do, and for the same reasons.

Even as spiritually-based people, we seek to *influence* others, through our behavior, into a more satisfying life.

What we *desire* means everything.

When a desire to influence leads to the desire to control, rather than positively affect, every effort is thereby corrupt.

We look at authority. A supervisor can control the workload of employees. An officer can order soldiers into battle. A police officer can control traffic. A judge can sentence people to jail. Parents can control the whereabouts of younger children.

There are always punitive repercussions for defying authority. One can be demoted or fired. One can face criminal charges or fines. Children can be punished.

All authority can be corrupt or be relatively free of corruption depending upon the *desires* of those in authority. Also, there are systems of oversights in nearly every form of authority, including parenthood, to assess, limit and even eliminate authority.

We look at deceit or coercion.

Unfortunately, this is all around us. We see parents bribing or threatening their children to behave. We see lovers react emotionally in order to gain the favor of a partner. We see supervisors and co-workers manipulate others to attain a certain end.

We recognize these in ourselves. Once we realize the harm, we can make adjustments.

But greater than these is what we see today in our media and our politics. There are so many who seek to influence us toward a certain perspective. Ironically, these play to our fears and ignorance instead our better understanding, our ability to think, reason, and especially our spiritual bases.

We hear the shrill, the opinionated, the accusers of others, the brazen, and we are engaged. Some even convince us they do *God's work*.

We see so many of us who are riled, angry, ready for battle of one sort or another. We find ourselves sucked in, while God is hidden in some dark corner.

So in the prayer-calm of grace, we should consider these *five elements*, and evaluate them according to what we know the spiritually-based life to be.

First, the one true power is God.

Our relationship to God and the function and purposes of grace is the **supreme** guideline for us in **all** matters. We should deliberate on **anything** that causes us to stray from this.

All earthly power is vanity. All influence is corruptive except to serve. We will find ourselves in seductive situations. We need not shun the responsibility. We shun the venal tug of temptation.

Secondly, we must always respect authority.

Even in disagreement, we respect the rules and guidelines of our society, knowing in principle they were designed to serve all, and those selected to administer these rules and guidelines are also, in theory, there to serve all, and should be given the respect of the position and the benefit of the doubt whenever possible.

These include our governments, our businesses, our schools, and even social structures.

We participate as we are required to participate and still keep ourselves focused toward the spiritual bent.

Thirdly, we recognize, without recrimination, how any person attained power and influence—not whether such is deserved, but whether it serves the common good.

We know people will be elected to office with whom we will not always be in agreement, but must respect the decision of the majority.

We know others will rise to positions in our societies by something other than their own merits.

There are also those who have attained status via wealth or celebrity or audience. Again, without impeachment, we can look to the fruits of their labors for the common good—and also if they are evident without them reminding us of their good works.

Whoever comes before us, and in whatever capacity, is the focus on themselves or others?

We are not to disrespect, nor even criticize, but we are able to examine what anyone purports to be, especially where personal enrichment is involved.

We are required to uphold the efforts of all toward the common good, but we are not required to blindly accept the status of those whose actions provide no evidence, except that all are equal inheritors of grace.

We will always be expected to *obey* the authority of rules and laws, just as we will always be expected to *obey* those who enforce them.

But we are never expected to submit to tyrants or abusers of these same rules and laws except to the *specific* nature of the rule or law, and we are never expected to *follow-the-leader* where there is no evidence of provision to the common good.

Fourth, we should reflect (kindly) upon those who *seek* power and influence.

Our wonderful democracies are still rife with vitriol and mediocrity. Our business hierarchy has many examples of avarice and snobbery. Our entertainments contain elements that are not thought-provoking or spiritually stimulating.

> *The irony is, those who seek power and influence, and are willing to do whatever it takes to gain it. Those who espouse innuendo, unkindness and even deception because it has become acceptable to many of us, forfeit all claim to the roles they seek on any kind of spiritual basis. In all these things, the ends can never justify the means.*

If one seeks support in any forum claiming there is a spiritual basis for it, and then behave in all ways contrary, we are right to deny support, except in direct, hands-on service for the common good.

We must seek positive outcomes that serve the common good while never abandoning our faith.

Finally, whether we ever seek it, or whether it comes our way, we know how we are to apply spiritually-based guidelines should we find ourselves in a position of power and influence.

We are to apply all the tenets of the spiritually-based life to seek grace and serve others, even if it means we must forfeit such power and influence in the process.

When people respond positively to us—our ideas, our proposals, our service, the evidences of our spiritual-based lives, we cannot help but be flattered and gratified.

Yet the spiritually-based person also knows we should never seek any power or influence that does not directly enhance the lives of others to a greater extent than ours, and we should never accept a position of power or influence unless we are willing to enhance the lives of others to a greater extent than our own, just as we should always be wary (without condemnation) of anyone who seeks any power or influence that does not directly enhance the lives of others to a greater extent than his/her own.

We know in the imperfection and vulnerability of our human psyches and emotions that we are incapable of exercising influence without some corruption, and only when others are served to a greater extent than ourselves do we continue to grow in the spiritually-based life.

THIRTY-SEVEN

Dichotomy

The generic meaning of any dichotomy is some action or thought has two opposing sides: right or wrong, good or evil, positive or negative. There is a duality in nearly every aspect of the human condition: should we or shouldn't we?

Of course, there are always discretionary, and even intrinsic elements to these. As humans, we tend to make decisions based upon our needs and desires at the time.

There is always going to be some measure of conflict in our thinking. However, as we grow in the spiritually-based life, we will become more aware of thoughts and actions that are adverse, with adverse results.

Another aspect of dichotomy greatly affects everyone, those on the spiritually-based path and those who are not, and for those who are seeking to nurture a vital relationship with God, it can become a recognizable standard in daily life.

> *In the simplest of terms, this dichotomy is allowing external circumstances to define us at any given time—to affect us to the point where these create an internal atmosphere.*

A rainy day may make us blue. Any setback may make us doubt. A spat with someone close to us may cause us pain and make us question ourselves.

Even people with strong ego-structures can be insecure—perhaps even because they have strong ego-structures.

We are also pushed toward one side or another by people and circumstances. Sometimes we may not even stop to assess if something is good for us or not. We may go with the flow, or participate in something because others are doing it.

So much sheer human energy in our world is used to influence others. So much of what is written, said and done is to make us believe we are either right or wrong when it comes to nearly every situation—we are, essentially, wooed, and then criticized if we disagree.

External forces can make us uncertain.

But if we allow any outside source to define who and what we are in any fundamental sense, even if only temporarily, then we have a problem.

Our interior selves must be so that we are not buffeted by extraneous influences. Our essences must be so rooted in God that we may return to peace-of-mind in short order. This is the way of the spiritually-based life. This is way we live. This is also the only way we can be solution-based and not problem-based.

How often do we allow outside forces to determine our moods or our frames-of-mind? Obviously, there are circumstances and events that can be crushing. But what about the smaller things we encounter from time-to-time? Does a setback cause doubt to linger beyond a day or part of a day? Does a disappointment stay with us long past its expiration date? Do we mull and brood until we believe we are less than nothing because someone or something has rattled our confidence.

Are we *afraid*?

Do we believe we are accident-prone, or have bad luck, or are jinxed?

Do we withdraw or collapse when something goes wrong?

Do we believe others are out to get us?

At times all of us are self-destructive. Many of us know people whose very personalities exhibit these traits. And yes, sometimes we do make poor decisions, very poor decisions, or shoot ourselves in the foot.

But in many cases, environmental conditions are not *personal* in the strictest sense; they are not *aimed* at us because of who we are.

If we are in a job we dislike, and perform in some substandard fashion, we should expect there to be conflict. But if we are good at our jobs, and then suffer some setback that is temporary and transient, it is not about who and what we are.

If we are in a harmful relationship, we have made a fundamentally poor decision. But if we believe a relationship serves all parties equally and well, and there is mutual respect most of the time, and we have a disagreement, even a severe one, it is not about who and what we are.

If we drive a car that is subject to breaking down at any moment, and it makes us late or ruins our plans, we have simply rolled the dice and submitted to the inevitable. But if we have an unexpected breakdown that sets off a series of unpleasant events, it is not about who and what we are.

If we are feeling vulnerable for whatever reason—perhaps even insufficient rest—and circumstances rise about us that make us feel even more vulnerable, it is not about who and what we are.

It is not personal, nor some lesson from the cosmos.

Who we are is *always* determined by us. We are either in a relationship with the divine, or we are not. We are either aware of our own foibles, or we are not. We either seek to remedy our own shortcomings, or we do not. We long for and make every effort, to have a spiritually-based life, or we do not.

No one or no *thing* can identify us otherwise.

As spiritually-based people we do not cast our fates upon the tides and hope for the best. We do not allow defeatism to become a self-fulfilling prophecy, and we certainly do not allow external influences, natural, interpersonal or other, to dictate or indicate what kind of people we are at heart.

We do not allow setbacks, disagreements or criticisms to make us feel unworthy of grace and good.

On the other hand, does it take some peripheral element to make us happy?

Are we happy only when there is some external stimulation or validation? Do we need the attention of a significant other to be content? Do we need the success of our work in order for us to feel good about ourselves? Does our outlook ebb and flow with the currents of outward experiences, positive or not?

Do we find no satisfaction and joy within ourselves regardless of the circumstances? Do we only relish the sunlight? Or can we find joy in a walk in the rain?

Is our inner constitution such that we are fundamentally content?

Do we allow other people to dictate our outlook, our sense of security, our very happiness?

The issue is not that we relish validation from external sources, but that this validation is a necessity.

It is our objective, and our good fortune, to find peace within due to our relationship with God. Despite innumerable and potent distractions, and storms upon us, the path to peace within and without can only be achieved by our faith.

On the spiritually-based path, we are to be anchored in our faith—our belief in grace and our ability to receive it. We should not allow ourselves to be fundamentally altered by any stimuli except for a foundation built through God.

We are not to be bipolar (in the strictly non-medical sense)—allowing the hills and valleys of extraneous events and circumstances to name us content or not content, nor are we to allow feelings created by these events and circumstances to linger.

This is not ego, and we should use introspection to assess where we are on the spiritually-based path so it does not become ego. We need to be mindful of how others may *see* us. Sometimes we are even buffeted by external events to the point of disbelief and must recover at a pace we wish we could better control.

But we *are* who we *are* through grace and grace alone.

Just as a cloudy day should not depress us, we should not *rely* on a sunny day to elate us. Our spiritual temperament is like a spiritual temperature. We do not run hot or cold because of what is going on about us. We have patience because we have grace. We *know* because we have grace. We are children of God, without vanity, in all occasions and circumstances, because we have grace.

It is a common theme, but bears repeating. Grace is the great equalizer in all inner workings of spiritually-based people.

We are not a failure because we fail. We are not losers because we lose.

Nor are we winners because we win.

If we make a mistake, we remedy it. We do not allow it to cause us to believe we are evil. We do not allow it to take us to the dark deep of aloneness. If we succeed, we feel a sense of satisfaction, but we do not blind ourselves to our own fallibility so when we stumble, we are crushed and overwhelmed and remove ourselves from spiritual sustenance and the immutable good of God.

One of the primary purposes of growth in grace is to rid ourselves of corporeal volatility. We are to entrench ourselves in the stability our faith provides.

Certainly, there will be times when events will cause us to retreat to a familiar step we had considered already behind us. Those of growing conscience always remember, much the same as hearing a once-beloved song transforms us into an entirely different time and place.

Our evolution allows us these digressions as we are able to recall them without temper or harshness, for ourselves or others.

In truth, we never really fall backward. Progress is progress, and we may stray to the side as if lost in some unknown environs, or stand upon the path afraid to move in any direction, or shuffle and stumble with little forward motion at all, but once we have absorbed divine good, some part of us will always know it is still there and still available.

Grace provides us an equilibrium that no superficial or transient inducement, be it tragic or seemingly glorious, can ever undo.

THIRTY-EIGHT

Spiritual Mortality

We have all heard the term **rock bottom.** Perhaps we have experienced it ourselves, maybe even more than once. Things have to get better because they can't get any worse. Our lives have become a swirling nebula of anguish and doubt. How many of us have abandoned all claim to faith because of it?

Most of us realize this will pass, even if only in some small, unnoticed place, even as we are engulfed in confusion. Eventually, and hopefully sooner than later, we will return to God to receive grace. We will nurture our souls. We will grow in the understanding we have not been singled out for disappointment, and the confluence of unhappy events occurs because of myriad elements.

We will acknowledge misfortune, though exceeding painful, is not *personal*. God did not wave a hand to teach us a lesson. We are not to suffer, as Job did in the Hebrew Bible, to test our faith.

However, there are those in our sphere of encounter, those we may or may not know, who do not believe or have forgotten this—who are unable to grasp that things will indeed get better, or who believe they are being punished for some transgression beyond the consequences of their actions and fortunes.

They may not even make the effort necessary to climb out of the pit. They may find themselves cloaked in a blanket of despair that has grown into the flesh until one cannot be separated from the other.

Admittedly or not, these are the believers in the *mortal soul*—death has come to the divine within them and there is no longer any connection to the divine goodness that is theirs to claim.

This is impossible, of course, and can sometimes be attributed to their belief God has abandoned them, due in some part to their misunderstanding of God's nature. Regardless, what they are experiencing is a kind of spiritual death.

As in all faith, however imperfect, what one believes is what is true.

Our recognition of this is crucial because as we know God's nature, we know just as God did not reach down to punish them, God is not going to reach down and save them: their own heart-wrenching petitions, or the pleadings of those closest to them who do not believe as we do, no matter how earnest or sincere, will evaporate into empty space, and no good will come of it.

We must make an effort.

We cannot change the interior workings of someone else. But we can help. We've discussed how an external stimulation can affect internal feelings. Do we not feel better on a bright, sunny day than a gray, cloudy one? Do we not respond to kindness differently than any perceived unkindness?

As we try to rid this type of dichotomy from our own lives, we may yet provide positive stimulations to those who are struggling mightily.

We are not to become pseudo-psychologists or therapists. We are not even to become teachers, except by example. But neither do we allow our limitations to make us idle.

There are several things we must do.

First, we must learn to recognize the signs.

Many expressions of grief and depression are obvious. There will be visible evidence of sadness. They will be lethargic, lack energy and focus, or wear the shroud of doom on their faces. We will often know if someone has had a recent misfortune: illness, death, divorce, loss of property or position, or financial difficulties. Many times someone in such pain will withdraw.

If the situation involves a close friend or family member, we may know first-hand.

Many other times signs are less obvious. Some may simply not seem to be *themselves*. They will be less optimistic, less open, less willing to let their guards down, less willing to talk at all.

What we know or do not know does not really matter in whether we respond.

We do so without presumption, even without acknowledging there are ongoing issues.

Whether a friend or stranger, we simply ask **are you okay?** People tend to be defensive during such a time, so even if the reply is *yes*, especially with those who do not know us, this is not the end for us.

We do not foist ourselves upon anyone. We do not try to commiserate uninvited. We do not offer advice. We do not push.

But we do not stop there.

Secondly, we offer.

Please tell me what I can do to help.

We may hear *nothing*. We may even be greeted by hostility or defensiveness, but we offer. If we already know at least a part of what the difficulty is, and what basic necessities need to be met, we offer them—food, shelter, clothing, transportation—we offer them sincerely, and we offer them with the expectation they will be accepted.

We provide benefit in whatever way we can.

We offer our friendship. We offer the *tangibility* of our service. We offer ourselves as if the service is for our benefit.

Some will respond favorably and tell us what is troubling them. We listen. We understand. We may even be familiar with similar circumstances from our own lives. We do not offer words, except those of comfort. We offer *action*.

In accepting our offer of assistance, they acknowledge lack. We enter into a covenant with them to share the responsibilities of this lack.

Obviously, *rock bottom* means different things to different people.

It's amazing how things relatively simple for us seem insurmountable to those caught in the midst of them. Someone we know has just gone through a painful divorce. Most of the creature comforts may remain intact, but they are devastated within. We take them to lunch. We offer to take their kids to a movie.

Someone else, for whatever reason, may be struggling financially, which piles misery upon misery. We can always help someone financially at some level. We do not offer them money unless asked.

We can buy them *gifts*. We can be diplomatic and still ease the burden. We can even claim we received a gift card we do not intend to use. We can provide assistance that cannot be denied.

If they need a job, we can help them update a resume, or hire someone who can. We can help them with transportation if that is an issue. We can actively search for them using whatever resources are available to us.

There will be times when we are in over our heads. There will be times when we cannot hope to provide everything they need. There are illnesses we can't remedy, medical costs we cannot mitigate except in small portions. There are sudden deaths and wrenching tragedies.

But the business of life goes on for them. We can tend to these while they are bearing their burdens until they are willing to let us (or others) help unburden them.

We can help with the smaller details.

Some may not respond favorably at all. They may want us to leave them alone. They may want us to mind our own business.

We make every effort to leave them with the understanding we are a willing and able resource readily available for them should they later decide to accept.

Thirdly, we still find a way.

The situation has not been resolved. The crisis has not passed.

Everyone *needs* in these experiences, even those who do not want our help.

It is difficult, and may even seem unwise, to aid someone without their permission. We can appear presumptuous and even callous.

If it is a close friend, or member of our family, we continue to offer. We do as a statement, not a question. *I want to help.* If that is rejected, we find other ways. *I'm taking the kids to the park. Would yours want to go? Let's have dinner together, etc.* There are always ways to tend to the periphery, even if it seems an opportunity to give the person in crisis more time to brood. If someone in the valley cannot focus on the peripheral details, we must.

Anyone close to us who rejects one-on-one contact still has responsibilities which require attention. We do these things hoping they will ultimately accept one-on-one contact, and in the mean time, some good has been accomplished.

For those who are not close to us—those we know but not so intimately—it is much more difficult. Whatever the reason, we cannot reach them even as we reach out to them. They may not *want* us to know them more intimately as then we would be privy to what they consider to be *personal* information.

Beyond gentle (and *extremely* gentle) attempts to reach out, there is something else we can and should do.

Everyone on this planet will accept the assistance of at least one other person.

This is who we need to know. We do not snoop. We do not impose ourselves into the lives of another. We do not ask for details not offered to us. We do not presume or claim to know what someone needs. We inch forward out of love.

You are friends with him/her, aren't you? Or *Isn't he/she related to you?*

I may be wrong, but I get the impression something is going on. I don't know him/her/them as well as you do, but would really like to help. Please tell me what I can do, and could I do something through you?

We will find this person. And we will know the words. And they will understand.

And if this *is* the person, and we are still rebuffed, then and only then can we pause for a time.

At all times, and in all cases, we come prepared to do what we are asked to do, just as we do what needs to be done without being asked.

Our *spiritual intuition* always allows us to provide external good to those in need. Whatever the circumstances, we do what we do until they realize the soul is still alive, and can claim their birthright.

No one **ever** need die an internal death. No one ever need surrender to it, suffer needlessly or suffer alone.

The fact is, there are such people in our relatively confined environments. They are there, close at hand, feeling as if their very spirit has died.

Always, we are there. Our hands-on caring attests to the degree of our love.

Grace is for all. The greater the number of those who embrace it, the more whole we all become. This cannot be so otherwise.

So we remember these four lessons:

We first do what we can to alleviate pain.

We make certain daily needs are being met.

We make certain (as much as we can) there is an ongoing process of recovery and growth—a brighter future in heart and in fact.

We do these things as proof the soul never dies. It merely strays. Divine good is always there and waiting.

THIRTY-NINE

Life As It Is

We must acknowledge there are people who endure overwhelming struggles every day—people in poverty, people with illness or chronic conditions, people in environments of conflict, people with emotional difficulties we scarcely understand, or have loved ones beneath the same penumbra.

We will also find ourselves in periods or conditions of need when it's all we can do to hang on. There may even be times when grace seems so distant we cannot calm ourselves enough to reach it, or so remote we cannot even sense it.

There are those whose lot may never improve except by the actions of spiritually-based people. There are people who do not have sufficient resources to even survive.

We understand this. We are aware of what we must do. We know what grace means.

Yet it is also important for all spiritually-based people to appreciate their *lives as they are.*

This is not when we are facing a major struggle or have serious issues in our lives. We need to tend to those even as they sap all our energies.

This does not mean a blind tolerance of things that are hurting us or hurting others. Just as it is necessary for us to reach out, we may find ourselves desperately wanting someone to reach out to us, and sometimes this doesn't come.

Nor are we expected merely to paint *happy faces* on the trials and tragedies we see or endure.

This means we are to find the good in the times of our lives when there are no wholesales changes—the common day-to-day existences we lead.

It is more than *stop and smell the roses*. It is to *see* the roses, and to *seek* them out when we do not see them.

Our *awareness* is focused in two primary ways:

First, through our growth-in-grace, we meet what we now recognize to be *minor inconveniences* with optimism, we practice our faith, and reach beyond potential obstacles placed before us.

How often has a *good day* been shaken by an unexpected event? Have we ever greeted the day with enthusiasm only to find a sick child, or our car won't start, or the weather is horrible, or our boss is in a really bad mood?

Have we ever started the day with a sense of foreboding, even if we can't put our finger on the precise cause? And then, we subconsciously make it happen?

The spiritually-based person knows the minor is minor.

We cannot always smile. We cannot always clear our minds sufficiently to receive the abundant grace available to us. It is our task and our joy to find the means to do this, of course, but it is foolish to believe we are never going to struggle.

But the divine is still there. It hasn't gone anywhere. What changes is our attitude toward it, and whether we find it or ignore it.

Our spiritual evolution requires us to *find the divine*. Even more, it provides the impetus through which this becomes second nature to us.

However, we must acknowledge it, just as we must acknowledge God to receive grace.

Obviously, this can seem trite. We've all heard some version of this so many times—find the silver lining, or make lemonade from lemons.

This is deeper than that.

The spiritually-based life requires us to find the desire, and the means, to alter our experiences toward eternal good. Regardless of the environment or circumstances, we must seek out something that makes us feel more a part of God.

We must find some joy in the immediacy of our lives, even as we endeavor to improve it. We must find some element of beauty in our environment, even if it is dark and gray. We must find some satisfaction in our work, even if it wears on us. We must contribute something positive to our relationships with no expectation of return. We must recognize the divine in others. We must do things for *ourselves* that enrich our souls and make us feel more *alive*.

As with *mountains out of mole hills*, we cannot allow what we *know* to be a speed bump become a barricade. Something can be found in every part of every day to enhance our spiritual selves. We must feel less threatened by temporary agitations or impediments and declare ourselves whole and open to the wonder we *know* is always there just below the surface of every hitch and hindrance.

Secondly, we must also find the means to relish the seemingly mundane and commonplace in our daily lives.

We so easily find the rut, the stagnation, the tedium of routine.

There is grandeur in the commonplace. Most elements of our daily lives contain beauty and nourishment. The paths we travel by habit contain charms we ignore. Many people we encounter have something to add to the ways of contentment. There are small epiphanies to be discovered in our homes, our families, our friends and our workplaces.

At times we cannot. Yet no matter the difficulty, the impossibility of it at times, we must take some pleasure in the moment-by moment passage of time, absorbing every iota of the external aspects of grace we encounter and recognize

We can continue to live for another day, or another event, or another turn down a different road.

Regardless of how often we have heard this before, in whatever form it has taken, the premise remains we permanently and irretrievably lose what we have chosen to ignore this day.

It may not always be profound. It may not be a rainbow, or a sunset, or the true meaning of the smile or touch we receive from another. It will never be a flash of light or a voice from above.

But it is there. We find more health than illness around us, more love than disdain, more abundance than poverty, more satisfaction than misery, more life than death.

And we are to always, **always** recognize this. Not with an *it could be worse* perspective, but a direct, apparent, and visible attitude. It's there. Right in front of your eyes, and you don't have to look very far to find it.

There are people who mean something to you. There are places, and books, and music and memories that mean something to you. See them, hear them, know them, find the treasure in them.

Then, where the opposite is true—more illness than health, more fear than hope, more misery than satisfaction, more death than life—we, too, are there.

We have the opportunity every day, in our hearts, and in the summer or winter of our hearts, the light and shadow of our hearts, the gladness or suspicion in our hearts, to help create the opposite of these, in whatever way we can.

We can go online and donate to a fund for some foreign peoples struggling for food, water shelter, and medicine. We can drop off a few cans of food to our local food bank or homeless shelter. We can donate clothing and supplies to our local women's center.

And the more ordinary; we do everything we can to brighten the atmosphere of every milieu we encounter throughout the day, and those who share these spaces, however brief and transitory.

Today may not be the day we grow in leaps and bounds. Today may not be the day when fruition comes. Today may not be the day when we find what we have sought.

Today is simply *today*.

Time is a rather arbitrary measurement, but it exists only for us. Only we are aware of it. Our *time* on earth is finite.

Each day will pass whether we are attendant or not. The sun will rise and set regardless of how we feel about it, or even acknowledge it. Hours will pass whether we weep or sing or sleep. We will move toward the ending of our earthly days no matter how we *are* or no matter what we do. Physical laws will play on regardless of us.

When we acknowledge grace daily, even in the worst of times, we grow. More, if we do not acknowledge these things, they, too, can become lost.

If we seek contentment, we will soon discover the expansion of everything that makes us content.

Accepting the reality and magnitude of our troubles at times, we also know if we wait until things get better before seeing good, we also postpone that which can serve us right now, at this very moment.

If there is no delight to be found in the present state, we must alter our outlook. If we cannot alter our outlook to find delight in any single thing or experience, what do we think is going to happen to improve our lot?

We must mark the moments with some sense of peace that these moments contain something valuable for us, just as we are a valuable part of them.

We do not count the hours. We do our best to live them.

FORTY

Judgment or Discernment?

Judgment is a reactionary response to someone or something based upon assumption.

We know we are not to judge anyone, especially when based upon any outward appearance or manner, even if there seems to be valid reasons. We believe we have an idea what a homeless person looks like. We believe we have an idea what a criminal looks like. We believe we have an idea of what a lazy person looks like. We believe we have an idea of what a dangerous person looks like.

We also believe we have an idea what a successful person looks like, or what a spiritually-based person looks like.

Many times stereotypes contain some common elements. They are based upon past and present media, as well as cultural bias. Jesus is often depicted as a saintly, almost effeminate individual, though as a Palestinian Jew he would have more likely been small of stature, dark-complexioned, and with short, wiry hair.

Suppose you looked at a group of photographs showing Enrico Fermi, Ted Bundy, Imam Achmad Cassiem, Mohandas Gandhi, Johnny Depp and Bill Gates, but you didn't know who these individuals were.

Which of these men are spiritual leaders? Which was a serial killer? Which built one of the largest companies on earth? Which was instrumental in the development of nuclear energy?

What if you were also told one was a thief, another was a terrorist, another was a vagrant, and another was a drug addict, even if it wasn't true? Which would you pick?

Stereotypes are rarely adequate indicators of a person's essence. Outward appearances are often useless. We see behaviors that may strike us in a certain way, yet even these are not sufficient to truly *know* an individual.

Stereotypes which cause a more *negative* reaction are more difficult to modify. We tend to respond very quickly to someone we register as offensive.

We do not judge people merely because stereotypes may be inaccurate, but because there is no spiritual-basis for judging anyone at all. However distasteful we find someone, there is no justification for judgment based upon appearance alone.

We echo the impartiality of God toward everyone.

In every instance of judgment there is an interpretation of facts, or an ignorance of facts.

Facts are not *truth*. *Truth*, by anyone's definition, is an interpretation of facts. A person in an automobile weaving in traffic is a fact. The driver is drunk is an interpretation of that fact. Of course, the driver could be distracted by something, ill, or the car could be malfunctioning.

The role of the spiritually-based person is twofold:

First, the spiritually-based person must withhold any judgment and deal strictly with the condition at hand in a spiritually-based manner.

Secondly, the spiritually-based person must seek to obtain all the facts before making any determination of the *truth*, also realizing one person's *truth* is another person's *opinion*.

Of course, we do make *judgments* about people every day, often many times a day, and certain judgments may even be necessary. Regardless of the condition of the driver, we want to avoid a weaving vehicle.

Judgment or Discernment?

We must learn the difference between *judgment* and *discernment* (or recognition).

Discernment, or recognition, is the way in which a spiritually-based person can assess a behavior, activity, or environment at any particular time, without partiality or condemnation.

Many times there will be a fine line the spiritually-based life requires us to explore, but we also understand *discernment* is necessary. Once we recognize something is awry in someone else, or some particular environment, we are required to respond.

There is a difference between two large men fighting in a parking lot, and two of our co-workers in a heated argument. But a spiritually-based person must respond to both. Certainly, we assess a risk to us and those about us. Yet we do not let *judgment* as to worthiness, deservedness, fault or ignorance respond for us.

We *judge* based upon assumptions. We *discern* based upon a rational assessment, prompted by a more spiritual basis.

There are two primary reasons we **judge** instead of **recognize. First, we feel threatened.**

There are many reasons we feel threatened, and there are many *real* threats in our world.

The key is learning the difference, and using our expanding spiritual constitutions to *discern* between real and imagined threats, we are able to grow.

If we are hiking and we come across a venomous snake, *discernment* allows us to realize a potential danger. Does venom make the snake evil? No, it means the snake perceives us as a threat and we are to give way. Angel's Trumpets have beautiful flowers but are deadly poisonous. If a child or pet comes in sufficient contact to make them ill, does this mean the plant is evil? No, it means there was not enough recognition of the danger

We are all wired to perceive threat. It includes behavior, activity and environment. This does not mean we cannot be cautious. Caution can be a form of wisdom. We may *discern* threat in everything from body language to hostile movement. But we cannot *judge* intent simply because we are afraid.

We also include circumstances in behavior, activity and environment. No one is threatened by those who scream at the tops of their lungs at an athletic event, but if we encountered that in a department store, we may want to run and hide.

Think of all the times *our* behavior is radically different from the norm; our behavior at a party and our behavior in meetings; our behavior eating dinner and our behavior at a rock concert; dressed for work and dressed for yard work. How often have we seen someone in a car playing music so loudly we can hear it through closed windows, and found it annoying. Would we feel differently if it was our children, or ourselves not so very long ago?

Of course, there are times and places for proprieties, but we cannot *judge* someone's nature because we don't always share the same sensibilities.

So what is the *real* harm in making a judgment about someone based upon their appearance or behavior? The worst that happens is our avoidance.

The harm comes in the lack of understanding. Ignorance is the bane of the spiritually-based person because our ignorance erects a wall between ourselves and those from whom there could be great mutual benefit. It certainly restricts our service.

Secondly, we judge those who are *alien* to us, or whose behavior is *unseemly* to us.

Someone inebriated or unkempt, or loud and boisterous, puts us off, so we want nothing more than to find an escape. We do not know how they would respond if we offered assistance, and the point becomes moot because we have no intention of doing so.

By not bearing their burdens, we share their weaknesses.

If we encountered two very similar people, one behaving *normally*, and one visibly trembling, and with ferocious body odor… which one are we most apt to look less favorably upon? And if we discover the second had just finished a round of chemotherapy, how would we then feel?

Judgment or Discernment?

We also tend to avoid people who are disabled or are physically different from us. It makes us uncomfortable. We could not possibly find things in common, or they could not possibly have anything to offer us.

If we cross paths with a group of people who do not look like us, or dress like us, or speak the same language, is our first action one of avoidance? Prejudice lies at the very heart of many of the world's difficulties. Unless people of different races and cultures, or even different personalities, realize the necessity of spiritually-based interaction and communication, certain ills will never improve.

Many conditions are exactly the same for everyone. If there are behaviors involved that unnerve us, then perhaps the onus for understanding is our responsibility, and not theirs. Understanding is the only way we can remove *judgment* as a knee-jerk response to situations where we do not have all the facts.

And upon any occasion where we must react without all the facts, it becomes our responsibility to eventually discover all the facts.

We **recognize** conditions. Discernment using this recognition is very far removed from **judging** a person or group or a form of behavior.

Familiarity does not have to breed contempt. It can and should breed love.

It is always easier to portray the spiritually-based life when we are familiar with behavior and an environment to the point where we are not threatened. So then, as we become more familiar with various behaviors and environments, we can become more productive and less threatened, and more in tune with who and what we are to be.

In the spiritually-based life, we also need to get our mental and emotional houses in order so we can relate to others in some positive fashion. A considerable part of our faith is service. We cannot possess the divine without distributing it, and we cannot adequately distribute it when necessary if a part of us desires to pick and choose who is to benefit, or deny benefit to someone who disturbs us.

It is up to *us*, through discernment, to reduce and eliminate all misperceived threat, alarm or disapproval that clutters our path.

FORTY-ONE

The Why of Who

As unfortunate and contrary to the core of our beliefs, and lacking in redemptive qualities, when it comes to our responses to those we encounter, the *who* does seem to matter.

Whenever, wherever and in whomever we find something lacking, a part of us cannot s help going through a qualifying process. It is often something we don't even think about.

This alone is an indication of our true progress (or lack of progress) along the spiritually-based path.

How much easier it is to give a couple of dollars to well-scrubbed person in the checkout line at the grocery store who finds him or herself short than respond the same way to a scruffy, unbathed person begging for change. How differently we view a person with an illness than a person with an addiction. How we are moved when we see the pain upon the faces of the family of a victim of a crime, and how indifferent or angry we are about the same pain in the family of the accused.

How we might rush to endow the parents of triplets with our gifts, regardless of their economic status, and scorn a single mother of three children under the ages of four.

How differently do we treat someone who agrees with us than someone who might not, or someone with whom we agree or disagree?

Often we cannot seem to help deeming the *desirability* of those in need, even though in the spiritually-based life, the *who* is not supposed to matter.

We make it matter for the same reasons we do anything else contrary to the spiritually-based life. We are imbued with prejudices and an emotional constitution that allows it, promotes it, and even encourages it.

What we have learned from experience is what we know, the gut-reaction of a multitude of cultural lessons, spiritually-based or not.

These lessons have become so imprinted upon our psyches we must examine every aspect of rote behavior to determine a spiritual basis for it, until such time as our spiritual natures react and respond for us.

This is important for those on the spiritually-based path because, literally, the health of our souls are at stake.

This internal, often instinctive *qualifying* process has three basic parts:

1) We have a negative (and visceral) response to anyone we deem *unworthy*.

That which is ugly or repugnant to us is to be avoided.

It is admittedly difficult for us to view all as children of God, born of the same soul, entitled to the same divine good. Obviously, as we receive grace and it becomes imbedded in us and our practices, our hearts do change. But how we have *learned* to view others can be as equally deeply-rooted.

Our psychic frames of reference run deep and have been reinforced over time. We know when we see a terrorist. Our media reinforces this. There is a profile in place for all who share a resemblance. We know *good* and *bad* when we see it.

We must discipline ourselves to recognize such thoughts and dispel them.

2) **We categorize people, and their current situations, even if unconsciously, by the degree of *self-infliction*.**

A ratio exists of the amount of responsibility we believe a person to have in his/her own adversity. A single, unwed mother created her own misery. An addict created his/her own misery.

A reckless person brought on his/her own misfortune. A criminal got what he deserved. A poor person does not have any ambition.

Our antipathy allows us to pigeonhole people who made poor decisions or acted rashly and are suffering because of it. Some of us have come to believe these results are a kind of cosmic comeuppance, even though in our best selves we know this to be untrue. We do not even consider the possibility of bad luck, or else we feel pity instead of compassion.

We have thought long and hard about cause and effect on many levels. Yet often we do not extend this to the behavior of others. It is a documented fact that the children of abusers are more likely to become abusers, the children of addicts are more likely to become addicts. Those without resources are always too close to the edge and simply do not have the same opportunities as many others.

Still, what if they have created their own misfortune…

It isn't supposed to matter, is it?

Also, we must delve deeply into the essence of pain. Our relationship to God is in part a solution to pain. But we must also understand there are many internal conditions that make this incredibly difficult. There are people whose life experiences have had so few redemptive qualities they literally know no other way. They have not *learned* wholeness because they have never *experienced* wholeness.

Perhaps we have never made a decision that affected our lives beyond that moment. Perhaps we have escaped long-term repercussions from poor decisions. Yet if we examine ourselves we can all recall a time when we made a choice, had a near-accident, did not verbalize what we were thinking, or succumbed to a temptation that would have had long-reaching consequences had we not simply been fortunate.

Sadly, there are those who are bent toward destruction and self-destruction, who are careless and irresponsible.

When our hearts and minds make no such distinctions, we are on the spiritually-based path.

3) We assess situations, again, knowingly or ignorantly, by our own level of ability to adequately cope with them, and whether we feel we can remedy or correct them.

We gladly donate money to a charity to help the downtrodden (as we should), but would shrink at the prospect of providing hands-on service: training for the homeless who long to re-enter the work force, or read to someone mentally broken, or help to establish a half-way house for recovering addicts, or reach out to prisoners on a personal level, or help an ex-convict find a place to live or a job.

Our comfort level may be so ingrained we cannot budge. But in order to be a spiritually-based person, it must expand.

We feel no responsibility if we do not believe we are capable of helping. We eliminate any compunction toward any type of service with which we are not comfortable.

The key is the spiritually-based life *calls* us to move beyond these assessments to a higher form of understanding. And with all understanding comes a higher form of service.

Our personal service will always reflect our model of the world. But the more we move beyond that, the greater our ability to be creatures of grace.

We are not expected to save the world. We are expected to improve the lives of those about us. Our presumed inabilities are due more to our own self-limitations than any real lack.

If our hearts do not evolve, we have not truly entered the spiritually-based life.

The reason is simple.

We *know* better. We cannot receive genuine good from the God of divine grace without knowing better. The revelations we

receive during such times are clear signals toward the life that *could* and *should* be.

All are equally deserving of our service, everyone in need is worthy of all good, and the joyful task of all spiritually-based people is toward these endeavors.

Also, we must realize on a deep, spiritual level, *all pain is alike. Pain is pain.*

The reality of pain is nothing truly matters except its alleviation.

Suffering is suffering regardless of who the person is, what prompted the suffering, or their own level of culpability.

Everything not whole in the entire human world is because of pain. Whoever treats pain, treats the world.

Any circumstance that injures two requires tending to both without regard as to who may have initiated, caused or is more *responsible* for the events which created the damage.

One of the divine fruits is compassion, and just as God does not differentiate between seekers, neither should we differentiate between anyone in need.

As we are able to overcome any internal selection process, we will also grow spiritually. The cycle of receiving, living more fully, and dispensing enables us. As we make ourselves aware of our own shortcomings, we open ourselves to the needs of others. As we grow in grace, these selection processes will dwindle.

When we truly become the children of God, we come to accept, in greater frequency and in greater profusion, that we are **all** children of God, and we believe it more certainly and without reservation.

And we behave accordingly.

That is living in grace.

FORTY-TWO

Not Like Us

Anyone who has found a spiritual path that has evolved into a conventional faith system has heard certain lessons that purport to translate God's disagreement with entire segments of our populations.

These are judgments, of course, and we understand God has no true hand in it, but it is still a powerful way to separate the *righteous* from the *unrighteous*. When confronted with the self-titled prospect that God is indeed a God of love, or that love is a part of *his* nature, the result has at times become a paradox:

Love the sinner but hate the sin.

Nearly every faith system adopts some version of this concept as a truism. All contain elements, and well as *consent*, that identify and allow for personification of something it believes is a *sin*.

This is difficult to justify on many levels.

First, it ignores the true nature of God. God does not have an opinion, nor the capacity to distinguish one from another.

Secondly, it ignores even what others believe to be the true nature of God. *If* God creates, would there not be some worthwhile purpose for all creation? *If* God has a judgment in these matters, who among us could possibly be qualified to *know* how God thinks? None of us are wise enough or good enough.

Thirdly, any judgment upon those who live or act contrary to what a group believes is a judgment actually created by the group, and not God, nor even the teachings of God, except as an arbitrary interpretation of what a group *believes* to be God or inspired by God. Most of these interpretations tend to be affected in the sense the character of the group is defined according to these interpretations. Again, it is a devotion to *things,* even ideas and concepts, that have evolved to a point where they shun further development.

Lastly, it evokes a *separateness* among the children of God, which already exists to the detriment of all. It is another part of the exclusionary process that segregates various forms of *believers* into groups. Perhaps this has no ill effects during worship, but cannot help but indicate and exacerbate separate ideologies that lie just beneath the conscious surface, and so densely that they are prone to erupt into something wholly ungodly.

We encounter this nearly every day—the *fruits* of sectarianism that has us devoted to so many separate *gods.*

Additionally—and obviously—it is a psychological (and obviously spiritual) impossibility to contain opposing feelings at the same time. One cannot love and hate simultaneously. One cannot be spiritual and anti-spiritual at the same moment. One can transition from one to the other, but contra-spiritual thoughts and feelings eventually and unavoidably lead to contra-spiritual actions.

When one identifies an act as a *sin,* the identification is actually an implication that what is a sin to some is not a sin to others, unless this act is one of the universal sins.

In fact, one cannot identify an action of another as a sin without committing a universal sin…deliberately harming another for harm's sake.

Those who identify *sins* retreat to the illogical, believing they can love someone despite this *sin,* because they are *of God,* instead of considering in true spiritually-based love they should have no such judgment at all.

The fact is, it is neither our purpose nor in our capacity to do this. Making such a judgment is presumptuous and tilts us toward thoughts of superiority. We have also made generic the word *hate*, and have actually applied it to God. God cannot hate. Only human beings can hate. We have skewed sacred texts and the teachings of prophets to incorporate the concept there are times, places and actions that we can *hate*. It cannot be done.

True hate is a very powerful emotion and serves no productive function. To hate is to separate ourselves from God. To hate is to lose all grace.

We know our own feelings. We know the truth in what is inside us. We either choose to deceive ourselves or we address it.

So we must know there is no disdain we can feel, hold or show that does not weaken us, especially in our relationship to God. Only in our lack—our superficial and utterly mortal viewpoints—do we make such appraisals of another. Only in some empty part not yet touched or completed by grace could any spiritually-based person allow such perceptions or gut-reactions to take root.

The mortal will always dilute the divine, and for the worst. We may feel exhilaration at a point of fear—adrenaline, or we may feel an uplifting at a point of sorrow—relief, or something positive from a negative—growth, but we cannot feel a positive and a negative at the same time any more than we can physically move in opposite directions.

What we are doing is creating pseudo-spiritual slag that keeps us immersed in self-righteousness and anti-spiritual opinions.

In the past, this concept has been applied to everything from what we might eat, to what kind of material we wear, to how we worship, to the roles of women in our cultures and our religions, to the value of certain calendar events, to hierarchies, and to the preservation and pious devotedness to physical icons, rites, rituals and celebrations.

It has also been applied to different races, cultures and varying religious practices. There has never truly been an integration of commonalities with regard to God's nature and function, except superficially. Our entire spiritual identities began with such differences, and have evolved to maintain such differences.

It is, and has always been, a doctrine of *us vs. them*.

Obviously, certain choices others make appear inappropriate to us. Free-spiritedness manifests itself in myriad ways: tattoos, piercings, clothing styles, makeup, music and all forms of outward behavior. There have been many periods in history where promiscuity and sexual experimentation have attracted attention. There have been claims of spiritual experiences through hallucinogens and physical items. There have been demigods who sought to lead from the depths of their own mortalities. There have been elements of mysticism in offshoots of every major faith system—that there are *magic* ways to God.

There have *always* been seekers, seers, and would-be prophets who have discovered some key to *nirvana* that all could partake.

There have always been existing conditions with the inevitable uprising of some opposed to those conditions, with those claiming to adhere to those conditions exerting their authority to maintain those conditions.

One of the more recent areas of focus, whether from a secular or spiritual sense, relates to sexual orientation.

So many of us simply do not understand homosexuality. How could such a thing exist? It defies the procreative rules of nature. More, it is at worst—deviant, and at best—unseemly.

Just as many, perhaps, believe it is a *choice* made by those who participate in it, and therefore have *chosen* aberrant behavior.

This has certainly been true in the past. Our world history is rife with cultures which practiced omnisexuality. Spiritually-based people shun this, not because it is unsavory, though it may be, but because it is *unnecessary*.

Sexual love is always to be private and personal, and between two loving individuals.

Even those who might believe one is *born* homosexual would name it a defect, and a serious one.

Anyone embarked upon a spiritually-based path understands two precepts regarding gay people.

First, all are to be loved. More, they are to be served. They are also to be understood, which may seem to be too much like work to some. Understanding requires educating ourselves to the alien.

Secondly, science and common sense has determined that for the most part, those who are gay were born that way.

Those who are born gay are drawn to members of the same gender just as the rest of us are drawn to the opposite gender. Humankind has progressed far beyond the genetic urge to reproduce. Our monogamous, sexual selves are a part of our spiritual growth in that we are to find our *better* selves through such partnerships.

Those gay-by-birth are not so different from those who are born left-handed, blue-eyed, dark complexioned, curly haired, or have any other inherited trait. We do not yet understand the meaning of our genetic code in its entirety. Obviously it is confusing as to why there would be those who cannot reproduce by natural means. This alone gives some cause to name it an abnormality.

Yet in our evolution toward seeking a more spiritually-based life, we also understand the contradictions in the *natural order* of things.

We are no longer born to procreate simply because we can.

We are still a people prone to anger, and capable of violence through anger, though it is no longer necessary—our survival is no longer threatened by others on a frequent basis.

We are still a people prone to greed and covetousness, even after our basic needs have been met.

We are still a people of wants who are slow to be satisfied, even after each of us has a personal, individual relationship with the eternal perfection of God.

The spiritually-based person must understand people among us are not required to change to fit in to any customary roles. And we must move into an even greater understanding that like left-handed people or people with heterochromia (different eye colors), those gay-by-birth are the products of the evolutionary process and are no different in spiritual substance than anyone else.

This substance must be nurtured, the same as anyone, enlisted and used, the same as anyone, and encouraged, the same as anyone.

We must advance the day when a gay person is treated no differently than any other soul, and a gay mated couple is treated no differently than a heterosexual mated couple.

The tendencies toward disdain regarding people who are born *different* contain the same cultural biases and superstitions as handed down from time immemorial. We cannot allow the well-intentioned ignorance of any past seeker to color the spiritual evolution we now strive to comprehend, accept and embellish.

We are not all born the same, except where it matters most and solely: our capacity to receive grace.

FORTY-THREE

True Justice

How sad, how utterly dispiriting, how incredibly pointless is the word *revenge*.

Revenge, in all its many guises: justifiable retaliation, reaping what one sows, the will of God, even certain aspects of law, is the sanctimonious and exceedingly purposeless response to a real or presumed hurt. And more often than not, actively or passively, we have a hand in it.

Someone has hurt you, or someone close to you, or even someone you may not know, but the action offends you, so you want to strike back, personally or by proxy. It's understandable. Perhaps it's even *natural*. But it's also terribly fruitless.

No matter how seemingly justified, how outraged and legitimized we may feel, a cruel response to a cruel act will only produce more cruelty. This, too, is part of the natural order. It can be no other way. We must find some internal means to diffuse the malicious so we do not make matters worse. A world of poison creates a poisoned world.

There is both intentional and unintentional harm. We nearly always recognize a difference. An assault is different from an accident, though the results may be the same. Even if the harm done is real, the intention to harm may not have been there. In every case, there has to be some measure of tolerance so we do not dissolve into rashness.

What if the harm done was deliberate? We have all seen examples running the gamut from spreading a rumor to a terrorist bombing.

The key is our response is to be the same. We are to tend to the aftermath and then seek to remedy the cause.

There can be no peace until the cycle of hurt and retaliation stops, and it is always going to be the responsibility of spiritually-based people to stop it. Though it may greatly pain our more human selves—a bruise to our sense of right and wrong, the desire to hurt with hurt—the self-righteousness of retaliation has to stop. Circumstances large and small will not improve until it does.

Ultimately, what is gained? Is there truly any enhancement of the spirit in such angry chaos?

We are all to be seekers of justice. And we believe when people receive *true justice* they lose their appetites for revenge.

What is *true justice?* There is no single definition.

For the spiritually-based person, true justice is even-handedness from a spiritually-based perspective.

The desire to seek retribution stems from a sense of loss. If this vacancy is not filled with comfort and compassion, the desire for retaliation festers and grows until it is acted upon. Perhaps we cannot replace a loss, but we can ease the *sense* of loss until the desire for requital has passed. We do this in ourselves and for others.

At times there is a *direct offense*. Someone has deliberately inflicted physical or emotional harm upon you and you want relief, believing, erroneously, seeing the perpetrator in pain will accomplish this.

At other times there is an *indirect offense*. Someone has gossiped about you and you find out about it, so you want that person penalized. Or someone has done something in ignorance that affects you and you want there to be consequences for them—perhaps even consequences of your choosing.

There is also a measure of envy in some of these situations. Someone has been given something where you have had to earn it. Or someone has received something you feel they don't deserve. Or someone received something you felt you deserved.

There are much more serious elements, of course. Dealing with the loss of life or the loss of property or the loss of function by another person is an extremely harsh aspect of life. We want the restoration of what was ours, and we want reparations. It is the same in an accident as it is in war—and frankly, with the same disastrous results.

In nearly every case, these desires are accompanied by the desire for the offender to be punished, and that desire cannot be separated from the desire for revenge.

No matter how we are hurt, or how much we have suffered, there is little spiritual basis for seeking, fomenting or supporting *a pound of flesh* from any real or perceived offender. Many times we feel the law is not enough. Many times we feel affliction-for-affliction will somehow help us heal.

As impossible as it may seem, especially in the loss of someone close to us, the only *spiritually-based* remedy would not only come to us through the nurture of grace, but we would also wish a greater spiritual evolution for the accused.

Of course laws must be enforced to protect the good of all. Of course there must be an accounting for all destructive acts, criminal or otherwise.

But those injured cannot be called upon to judge the accused. The cycle of resentment inflamed to ill action would only intensify.

Look at our world today. Look at all the corners of dissension. Look at all the attacks, the response, the counter-response, and so on. How could it possibly end without so many of us emerging from a spiritual basis to say *enough*?

And though it is true we will never agree on what true justice is, the spiritually-based person knows what it is not, and thus should have the impetus to participate in its manifestation.

We must bandage and restore those who are hurt. It, too, may seem ineffective, as we seek to heal those bent toward a return to battle, but it must be done in the hope at least one will see the futility of reprisal. At times it will be like refilling a leaky tire. It will inevitably need to be refilled again. We patch it and hope the patch will hold.

We treat the innocent and the accused with the same care. We treat the innocent so they will not hunger for revenge. We treat the accused so they know everyone is not an enemy. We treat all with love so none succumbs to the urge to strike back.

This—the seduction of reprisal—is the true foe.

We also do this in ourselves. We treat our pain, we go within, we seek help, we rid ourselves of the same temptations.

We begin this in our hearts, in our relationship with God. We reach out in real and tangible ways. We replace the tire. We work to make environments safe. We work to give everyone the means to feed and clothe and house themselves and those closest to them, to be productive in the ways acceptable to them, and help provide them the tools to find internal and external peace.

We ask the simple question that, for whatever reason, rarely seems to be asked: **Why did you do this, or why do you think this was done to you?**

Many times *offenders* do not even know the beginning. Other times a fundamental need is denied them. Would you steal food for your family if you had none? Would you assault anyone who tried to stop you? Would you hide the truth of your *crime?*

And what if we treat the hostile, the belligerent, the irrational in the same manner? Would this merely be naïve? Or is there a chance they might understand not all are enemies. Is there any chance those within their influence might find the cause less just?

We befriend, we provide resources, we commiserate without stoking the fire or joining the fray.

Incidences can range from the seemingly trivial, such as a harsh word, to the inexorable, such as armed conflict. Events can also spiral out of control in a whisper.

Regardless, the solutions are the same because the sources are the same. We must address and be prepared to remedy *feelings* of inequity the same as the inequity. Further, we must understand perceived inequities from the perspective of those who are suffering and not our own.

Remember when you were a child. Someone pushed you or took something away from you. You wanted your pain to be noticed and you wanted the offender to know the same hurt.

Though infinitely more vicious and the scars far more permanent, the roots of all wars are the same.

All attacks are the result of virulence. All reprisals, by their very natures, are the same.

One person's justice may be another person's revenge, but on the whole, the more we can deliver and restore equanimity to all, the less the likelihood those same people would ever resort to conflict.

If a hurt is diminished, the desire to respond is diminished. When the source and the result are in agreement as to the potential for harm, the urge to harm is abated. When all are more satisfied in the fundamental qualities of their lives, the lure of conflict is reduced.

Also, in ourselves, we forgive quickly and fully, as we have learned.

When more are understood, greater will be understanding, and the potential for any perceived harm, or retribution, will be eased. The more it is eased, the more peaceful the environments we share.

Again, it is the math of God. The more that good fills us, the better off we are. The greater the number of people who receive good through grace, the better off we all will be.

The more who receive justice, the more justice there is.

It is a part of our purpose, and a considerable part, to initiate these principles, to enable them, and to prove them.

FORTY-FOUR

Spiritual Paradoxes

The world we inhabit, and our place in it, contains many paradoxes. Rain which benefits one can flood and ruin another. Our good fortune may come at the expense of someone else. Any hardship that befalls one can be a benefit to someone else.

Of course, there are matters of perspective in all these things. There are lessons to be learned in every situation we encounter, whether the initial result seems good or not. We know there is a randomness to things even as we understand cause-and-effect. A hailstorm may strike a home and leave others in close proximity virtually untouched. Someone may be more susceptible to a virus and suffer more greatly than others.

Life, without the intervention of spiritually-based people, is not always equitable.

We know how we should view these things, how to respond and what we are to do, just as we know God had no hand in it except through us.

Again, and always, this is living the spiritually-based life.

There are other paradoxes, however, that require more reflection as to the true welfare of the spiritually-based person and the environment he or she helps to create.

There are fundamental paradoxes in nearly every sector of our lives—where we live, where we work, where we play, what we do.

It is also important to meditate on these things with no sense of superiority or sense of bias.

In times past people could not live in the same neighborhoods, attend the same schools, even work at many of the same places, simply because of their race. We all know the extreme malignity inflicted upon Jewish peoples throughout history, culminating in the events of the Second World War. Exclusionary practices are found in all cultures even today.

Similar divisions exist by ethnicity and relative prosperity. *Friend* or *foe, associate* or *outsider* can be determined by such divisions. Some may even seem rational, like the manner in which a Christian, Jew or Muslim worships. Each to his own.

Schisms between various groups and sub-groups in every society have grown to the point where so much potential commonality is ignored. The term *class warfare* has been used to illustrate political differences.

Hopefully, and with effort, we are growing away from such superficial classifications.

In other cases, differences have escalated into something contentious and threatening, or at the very least, contribute to a kind of communal cynicism. The louder one is, the more he is heard. The more violent one is, the more attention he receives, the more vain one is, the more enlightened he appears, the more egocentric one is, the more seriously his words are taken.

In so many venues, these would not be tolerated. No employer would hire someone whose primary course of action has been to disparage others. No sports franchise would want a player who *claims* to be better than anyone else on the team as his primary asset. No one wants to be excluded (and should feel the same way about being included) because of physical unattractiveness (or attractiveness), no matter the situation.

Spiritual Paradoxes

Yet many of us somehow accept these as fixed and inalterable.

Every spiritually-based person *knows* what conforms to our principles and what doesn't. It isn't a matter of judgment, but we can and do recognize behaviors that are vain and self-serving.

> *We do not have to accept the behavior as right or correct to befriend or provide service. We can, however, choose not to uphold the actions. We do not have to vote for any candidate, support any form of entertainment, participate in any group, or any other activity for public consumption, that opts to degrade others for gain, or advances any kind of exclusivity based upon inequality.*

We are not required to buy, consume or bolster any one or any thing that generates conceit or narrow-mindedness toward others. We are not loud about it, or provocative about it. We simply choose not to take part in it, except through service.

Other paradoxes are more abstract, or may hit closer to home.

What if someone works for an arms manufacturer? We love our country and believe it has a right and duty to defend itself. Yet we also acknowledge the product we help create, even if we are a mere bookkeeper or factory worker, can be sold to others whose sole intent is to use these weapons in aggression.

Suppose someone is a farmer. No endeavor is quite as noble. His livelihood depends upon a successful harvest. Yet he also knows prices rise when others experience drought or other hardship, enriching him, and sells his abundance at a greater profit even as there are others who suffer.

Suppose someone imports goods that can be offered to the consumer at a savings, though it may put some of his neighbors out of work.

Suppose someone works for a company that pollutes our environment on a major scale, and the pollution is obvious.

Suppose someone is in the legal profession whose practice is devoted almost exclusively to those who file claims against insurance companies, realizing many would prefer to settle the issue than drag it out, even though there may not be any legitimate wrongdoing to their clients.

Suppose someone works for a medical entity that overcharges for medical procedures covered by insurance, or prescribes certain procedures *because* the patient is covered by insurance.

Where is the spiritual basis for any of this? Can we still claim to be spiritually-based people?

Of course. Anyone can approach God and receive grace. We've discussed several times what is required to open the way without internal obstructions. Stubbing a toe can affect this process just as adversely as engaging in duplicity.

But there is always more.

The spiritually-based person can and should find some of these paradoxes troubling.

As we consider these things, with as little bent toward criticism as possible, there are three questions we must ask ourselves and prepare to respond to the answers we receive.

First, who truly benefits from an endeavor?

If the answer is *all* or *most* then there is great benefit. An attorney who defends the accused, even if the majority may indeed be guilty, serves us all through maintaining a presumably equitable balance.

A political aspirant who wants to serve and presents him or herself in the best possible light without making negative claims as to the worthiness of an opponent can benefit many he or she represents.

The manufacturer of a product which can be used for destruction, though this is contrary to its primary function, can be aware of this. Taking action to prevent its ill-usage produces far more benefit than risk.

A company that produces harmful waste, whose products benefit many, and who is sincerely determined to reduce or eliminate the negative impact on the earth, can provide a positive influence.

On the other hand, any person or entity that seeks to serve only *one*, or a *few*, should be subject to consideration as to whether we participate as a patron, employee, or consumer.

Far too often the lure of economic prosperity clouds rationale as to whether we should or shouldn't.

Secondly, we must ask ourselves the true value of what is gained, and whom does it serve?

Do we feed the beast by responding favorably to those who espouse the gospels of animosity or contention to rouse us?

A media personality whose wealth and standing comes from seeking and exploiting presumed flaws in leadership (or anyone else), and does so indiscriminately, and without any real solution except to the propagation of the same, preying upon the anger and resentment of those who cannot rise above it, primarily serves only himself and those of like-minded malice.

People who provide sub-standard housing to the poor do serve a purpose, because that is all some can afford. But if the standard is lowered in order to create a certain profit, is anyone truly served beyond the ownership?

How much of our entertainment truly enriches us? In the past, would we have been one of the many present at gladiator competitions, public executions or riots? Do we need carnage, literal and figurative, to liven something within us?

Is creating a fine rifle, with a multitude of uses, regardless of how we may feel about guns or hunting, the same as creating a submachine gun whose only real function is to destroy human beings? What is truly enriching about a weapon that can fire ten rounds-per-second? How would we feel if everyone over the age of eighteen possessed one? How would we feel if everyone in our neighborhood owned one?

Does a company whose product can be made safer but does not and will not because they are not *required* to truly benefit the greater good? What about a company which produces poisonous residues, but hides them or denies them? Is it worthy of any support, even as they employ some of the citizenry?

Though it is a near-impossibility to make certain judgments without being judgmental, we **are** able to assess the common good.

We *know* if something creates more harm than good.

We weigh such things in our own lives every day—many times a day. We may not think of it in those terms, but we do. We know if an action creates harm. We know if we are reckless or inconsiderate. We are well aware of the potential for damage.

Each of us represents *one,* and we know when what we do, even indirectly, adversely affects more than one. The spiritually-based path can call our every participation into question as to how we enrich or are enriched.

Thirdly, does any effort we participate in, actively or passively, create a quandary for us in maintaining a spiritually-based life?

Are we supposed to leave a position that feeds and clothes us because the industry may create as much harm as good? Are we supposed to deny ourselves entertainment because we cannot find a spiritual basis for an activity? Are we supposed to try to alter that which is and has been for far longer than we've been a part of it?

Again, the spiritually-based person *knows*. And our first instinct is to seek ways to avoid any responsibility in these matters. This, too, is a part of us. We do not want to be one of those people picketing for equality or against pollutants. We don't want to miss an entertainment we've grown to enjoy. We don't want to run afoul of anyone if we lament certain political processes. And we certainly don't want to rock the boat when it comes to our jobs.

Yet as we move along the spiritually-based path, we still **know.**

Our relationship with God is solitary and internal. But we all know it doesn't end there.

We've made great strides in recent years. Nearly all manufacturers are aware of the byproducts of their industries, and are making efforts to reduce the adverse affect of them. We have come to know the futility of armed conflict, and the price paid for arming those who seek to do damage above all else. Many of us are beginning to understand the damage that dissension-for-profit is doing to our society and our government. And we are learning what greed for greed's sake can do to the common good.

But as spiritually-based people, we must also participate. Not only that, we must seek to do so without inflaming the passions of those who may not agree with us.

We cannot allow harm to persist in equal relationship to good, and in our hearts, every spiritually-based person knows the difference by looking within.

We do not participate physically, emotionally or financially in any endeavor that creates more harm as good, and no matter how much we argue with ourselves about that ratio, some part in every spiritually-based person knows the difference.

In such situations, we must seek to **positively** influence the impact such things have on our world, our communities and our fellows. We must strive to help create equity among the downtrodden. We must seek the means and methods to preserve our planet. We must find areas of entertainment that can enrich us. We must make our work count for something more than *paying the bills*.

The irony of the spiritually-based life, though often discomfiting, is once we know a thing we cannot *unknow* it. It compels us to a greater calling because of the benefits we have reaped from God's abundant grace. And to sacrifice one is to lose the other.

There is no such thing as a *necessary evil*.

Ultimately, there must be good.

FORTY-FIVE

Spiritual Modesty

To examine what modesty really is, we must first dispense with any part of any ideology that suggests or purports this current era is one of decay—or at least, more decadent than some other era.

Every successive era is going to be deemed by some as more corrupt than the previous one. This is important because we are never to substitute priggishness for spirituality. This returns us to the concept of *necessary behaviors* in the guise of piety. Spiritually-based modesty has little to do with any presumed past proprieties.

Consider this. A single god is a relatively recent concept. Monogamy is the same. Sacred texts are filled with characters who are brash, brazen and egotistical, and are revered for it. Trickery, lies, deceit, lust for power and influence, promiscuity, gluttony, drunkenness—every fault ever named—have been with us far longer than our acknowledgement of God, accepted, and even admired at times by different cultures. Even our current societies tend to appreciate pretension as a strength.

Obviously, there is much over-consumption in the world around us. Yet even in times of so-called spiritual renaissances, there were inconsistencies in what was good, true and just. We do not *return* to the better, we move *forward* to the better.

> **As every other spiritually-based consideration, true modesty is an examination of our behavior in that light.**

In some instances, modesty is a vanity, especially when we desire for others to see us as so, and not for its own sake. Modesty is not to be an affectation. Spiritual modesty is another means in which we choose to conduct ourselves.

As all our spiritually-based desires, it is also difficult to name anything a *virtue* without seemingly indicating the lack of it in others. We cannot seem to want a thing, or do a thing, without distinguishing our acts from the absences of it in others. This belies the very definition of modesty, and we must be aware of that as we ponder it.

Again, we conduct ourselves as our spiritual bases require, and do this without advertisement.

Spiritually-based modesty has two primary elements.

First, modesty is any *mindset* that exists without the desire for or expectation of recognition.

We already know there is spiritual footing in doing good for the sake of doing good.

To do this with our hearts and minds free of any need or want of outward affirmation is spiritual modesty.

This grows the spirit and enhances our personal relationship with God. When we are able to maintain a perpetual attitude where this becomes second-nature to us, all our focus is pointed outward. It is almost as if we become an echo of divine good, where we act as a conduit, relaying what we have received.

When we do this without any *desire* for appreciation, our *desire* becomes more pure, more genuine, and motivated by love.

Secondly, modesty is any *activity* for the greater good without any desire for or expectation of recognition.

The performance of any activity for good is not a *show*. We do not seek recognition for deeds, and once our attitude is such that we do not desire it, our work reflects this. We do what we do and move on. Spiritual modesty impels us toward anonymity.

We can feel good about ourselves and good about our service without bowing to vanity. We can act for the sake of action.

Obviously, and with nearly everything else involved in the attitude and work of the spiritually-based life and the human condition, our mortality will impede us. After all, do we not *deserve* recognition for the positive results of our actions?

Perhaps. But the closer we draw to God, the more we realize such desire, and even such acknowledgement, would spoil us, leading us to the expectation of such awareness in others. Then, the awareness of others becomes the focus and not the action itself.

Also, if such awareness does not come, would we then lose our incentive for such actions? If the action is its own cause and its own effect, then it remains more true to the cycle of divine good.

The desire for importance is perhaps the most immodest thing one can do.

There are those among us, regardless of what they believe, who seek to nurture, protect and enrich the lives of our neighbors every single day, and who do so with no desire for praise, no expectation of any recognition or reward except the enhancement of their spiritual selves and their individual relationship to God.

We should be modest in all our actions, even to the point of resisting praise. We should be circumspect about every endeavor so ego does not impair us. We should reveal divine perfection and perfect good in whatever we do, knowing *a single act of vainglory will be remembered far longer than ten acts of grace.*

Above all, we are to embrace humility, understanding we are fortunate to have found the way to goodness and grace, and those of our kinspeople who have not found such a way, are to be viewed and treated with even greater love and care, not disdain. Nor are we to be *proud* in any successes, but grateful to have found that God exists for us.

Also, we must redefine what we believe modesty to be, without vilification, of course, but again as recognition of what better serves our spiritual natures.

We are virtually bombarded with the seeming lack of modesty of others. There are *experts* who tell us how to feel. There are people in our workplaces who want us to think as they do. There are politicians who want us to believe they are *true* and anyone else is *false*. There are athletes for whom it is not enough to simply succeed without bravado. There are celebrities who try to influence what we wear and even how we smell with no greater foundation for it than being in the public eye. There are entertainers whose seeming objective is to draw attention to themselves as much as or more than their performances.

Just as what we imbibe determines our physical health to a considerable degree, our sensory intake can affect our spiritual basis. As always, we can decide *this is not good for me* without being critical.

Are we to be blind to those who demand attention merely to have attention? In fact, we are, in that we can ignore it and direct our attentions elsewhere.

Are we being judgmental if we believe we see immodesty in someone else as vanity? Yes, if we view it with scorn. We can if we still love and serve those whose actions we decline for ourselves.

We consider two factors in these conscious decisions we make about what we consider to be the absence of modesty in anyone else:

First, we ask ourselves if we are genuinely uplifted or nurtured by an action beyond the call to serve. Any action we witness that is overtly self-serving has no spiritual basis.

Secondly, we search ourselves for prejudices and unkind feelings toward any action we witness, considering every possible benefit we can imagine, before we conclude we can play no part in it, again beyond the call to serve. If we prejudge or misjudge the *who* then we cannot help but ill judge the *what*.

Finally, we should consider modesty of the body, and if this matters at all.

We all exploit certain assets. God is the greatest asset of all, and we seek to exploit divine energy for our own well-being and the well-being of others. We use our minds to solve problems and create solutions. We use our bodies to improve the conditions of those we serve.

Our bodies are ours. We use them for everything from simple movement to the ways we love. It would be hypocritical for us to claim any *moral* high ground regarding anyone else's use of his or her body. We all use our bodies to accomplish certain ends. Our bodies are tools. Everyone uses the body for work and play.

Our bodies are assets. Many people's bodies are their primary assets, beyond their minds, of course. Athletes, actors, models, dancers, even traffic cops and construction workers use their bodies to exercise their particular skills.

So are there any spiritually-based limits to using our bodies as tools?

Without negating the essential constitution of any other human being, it is something to be considered, if only because of the internal environments we seek to create, and there *is* a difference between those who use their bodies to utilize their skills and those who use their bodies to provoke.

Everyone wants to be healthy and fit. Physical activity can feed the soul. Everyone also wants to be attractive and desirable to a mate. It is part of our humanity. It can also be a part of our spiritual selves when our highest and best is exchanged between adults committed to such a partnership.

> **Yet those who exploit their bodies to the many, and as a source of titillation and desirability, or to exhibit physical superiority over others, simply because they possess these traits, do present a conundrum to the purposes of the spiritually-based life.**

We cannot blame them for doing this. But we can decide for ourselves if such a function should hold any interest for us.

Is there anything amiss when an actor disrobes or dramatizes a sex act in any frivolous sense? Is there any fault to be found in an athlete who preens after a success or belittles an opponent? Is there anything fundamentally awry in being a stripper or a prostitute?

We may ask ourselves, and again, only in the purest of thinking, to what purpose is this done?

What *art* is there in a sex act without love? What inherent substance is there to provoke *desire* in anyone we do not care about? What true, real, and substantive *goodness* is there to use one's physical form to sell a product for profit, or to capitalize on it for mere arousal?

We are to be modest in all we do, and seek modesty in its every form. All accomplishments are to be celebrated, but as a part of what God is and what God provides. We are to never seek glory for ourselves, or unique recognition for our efforts, but seek to serve for its own purposes, and we are to never allow the *apparent* immodesty of others to influence us, alter us, or dissuade us from these principles.

FORTY-SIX

Spiritual Secrecy

The spiritually-based person is always aware and open to areas of service. We have a co-worker who is having a bad day. We have a friend who needs a friend. We see someone whose need is obvious.

We also know there are people in our communities struggling to get by, and we respond in whatever ways we can. We see people around the world fighting for their very survival, and we respond in whatever ways we can. There are always areas where our help can mean something.

We have discussed the premise of providing hands-on service at least three hours a week to serve as a reminder the grace we receive must be dispensed, even as we know grace is available to us in greater abundance, and more opportunities will present themselves as we move about in our daily lives bearing the seeds of grace.

We also understand we must approach these things with an affirmative attitude and grateful heart, even though our efforts can still bear fruit when we cannot.

We know those who recognize our efforts should see through us our purposeful relationship with God, and that grace is equally available to them, and that we do not desire recognition or praise.

We have come to believe in service, the glorious cycle of grace continues as we acknowledge, absorb and dispense. The process is as it is for a reason; the last leads us to the first. We cannot circumvent it.

So it may seem puzzling, or even conflicted, but it is equally important for us to do all we can do in privacy and secrecy.

Why?

To preserve the integrity of actions while removing as much *self* as possible from our service, just as we seek to rid ourselves of such desires. We do this so our motives remain as pure as possible.

To help someone and receive appreciation fills us with a great sense of contentment and purpose. We do not have to ignore these feelings. We can and should feel a sense of accomplishment.

But what if we don't receive the appreciation we feel we should. What if someone does not respond the way we expect? What if the person we are trying to help does not appear thankful enough?

Our thoughts then turn to disappointment and even disdain. Our egos become involved. These are the fruits of acrimony. And despite the knowledge we do what we do because of our spiritual basis, our human emotions lead us back to the age-old thoughts of *well, if I'm not going to be appreciated, I'm not going to do that again...*

We must serve for the good of service, and because it is our purpose. More, it is our **right**, and there is a great element of self-ness in that the more we impart the more we can receive. The more we receive, the more our soul absorbs and the happier we are. There is no ego in this. There is the divine reciprocity of grace, which transcends all secular rewards, the desire for such rewards, and the expectation of rewards.

However, we should contemplate the true *delight* in service is when the act is known only to ourselves (and others only when we might enlist assistance).

Imagine ourselves as defacto *Santa Clauses*, leaving anonymous gifts for the cause of grace. We give simply because we are aware of need. We give simply because we want to, and because we can. Would not the anonymity of our actions be just as, if not more, delicious, than if we were on the local news?

Suppose we become aware of someone struggling to pay a heating bill in the depth of winter. Should we call, declaring our intentions? Should we show up at the doorstep with check-in-hand? Should we make sure everyone knows of our good works?

Or should we simply go to the utilities department, explain we wish to pay the bill on behalf of this person, and pay it.

What about leaving a bag of groceries and slipping away unseen?

What about leaving a dozen blankets at a local shelter without a word?

What about contacting a local college or technical school and ask if there is a fund for those who are truly struggling to pay their tuition?

What about anonymously giving money to someone in prison to afford a few modest amenities?

What about donating to various charities and causes with certified checks or money orders so no one knows who we are?

What about sending gift certificates to schools for coats and shoes?

To provide in secrecy is to fulfill the potential of God. To provide in secrecy is to acknowledge the truth of our beliefs. To provide in secrecy is to exhibit to others we need no recognition. To provide in secrecy is to allow others to realize there is a higher place in **all** that needs no identification, save God.

All rewards come from God in the form of grace. Not only should this be sufficient, but grace cannot be procured without it. It is a physical law that energy cannot be stored without degrading. Water evaporates, whether used properly or not. Batteries drain, whether utilized or not. Even *perfection*, as received by us through the veil of humanity, erodes—unless regenerated through grace.

> *A single act of goodness done in silence is more powerful than a thousand acts by a thousand people done transparently.*

How can this be? Sheer mathematics proves otherwise. Even if the process of generosity is not continued by all, surely at least a few will continue on. There will be a ripple effect from one to another. If so, wonderful.

However, and unfortunately sooner than later, the light will dim, people will forget, life as it has been will continue. Only those truly committed will remain, and the cause will fade, because the reason for the cause has changed.

Should our spiritual selves be so transient? Of course not.

Nor should we ignore or fail to acknowledge the millions of people in our world who strive every single day to bring goodness into the lives of others. Millions of people who want to bring light to these imbalances. Millions of people who devote their time and energy to creating equity amid the inequities of life. These people should be honored, supported and praised, and given our appreciation.

The difference is for us, as individuals, who share an ideal with all who serve, but serve on a smaller scale, do this consistently and privately because the path to perfection requires it. This does not mean those who serve are vain. This means we want to insure the absence of vanity in ourselves.

We do what we do simply because we want to have a personal, individual relationship with God, and are compelled to do so by grace. We do what we do because it is *ours* to do, and a part of our worldly lives.

Certainly, people are rallied, and wonderfully so, by an event or a focused need. People convene and seek to improve the lots of those affected by storm, or fire, or illness, or other catastrophe. Eventually, these things are resolved to a conclusion.

These works are important, crucial, and vital to the common good. We should always participate in times of community or individual needs. Many of these events require armies of helpers.

Spiritual Secrecy

Yet the spiritually-based person, full of grace, desiring only grace, working as a solitary emissary of grace, will perform acts of good time-and-time again. It will be a way of life. It will be a testament to faith. It will be a permanent, tangible and absolute existence.

Still, perhaps, it doesn't add up. Even the most devoted of us would take years to perform a thousand acts of goodwill.

Yes. But how many of those anonymously assisted will forget? Nothing was asked. Nothing was expected. Nothing was brought to light. It was simply *done*. How much more likely are these to respond-in-kind? How much more likely that a certain percentage of these, even if a minority percentage, will reclaim more of their lives, heal, grow, move on and move upward? How many of those aided in secret will recognize the validity of such actions?

And in doing so, how many will wonder the *why* of it, eventually discern the *good* of it, comprehend the *need* of it, and wish, in whatever way, to emulate the *truth* of it?

No matter how noble, how keen, how genuine the service, there are always implied expectations which affect the unwary. Is the act itself sufficient? Of course. Are the motives pure? Of course. But those not upon the spiritually-based path cannot long uphold such ideals without bending toward some self-regard not of grace. And that *is what distracts us.*

It is not a child's fairy tale. Perhaps we've never received anything similar anonymously, but more than likely we have received such a thing, however small, *unexpectedly*, and from someone we did not know—someone who did not stick around to receive our admiration and praise. Do we remember? Of course we do.

Moreover, if we have not received such a gift, we know how we would have felt if we had, and if we opt for a more spiritually-based vision, we will crave to do this for others.

Our presence in the face of an unseen God is how we receive grace. Our unseen presence in the face of others is how grace is discharged.

FORTY-SEVEN

The Cloister

There are some among us who have abandoned this world in order to attain a higher level of consciousness—those who have forsaken as many of the distractions of this world as possible in order to concentrate on spiritual matters.

Every major faith system has groups that live hidden away from the rest of us, who seek only communion with God.

These share an enormous commitment to the causes of the soul. They believe the key to finding God is in the cloister—the quiet calm of a structured environment devoted to the *search*, and ultimately, the *recognition* of the spiritual. They make sacrifices in order to discover the best in what remains.

At times they serve. At times wonderful gifts emerge from these environments. These cloisters delve into the material world to bless it, to contribute to it, even to benefit from it. Yet there is always a retreat to the hidden walls.

What a wonderful thing to be so committed to the causes of the soul. What a blessed mindset is created to touch the face of God. What truths are uncovered in such dedication to eternal intimacy.

But…we must also ask ourselves if this truly serves the causes of grace, especially over the course of time.

The very disorder of human existence breeds the divine purposes.

Without the chaos and calamity, without the bluster of so many struggling to survive, grace would have no meaning. Not only physically, socially or economically, but also to have any real sense of spiritual equilibrium or purpose beyond the soullessness of routine practices. We would be born spiritless, with no hope to correspond with eternal perfection, no desire to know the *more*, no compunction to *be* more.

Wouldn't this be a good thing, a move toward a more perfect world? It would if it had any basis in reality. Human evolution without the instinctive drive to seek and discover divine goodness, its purposes and its fruits, is what has created all this disarray. And because humankind evolved in such a wholesale fashion without it—so few to grasp God's true nature, so few to be thus inspired and to inspire others—our world has become what it has become, less of the *more* and more of the *less*.

So, the world *is* chaotic and disruptive. Real life is always calling and has many demands. It is often difficult to find a quiet time and place to go to God, though we must, and it would be much easier to cloister ourselves in an environment that would simplify the process. This would certainly make things more convenient.

At times we seek our own *cloister* to recharge and regroup. We must retreat from the uproars of our daily lives. There are times when it is desirable and necessary to find a retreat where we can simply commune with God.

Whether it's a room, a park, a quiet place in our own backyards, or even a spot farther away from our front doors, we seek places where we can *hear ourselves think*. Otherwise, we procrastinate until we find ourselves removed from our spiritual practices.

The Cloister

Yet we invariably return. We come back to *reality*. Perhaps this is a necessity of the environments we've chosen. It is almost certainly a necessity of the world in which we are a part—the world of spouses, children, significant others, friends, work, entertainment, stimulation. Most of us could not escape even if we wanted to. We have made commitments and there are people who depend upon us.

But beyond this necessity, it is the world *as it is* that needs to grow and only our habitation of it, and service to it can accomplish this.

This is of our creation. And only grace can influence anyone toward perfection. What has been created, and sustained by us, requires our attendance. What also exists despite us, requires our action.

Our desire to serve cannot be accomplished without the want of the spaces we inhabit. Too much effort is already being made to hide from it. Too many of us have already surrendered to the immensity of it. Too few have taken it upon themselves to improve it. There will be times when the magnitude of struggle and suffering in our lines of sight will seem more than we can bear. We become insulated from its call, numbed to its existence.

We will continuously find ourselves up to our elbows in *messes* that thwart our every spiritual bend. We will be frustrated to find adequate time for our own spiritual nurture, much less the needs of others about us.

It is an irony, of course, that in order to gain divine good we must somehow block out the commotion, yet to administer divine good we must be knee-deep in it. Nonetheless, it is our function as spiritually-based people to bring a sense of calm into it, to salve it, to enrich it and to illustrate in some small part what it potentially could be.

Through our relationship with God, we find the energy to do this.

Sometimes our schedules are filled to capacity. The expectations upon us are enormous. How we would dearly love a tranquil place, even a tranquil few moments. How often can we rightfully claim we are at our wits end, are burned out, and desperately need a respite from so much responsibility.

How justified it is that we scarcely have time to keep our own houses in order, much less those of others.

At times *three hours a week* may as well be a month.

Yet this we always know, and cannot dispute, as we seek to claim a spiritual basis for our lives: *we* are the only ones who can positively affect our collective environments. There is no other way to accomplish it. God is made manifest here only by and through us. If not for us, it will not be done.

When we are still, and receive grace, we *know* what we are to do. Yet how long is it before some distraction challenges us?

In the cloister the relative calm may make it easier to reach God. It may even make it easier to receive good in abundance.

But there it melts away. There it stagnates. There it becomes something less than grace—the law of diminishing returns.

We simply cannot serve from the cloister. Neither can we *hide* from the world in order to find spiritual bearing.

Despite its benefits, and the utter sincerity of those who seek to remove themselves from the rest of us, the quiet insistence of grace causes us to remain in the midst of *the rest of us*, as noisy and unproductive as it is.

So, we seek to bring peace to our own small spheres. We know how to do this. We know how to receive divine good. Regardless of its strength or lack thereof, regardless of how our routines and awkward surprises of our existences make us stray; we bring peace to ourselves. We do this not only because it is desirable, but also because it is necessary. Without some measure of peace, grace is a phantom to us.

In the beginning, we find that place without, wherever there wis calm, wherever there is quiet. With practice we begin to find that place within, bringing calm to ourselves, bringing the quiet to our thoughts.

The Cloister

This is our first practice.

In doing so, we bring serenity, if imperfect, to those for whom we are responsible—our families. We do this even with the knowledge there will *always* be times of dissension and discord, and individual paths for every soul. We do this because it can be no other way if we desire a spiritually-based life.

We find the strength of grace, knowing the value of grace, intuitively giving ourselves to grace, so those about us understand this also, and will seek to know its benefit, because they have seen it in us. They do not see us as holy, righteous or pious, but held together by something strong within us.

This is our second practice.

We do this not as preface, but because these mirrors are what we see ourselves in every day. We do this not as rote, but because our hearts know no other way. We do this because it is our pleasure, and all who can see will see this in us. The practice of receiving and dispensing grace is our contentment even when all about us is in discord, and our confidence in the ultimate goodness we help to create illuminates the spaces we inhabit.

We serve. We serve even when our efforts with ourselves and our families are lacking. We serve because it is ours to do, because grace exists in us regardless of volume or purity. But more, we do this because we *want* to, are moved to, as if our very nature has been altered, as if such acts are as natural parts of our constitutions as deep breaths to clear our heads, stretches to awaken muscles, rinsing our faces to come alive. We *know* always the perfection of grace in the corporeal world.

This is our third practice.

The disposition of our near-world cannot improve from a distance. The disposition of our near-world cannot improve without the divinely inspired amplification of grace. The disposition of our near-world cannot evolve except randomly and haphazardly without the loving actions of grace-filled people. The disposition of the entire world will not grow except through the proximity of those who desire the *more*.

We cannot accomplish any of this while hidden away.

Ultimately, this will spread. Eventually, we will see the yield of good.

To best the crush of the real world's call, to find ourselves thriving in it and with increasing patience reveling in it—to join ourselves to it in hope and the certainty of good, and then to get our hands dirty, is to multiply God-on-Earth.

FORTY-EIGHT

A Competitive World

How often we have heard what a *competitive* world this is. We compete for jobs. We compete for promotions. We compete for the affections of a potential mate. At times in our history, and some even now, we compete for food, shelter and other components of mere survival. And no matter what the outcome, we compete to win.

We cannot avoid it. So many situations require us to vie to get what we want, to go where we want, to gain what we want or need. It is a part of our natures. How many of us have raced to a particular parking space, or across the tarmac even though our seat is already assigned and secured? Have we ever eyed a platter or a bin or a shelf, or any other communal server for a *specific* item we are willing to literally knock aside anyone ahead of us to obtain it? How many times have we seen children fight over a book or a toy or a space?

There are obvious flaws in this process. Rare is the situation where one can prevail without another being deprived. It is nearly impossible for someone to gain without there being a loss as a counterpoint.

At times this seems relatively harmless. At times the *prize* is so trivial that any sense of gain or loss evaporates within minutes, even seconds. Our cultures tend to reward the aggressive, the loud, the boisterously persistent. At time this may even seem like a necessity in order to fulfill a basic need.

So what does any of this have to do with a spiritually-based life?

The key is simple, and should come from the heart. Do not contend in anything if you seek to do harm.

It is not the competition that determines the existence or measure of spiritual basis, but the soul of the competitor. Of course we can brainwash ourselves, or provide ample excuses to ourselves as to why it's okay to gain an advantage, knowing at the outset someone is going to be harmed in the process. Anyone who competes must be prepared to lose and they assume this responsibility, just as we cannot avoid competitive behaviors in certain arenas.

Still, we also know what is *inevitably damaging* and what isn't. We know internally, through conscience, and through the ameliorations of grace. If the competition itself appeals to our lesser selves, or if in doing so our main focus is to seek and exploit weaknesses in others instead of measuring ourselves against the *course*, or if the process makes us more narcissistic, we *know* the absence of spiritual foundations.

Life is *survival of the fittest,* and *I didn't make the rules*…right?
In the spiritually-based world, we *do* make the rules.

Any aspiration, intention or deed we enter into where we possess even the slightest desire to harm another is contrary to the spiritually-based life. Nor are we to contest in anything where the natural and obvious byproduct would be harm.

Two people on a track or in a pool trying to reach the finish line first is pretty basic. Each is aware of the possible outcome. One does not have to injure or impede another to succeed. One gives his best.

But let us examine so many other aspects of our lives, many of which we've already discussed.

If we have to sabotage a fellow employee to gain the favor of a supervisor, or someone in a position to elevate our status, where is the spiritual basis in that?

If we have to decimate the character or skew the decisions of an opponent to win an election, or support those who do, where is the spiritual basis in that?

If we have to devalue someone to win the affections of another, where is the spiritual basis in that?

And if we have to physically injure another to prevail, where is the spiritual basis in that?

Any time we must rely upon the decisions of others for our successes, there will be the temptation of moving beyond simply exhibiting or articulating our assets to diminish those of someone else.

In the circumstances where certain competitions are physical, the temptation, and even the acceptance of injuring another competitor should bring pause and introspection to the spiritually-based person.

A boxer, martial artist, or any other physical combatant **cannot** be successful without harming an opponent.

In American football, ice hockey, and other sports, it no longer seems sufficient to thwart an opponent, but to eliminate his effectiveness by injury.

More, our participation as spectators in these things helps create these environments. We feel the adrenaline and live the violence vicariously. We crave it in video games and fictional entertainment. We watch political and social commentary with delight when someone else is flayed. We enjoy the carnage, however harmless it seems, not because we desire to be a part of success, but because we desire to view the destruction of someone else.

In everything from business, to politics, to recreation, to entertainment, to social encounters, the most effective and expeditious way to gain the upper hand is by maligning someone else. And the opponent does not have to be willing. It could be someone who merely doesn't share a point-of-view, or is apt to have a different perspective.

It does not even have to be accurate to influence some.

How we delight in the fall of someone else. And yet we still feel sorrow when they are laid low and cannot get up, or seriously injured in body or spirit, as if such hypocrisy is validated by the commonness of practice.

We vicariously absorb the struggle of combatants every single day, even as we know the feelings that rise in us are not spiritually-based. How can war be the same as a mere game? It is when any part of ourselves delights in abject destruction.

At times our adrenal glands are our worst enemies. Adrenaline represents the seats of our lesser selves, the drug of choice for the frustrated and unhappy. We have a guttural and visceral response to skirmishes of any sort, from the mere to the deadly.

When we discussed *universal sin,* we made the connection to the deliberate harming of another. It is so easy to agree with this principle. Yet we somehow validate so many areas of contention where the real, true, inevitable, and even *desired* result is the disabling of one by another.

We have discussed paradoxes and how our relationships to societal influences need to be re-examined. We know how difficult it is to appraise our spiritual bases with respect to all types of activities, even those we enjoy.

But there can be no doubt here. We have at times relished the downfall, the *comeuppance* of others. We have reveled in another's defeat. We have even provided the foot upon which others have tripped.

We have celebrated violence and destruction in all its forms.

We have reveled in the stumbling, falling, and resultant hardship of one we oppose.

Whatever is within our control, as direct participants or as spectators, we must not *willingly* engage in the deliberate harming of another.

In fact, it is a part of our function to help create an even playing field for those in our spheres of encounter. Often times there will be very little we can do. We make the effort based upon what we *can* do, or what we earnestly *try* to do.

We do this in our thoughts, words, deeds and patronage, or absence of patronage. This is *always* within our control.

So why is it more difficult to remove this aspect in situations where we might contend? Or why does it bring some corrupt pleasure as we watch others contend?

Because in some perverse way, it makes us feel less vulnerable.

Whatever we desire or *need* at the time, and cannot have…a better job, a better home, a special someone to place us above all others, even basic peace-of-mind, infuses us with such a sense of lack we find relief in the lack of others. And the farther unreachable this is at the time, the greater our desires to witness the suffering of another.

We *must* acknowledge the satisfaction of winning (above the satisfaction of participating) is a conceit and cannot help but lead to treachery.

We *must* acknowledge the myriad guises of what is essentially warfare, and that the thrill of watching any form of this is superficial, perhaps even involuntary, and not a part of our spiritual processes.

We must understand in our evolution as spiritually-based people, we are to countermand that which has not fully evolved in our species. There is absolutely *no* gain for us as a world community in competing for the sake of harm, whether the opponent is a willing participant or not.

It is better for us turn away, except in service. We do not incite. We do not respond in kind to those who might incite us. We do not seek to elevate ourselves when others may fall short, and we certainly do not seek to bring about their harm.

In any environment or circumstance, what real gain can there be in climbing over the bones of another, as a direct or indirect participant? What good is there for our spiritual selves in attainment at the deliberate expense of another? What good is in the passions that arise out of being witness to such things?

Nothing. No *good*. No redeeming qualities at all, unless the fruitlessness of such actions brings us to a more spiritually-based conclusion.

Perhaps we may not always cast the most positive light.

What we cannot do is darken the room.

FORTY-NINE

Profound Faith

We have all been confronted with profound faith, though often we do not name it as faith at all, sometimes to our annoyance, even horror.

We have answered the door to people who wish to share their literature or beliefs.

We have seen examples of *righteous indignation* toward the behavior of others, specifically those who do not share the same elements of faith.

We have also seen treachery and destruction purportedly as acts of *faith*.

We have even seen people give up their lives as suicide bombers while destroying the lives and property of others, all for the causes of *faith*.

We have seen wars among people upon the same land with its foundations in different faith systems—even different sects of the *same* faith system.

History is filled with those who have persecuted others to preserve their *faith*, just as there are those who have been martyred for their *faith*.

There have always been zealots and extremists who claim violent actions are validated by their faith.

> **The genuine spiritual quality of any faith system can be discerned by one simple trait: the willingness or unwillingness to harm another. The spiritually-based person must exhibit and engender the absolute unwillingness to harm another.**

We know our way. Our way is not confined to stipulations. Our way is not aggressive toward anyone. Our way is not to sway others into capitulation, or even simple agreement. Our way is certainly not violent in any form.

Yet we should also consider what motivates some to what we could name *extreme*. We understand the claw of superstition. We understand the clutch of dogma…*things*, be they in rites, thoughts, language or behavior. We may not understand, but we have all witnessed acts of self-mutilation as examples of faith.

Some believe in swords as fruits of grace even as we believe in service as the fruit of grace. Some believe in expulsion as a fruit of grace even as we believe in inclusion. Some believe in separation as a fruit of grace, even as we believe in intercommunication and rapport.

Yet this is not the lesson.

What we are to learn is not how to deal with such people, though at times we must. What we are to learn is not how to discourage the more innocuous of practices, nor how to cope with the most irrational and devastating of these practices, though as long as such concepts exist, we will be confronted with them, and become heartsick because of them.

> **The lesson for us to consider is what our environments would be if our faith in the power of good was so embodied for the causes of grace—if our attentiveness was as strong as others.**

Injudicious though these may be, we cannot doubt their commitment. Certainly we may see a kind of blind supplication that creates far more harm than good, and we may feel we share nothing except blood, bone and flesh. We may rue that we belong to the same species, or live in the same space.

Yet we must stop to consider, with eyes open, the sheer potential of commitment in profound faith.

Commitment is the impetus behind all spiritually-based activity.

Our efforts to seek God require commitment. Our efforts to receive grace require commitment.

And our efforts to be true implements of God require *great* commitment. Otherwise, nothing is done.

We learn in the examples of history of great sacrifice. We learn the gains in ideas and ideals through the sacrifices of others. Yet the spiritually-based life also demands we consider sacrifice, however noble or ennobling, is far easier than genuine commitment.

Genuine commitment requires the desire to *be*, to remain, to do, to continue. Genuine commitment requires the stamina to *live* when sacrifice offers an exit. Genuine commitment illustrates the world-at-hand is not a proving ground, but rather the stage upon which all elements of profound faith are played. Genuine commitment adds the *regardless* to all our beliefs and actions.

When we believe we sacrifice, we cede what we do not possess, or yet possess, so we truly lose nothing. When we believe all is better spent in spiritually-based pursuits, there is no sacrifice. When we commit, we make a solemn promise to ourselves to advance the causes of grace, aware of the barricades we will face…aware of the murkiness contained in every corner of our experience.

Our faith is not rooted in volume. Our faith is not rooted in *things*. Our faith is not rooted in the desire for visibility, nor even a fair hearing. Our faith is not rooted in numbers in the strictest sense.

Our faith is rooted in what one might accomplish here as an acolyte of the spiritually-based life.

Our faith is based upon our own internal well-being and the well-being of others. Our faith is based upon us, as the recipients of grace, to be the centermost part of all we can see and reach and touch, a single cell in the heart of all the humanity about us.

The more profound the faith, even in silence, the greater, richer, and more beneficial the service.

Contemplate this:

Sound travels in waves. These waves travel through mediums such as atmosphere, and affected by physical laws, diminish with distance. How close we are determines the clarity of our hearing. Certain factors can mitigate proximity.

Have you ever been near a lake on a quiet morning when the water was placid with hardly a ripple? Have you ever called out just to see how far your voice would travel? Have you ever been at the edge of a deep ravine, or the mouth of a cave, or atop a hill, and announced yourself to hear the echo?

How near one has to be to hear us is also based upon these factors…how loud we are, ambient sounds, objects between us, the complexity of the message.

Longer-distance communication has been the antecedent of technology since the initial urge to communicate farther than our individual voices allow. Today, there are billions of voices longing to be heard—and many who desire to be heard above all else see no other way than to raise their voices, or commit acts to draw attention to their plight.

Though it may seem counterintuitive and even primitive in the technology of this age, our commitment to faith—a profound faith—returns us to the beginning. A beginning where we need never shout.

Imagine those who are within the range of hearing regardless of where we are. We may have to draw nearer, certainly, but at various times of every day, many are close enough to listen to us.

We simply speak *I am here for you.*

Suppose those within reach of hearing, sharing the same commitment, would also utter *I am here for you.* The sound would overlap for some, but still, it would spread farther and farther as each within earshot heard and then spoke.

Profound Faith

As many as there are those willing to speak, willing to hear, willing to act, the progression would continue.

How far would it reach? How often would we hear?

That is the power of our commitment to such profound faith. We are to be the gentle voice, the tender touch, the very echo of God.

So...our commitment must also be profound.

No matter how far our individual ranges, the potency of our faith will affect those within that range. With full hearts our song goes forth. With willing hands we touch. With gentle voices we repeat..._I am here for you._

To grow our faith is all we are ever to be in this life.

Regardless of all our endeavors, our accomplishments, successes and failures, our identities are be grounded in this.

If we are to believe in God in any capacity, to believe in God's function and purpose, and to then seek an essential relationship with God, the nature, validity and strength of this relationship is all we could ever hope for. All we are ever able to control are the times we find to go to God and accept what we can contain.

There is simply nothing greater. To absorb purity and perfection, to return again and again, to know it exists for us and enables us to go there as long as we draw breath of life—to understand it is boundless and unfailing, and holds no judgment for us—is more valuable than any single thing or any combination of things, or even _all_ things to be found in this world. No act will ever be as powerful for us.

— — — — — — — — — — —

To have a profound faith is to grow, to continue, sometimes slowly, sometimes laterally. To have a profound faith is to find our souls aloft and light on a higher plateau far removed from where we once were—to begin each time from steps farther along the infinite path to perfection, and lose sight of the creatures we have been.

— — — — — — — — — — —

Commitment is our engine. Grace is our fuel. Goodness is its residue.

FIFTY

Thirty Seconds Can Change the World

Early on in our spiritual practices, we will be tested. Even as we grow and the process becomes easier, more fluid and more dynamic, we will continue to be tested. These will be the same difficulties we have experienced before, now to be viewed and dealt with from a spiritually-based perspective. At times only our perspective changes until we are able to impact people and environments by our own goodwill.

In the past, our reactions have either been quick, evidenced by some anxious response, or slow, as we choke and swallow our tension until it inevitably rises again. Our habits are implanted like the roots of great trees.

Our personalities were formed long ago. We cannot change our natures in one fell swoop. Some aspects of our personalities can never be changed. That is the human condition. That is why we feed our souls. If we are outgoing, we will probably continue to be so. If we are shy, we will probably continue to be so.

By the time most of us start school, our personalities have taken hold.

We are not tested by some cosmic force. We will be tested by our own former, ingrained selves.

There is a vast difference between our *natures* and our *mindsets*. If we are outgoing because we are friendly, why should that change? If we are outgoing because we need to be seen and heard, that can be mitigated. If we are shy because we enjoy the quiet, what is the harm? If we are shy because we bear scars, this can be eased. When we begin to view ourselves from spiritually-based points-of-view, not in vanity or pride, but in the desire to be *more*, this is progress.

Our emotional constitution is often like a weapon we use to respond to stress, and only we control the sensitivity of its firing mechanism. How quickly it is used, its intensity, or whether it will be used at all, is within our control, even if such acuities never completely evaporate.

This is not to say we should clamp a lid on a boiling pot. We are not all made the same. Self-control comes easier for some than others, or in different venues than others. What provokes one might seem harmless to another. Sometimes even outrage can seem warranted, though ultimately it is found to be counterproductive.

Our bodies react instantaneously to sudden fear or any perceived threat. We have normal defense mechanisms that create responses to unpleasant surprises or provocations. We have all felt visceral reactions before our brains begin to function.

Regardless of the source, or how we tend to respond, we must deal with all potentially damaging reactions before they escalate, and **the most crucial time is when we feel that initial surge of alarm that pumps adrenaline into our systems,** even if in a seemingly immaterial amount or only for a brief time.

We deal with *life* from a spiritual perspective *because* of our natures.

The grace we receive may be instantaneous, and the goodness we derive from it may be instantaneous. But even as we do not see the results of feeding our bodies at the same moment we eat, we do not always see the complete benefits of grace the moment we receive them.

And it is at such times when our former natures allow external stimuli to corrupt the soul, though it may be slight, and almost certainly temporary.

There are extreme shocks to all of us: untimely deaths, acts of violence, major events with unexpected consequences, horrific accidents, loss of a relationship, loss of a job, crisis for someone close to us. These occurrences tend to stay with us, often playing out again and again, and require consistent effort and reflection and development of coping skills. There will not be instant healing, nor should we squelch any throe until we can process it, though this must be done as quickly as possible or else it will fester.

However, the relatively minor things, things we all encounter periodically, undo us in smaller, though equally septic doses. A child running out into the street in front of us, a situation that makes us late, criticism suddenly cast in our direction, a disagreement with a loved one that escalates quickly, any unforeseen setback, are all examples of things our minds and bodies respond to before the positive natures of our growth experiences take over. Our pulse quickens, our thoughts rise up and our brain tells us to respond quickly (and often harshly) or we will burst.

This is when we must allow our conscious, spiritually-based self to overtake our subconscious responses. It is not easy. We are still wired with the *fight or flee* responses of our earliest ancestors.

But as spiritually-based people we are compelled to a higher level of self-control and a more constructive outcome.

Imagine 30 seconds of self-enforced patience and self-control.

It's easy when we're calm. And during some calm time, we should take a few minutes to look back over our recent history and find the events where 30 seconds of patience and deliberation would have made a world of difference—if we had been able to exercise 30 seconds of non-response, or a non-negative response to a situation. Even if we could not find perfect tranquility

within, even if our brain was flooded with every angry and sour thought and feeling, even as our heart raced, had we consciously drawn grace into our consciousness, what might have changed?
We will find a lot.

> **Consider how many times in our lives (and the lives of others) we would have been far better off if we had simply paused and sought grace for 30 seconds in any and every provocative situation.**

How many regrets would we have avoided? How many disagreements? How many hard feelings?

> **How would our world be changed if every angry person, even those who have not sought grace, took 30 seconds to allow temper to settle and sanely evaluate their responses before acting?**

Think of all the hardship and sorrow that would have been avoided. Ask anyone in prison convicted of a so-called *crime of passion*. Ask those who have experienced road rage, or disagreements over ultimately trivial matters that surged out-of-control, friendships lost, family ties severed, disagreements escalated into something more lethal. Ask those who have said something they desperately wish they could take back, and perhaps are still haunted long after the event.

Wouldn't it be worth it even if all we gained was the absence of regret?

There are four basic parts to this process.

First, we make ourselves *stop*.

Everything that follows is contingent upon that. No matter what has initiated the tide of harsh feelings, we stop, realizing what is happening to us. In that split-second when something has made us afraid or angry or hurt, we stop. If someone cuts us off in traffic, we mentally stop and do our best to ignore them. If we are face-to-face with someone and an argument ensues, we physically stop until we can mentally stop, apologizing if we must, promising to resume later if need be, but we stop. If for whatever reason we cannot physically remove ourselves and find ourselves in the middle of a potentially volatile situation, we stop within.

Event triggers are commonplace. Some event has transpired that threatens whatever environment we inhabit at the time. It is a part of our humanity, though we do not allow them to rule us. We take a breath.

The thirty seconds begins.

Secondly, we *recover*.

Whether we say it to ourselves or aloud, *I need a moment* is a necessity. There are rarely instances when this is not practical or possible. It doesn't even matter if we are understood. We must recover. Feelings become actions and only when our feelings are more positive are our actions more of what we desire–what is healthier for us and more beneficial to everyone involved. We recover by remembering who and what we are. We recover by remembering we are children of God made of grace and on the path of *perfection*. We recover by letting those around us know, if need be, we are uncomfortable in the situation. Even if at the time it seems like surrender, we take the time to turn inward. Soon we will discover that this process only takes a few seconds.

We simply wait until we are calm.

Thirdly, we *disperse* psychic infection.

These are a part of our physical form and not our spiritual form, and much of the time serves no worthwhile purpose. As we recover who we want to be, it is easier to recognize all obstacles. The initial surge has abated. Our physical responses are more manageable. Angry thoughts and feelings are simply replaced by more positive ones. We recognize the potential good in ourselves and that makes it easier for us to recognize the potential good in others.

This is a rational process, and the return to rationality is a return to our spiritual selves. When we are able to recognize and return to the prospects for good, everything is clearer. This can only occur when we let go the things that are poisoning us.

Even if the process is not complete. Even if we recognize the possibility of more vitriol. Even if there is not adequate time for us to deeply cleanse ourselves, we allow the hurt to blanch as much as we can and deal with it later in solitude.

Finally, we *resume*.

The thirty seconds has passed. Are we perfectly calm? Of course not. But we are more in control. If whatever provoked us has moved on, we can resume our course much the same as we began. If there is an ongoing issue involving someone else, we are better prepared to diffuse the situation. We are better able to help solve the condition instead of making it worse. We are better able to be an advocate for good instead of fuel for bitter escalation.

Our daily lives are in fact conducted in how we respond to stimuli of all kinds. Seldom are we able to move through the world as a strictly internal process. Our lives won't allow it, and it should not even be something we crave. We are to live among our fellows and nurture each other as we are nurtured.

Until such time as our reactions under stress are no longer weapons, we can still manage this successfully.

Controlling the trigger is controlling the weapon. And a weapon is not a weapon until it is used as some destructive force.

Thirty seconds of introspection removes our finger from the trigger.

The Price of Redemption

The key to the spiritually-based life is the heartfelt distribution of God's goodness to all. This is the mark and product of our redemption. As we become more whole people, seeking a sense of *more* in all we do, no matter our distance from it, no matter how many times we err, we will ever realize the validity of our faith: the eternal grace of God is always there, always ready for us to absorb, always in limitless abundance.

We seek this perpetually. We learn to receive. We learn to convey it.

We are to be both beacons and guides. We are to be living examples of these tenets, and shine forth through the dusk of our humanity. We do this through conduct and activity. We do this because we have no doubt as to what we are, what we are to be, what we are capable and bound by love to do.

As we live, as we proceed, the spark of God within us capable of so much expansion, awakens us to a simple prospect. It is not a measure or guidepost. It is not a goal where we succeed or fail, nor an ambition. It is not a gauge or evaluation. It is not even a reminder, though that is part of all we do.

It is a *purpose*.

We have the power to redeem one another.

This is not a vanity, nor any seeming belief in our own betterness. This is the fundamental desire to improve the lives of those about us, however small, however apparently immaterial at the time. When we say we may provide *redemption*, we are not speaking as those who believe in spiritual redemption achieved by adherence to other faith systems. We are speaking to the identification and response to the wants and needs around us.

That is the sum of what we have learned, the logical and spiritually-based conclusion of our lives upon this earth. God cannot truly exist in us otherwise. *We* determine God's reach, depth and potency. The very existence of God is proven by us. The infinite goodness of God is exemplified through us.

We will daily face the validity of our faith, ever and always. We will move forward without counting every stone along the way, or looking ahead to see no end. We will move forward simply because it is the only way to go.

Our purpose is not a chore. Our purpose is not a task. Our purpose is not even a means to an end. Our purpose, like our path, is not something we complete. Our purpose is a single step, and then another.

In these steps, not matter how short, no matter how often we stand motionless, no matter how weary we become beneath the weight of our troubled world—no matter the sheer audacity and fervor of the creatures who bear the burdens of so much cultural detritus, so much disappointment manifested in lashing out instead of reaching out—we are to be *there* in kindness and gentility. When we acknowledge the virulence of so many of our race, without being overcome by it, we may relish our lives upon the spiritually-based path.

We are to *become*. We are to *be*, even as we find new enhancement when none seemed possible, or even desirable—even as we attain levels of comfort and contentment we are reluctant to leave behind for the uncertainty of *more*. We may fully believe in the *more*, yet fear its persuasion because we have advanced such a distance already. Even if we have found *enough* to be an adequate state-of-being, we are to *become*. We *become* because it exists for us just beyond the next step. We *become* because we are compelled to *become* in every state of grace we discover in each step.

This is our function, and we are blessed because of it.

And so...we must also know, in the spirit of love and generosity, even in the knowledge of the seemingly unobtainable, and again, without any recrimination to ourselves or others, always, always in the everlasting nurture of grace, no one upon the spiritually-based life is *truly* redeemed unless *all* are redeemed.

No one can claim the ultimate value of his redemption until every nation, every bloc, every city, town and village, every one upon every road and in every place...every man, woman and child... is redeemed.

We are still whole. We are still the children of grace. We do not forsake the utter joy of our experience in this singular consciousness of mortality. We do not fret or create difficulties for ourselves to manage. We do not despair at the sheer weight of such embrace. This is not a measured end, nor is it a pretext to the premise we may never rest, never savor, never delight in the peace grace has brought to us. This is not a call to march upon the ills of the world until the day we rest eternally.

We do not know this as an impossibility, though it may be so in our lifetimes. We do not look to results, though obviously we hope to find the *more* among our fellow beings. We do not know it as aspiration, though it is an aspiration, lest we believe all has been accomplished. We do not know it as a tally in our favor.

We know it as a *truth*, as a logical, rational, sane and divine end to fact and premise...no need may go unrecognized in the midst of spiritually-based people. No need should ever be ignored.

This is our inspiration born of eternal perfection and divine good. This is our *love* enhanced and unmeasured.

We cannot ignore what is visible. We cannot ignore what is felt, as we recognize all derivatives of struggle. We cannot even ignore the invisible and intangible, if through introspection we embark upon spiritually-based matters, or cast a spiritually-based eye upon all we think or do.

We are not required to forsake our lives, except to live in the understanding we cannot be whole without executing some part in such a purpose. We need not remove ourselves from our friends and families, even as we serve, nor are we required to abandon positions in our societies, except where they no longer serve us or others.

We begin inwardly and move outward, even as we still founder. If we wait to move outward until we are *complete*, then we will tread water until we drown. But we do move outward with the desire of goodness for all, the will to make it so, the effort to see fruition.

We believe every good thing will spread, like the dawn, and *everything* will improve. That is all we can do, though this we must do.

We are upon the eternal path to Perfection. And to so desire with our hearts and minds, our hands and feet, for all to claim what is rightfully theirs, is in the footprints before, the footprints after, the footprints we leave behind.

The path is consistent and perfect. It is we who stray, we who wander, we who find other courses, believing they are alike. Yet we are to be ever heartened by the realization God is everywhere upon the path. From our very first step, God is there. When we pause, God is there. When we are drawn to some other, no matter what lures us, God remains, available at all times no matter in what condition we find ourselves, or how frail the first step back. There is *always* a step back.

The God of eternal perfection and divine good is *always* there.

The path does not wind, but neither is it narrow. It is as broad as the night sky so we may always find it, or know in what direction we should move when we stall, or know without doubt where it leads. All we need recognize is that it leads to progress…the progress readily available to us, yet only in the spiritually-based life.

We may always know perfection at any point. For it is not the path itself that is imperfect here and more perfect there. It is us.

What we are to find is grace. What we are to learn is simple.

We will never be truly successful at anything, so far as our spiritual selves are concerned, until we are committed to doing the least of things we know need to be done, and stop doing what we know should not be done.

Are we lost if we fail? We are if we abandon God. What we fail to see, we cannot have. What we fail to consume, cannot nurture us. What we do not have, we cannot share. Only when we swallow as common practice are we fed. Only as we continue, is there abundance. Only in abundance can we share.

As every spare soul in this world is entitled to divine good, none of us can claim complete wholeness until this has been accomplished. This is not our burden, our onus. This is our birthright, knowing along the way there is much enchantment.

All kindness shared adds energy to the kindness, so that it will never die.

We know this not as proverb or Sisyphus stone, but as a calm, firm conviction in the great potential of goodness in every mind, love in every heart, affection in every face, and gentleness in every hand.

We know this as hope, a hope with function, a hope with direction and determination, a hope we will be one, accomplishing what one can do, and a hope we will be one among many, accomplishing what many can do.

We believe in each other.

It is always ours first, then through us, to others.

The recognizable, though an ideal, makes it possible.

The possible, though difficult, makes it accessible.

The accessible, though daunting at times, makes it so.

Let it be so.

Author's Note

When a movie or recording is issued to the public in some form other than its original version, there are *extras*—this to lure potential buyers with things they didn't have access to before—deleted scenes, deleted songs, different versions that did not make the final cut.

Ah, marketing, that indispensable tool of all things creative.

I began this exercise with over ninety concepts. Many were easy to fold into others. Even at fifty there is some repetition. It cannot be otherwise. In anything, as in all things, once a premise is established, and basic fundamentals are designated—and in all philosophy there are only a handful of fundamentals—the rest is elaboration upon the same themes.

Of course I may have missed a few keys that make as much, or more, sense as those I listed. This is not a perfect endeavor. My greatest hope is that my sincerity is acknowledged, and that you find some value in this. That is all I really care about for my part in this.

However, there are a few snippets I could not find a place for in this little book. Many of these are also repetitive, but did not fit so neatly into context.

They are random, though they fit into the themes of this text, and I have decided to list them if for no other reason than my desire some may find a sense in them perhaps absent elsewhere.

I thank you for your patience…

~
~

Every sacred text, every business training program, every person who speaks or writes about human interaction, ventures into the area of **dealing with difficult people**. It's valid, of course. There will always be those with whom we cannot seem to get along.

It's also presumptuous, because who's to say *we* are not the *difficult* one, or at least we are an equal contributor to the lack of harmony? Who ultimately makes the determination as to who is the most reasonable or most sound?

No one.

Their constitutions are constructed from the same process. Only those born with certain mental defects are born disagreeable. The rest is learned.

Regardless, and admitting for whatever reason, there are those who just rub us the wrong way, we must understand a couple of things.

First, there are *negativists* in every environment—those who seem to disagree with everything, discourage every effort, and bring very little positive input into anything.

No matter where we are, or what we do, or the venue in which we find ourselves, we will encounter such people. And we must be ready to deal with them from a spiritual-basis.

Generally, negativists are afraid. They are afraid of change. They are afraid of not being heard. They are afraid of losing their position, or their perceived position. They are insecure in their own beliefs. They carry past pain.

We do not judge them. We simply accept them as they are with the knowledge they possess the same right to good and grace as anyone else. They may not seek it, but it is theirs to claim. And should they struggle, as these invariably do, we do what we can to alleviate their suffering, self-inflicted though it may be, without any judgment or expectation they will change.

We treat them with the same kindness we would someone we deeply care about.

As difficult as it is, we must not shun them, avoid them, or exacerbate the more virulent aspects of their natures. We do not always agree with them, of course, but we listen, we take to heart, and we respond in kindness.

Author's Note

> ***We must also understand and accept no one ever wins an argument.***

The object of any argument, by its nature, is to win the upper hand, to succeed in making a point that neutralizes someone else's perspective. And, of course, it doesn't end there, because no one wants to have his/her point negated. So it escalates, becomes more harsh, more shrill, more adversarial, more antagonistic.

And it *never* ends. Retaliation becomes a kind of warped dictate of honor. Anyone who is insecure, feeling *put down* will nurse the wound and seek the means and the opportunity to *get even*.

It is in every real way an ailment, a desire to not necessarily be *right*, but to be heard above everyone else. And when these feel slighted, they will plot a response born of the same fear, doubt and anger.

On a larger scale, this is how armed conflicts begin. This is how massacres begin. This is how divorces begin. This is how tension and the complete absence of reconciliation begins and decays into hostility.

Disagreement is not only contrary to the spiritually-based life, but is simply not worth it.

Spiritually-based people seek to disarm these situations with a greater sense of understanding from the outset, so there is less reason and cause for them to intensify.

Secondly, our reaction to people we deem as negativists is far more basic than we ever admit or articulate. We simply don't *like* them.

If it seems an oversimplification that we simply don't *like* someone, think again, because it really is that simple.

All of us know someone we took an instant disliking to. Perhaps as we got to know them better, things improved. More often than not, however, our dislike remained until we, too, were poisoned by it.

We don't like their voice or tone-of-voice. We don't like their demeanor. We don't like how they do things. We don't like their shape, their color, their ability to get the better of us. Perhaps we are even envious of them.

She talks too loudly. He got that job because he knew somebody. You know why she got promoted, don't you? He has a weird accent. She dresses like a floozy. He inherited all his money. Her husband is rich and she doesn't have to do anything.

Perhaps our own vanity, or our own fear of revelation makes us give lip-service to someone we simply don't like. We just don't want to say it. *I just don't like him (or her).* We would rather fool ourselves and others around us into believing we possess some ascendant quality that doesn't allow for such admission or candor.

This is lazy and dishonest. The transgression is not merely we do not like someone, but that we refuse to acknowledge it as fact. How differently people would respond to us if instead of seeking support for our attitude, often to enhance it, we admitted we don't like the person we're talking about—and that such dislike is a spiritual struggle for us.

How refreshing (and productive) it would be if we admitted this to ourselves. How revelatory it would be to our presumed spirituality if we thought deeply into this and realized the people who *push our buttons* or *get on our bad side* is someone we just don't like.

But it's there. And often times we avoid what the spiritually-based life requires us to do because it's too much like *work*, or takes us to places we don't want to go. After all, our encounters with God are serene and filled with grace. We step off as if on a new land. Why tempt harsh feelings? We want the solace of grace to last.

It may not come easily or naturally for us. Introspection can be an arduous process if we're unaccustomed to it. Why dig up all that unpleasantness if the point is to feel better?

Why is it necessary? Because the spiritually-based life cannot exist without it. We are not to be confined and insulated. The world out there can be messy, overpowering, fractious and impatient.

Author's Note

And one of the elements of the spiritually-based life—perhaps the greatest element—is that we are able to transport grace to every environment in which we find ourselves, and in every situation we encounter.

So we make the effort to understand ourselves—to understand why our impression of someone is as it is. Calmly, studiously, we nonetheless dig deep to discover what about this person causes us to react in such a way. What is the *real* reason we don't like someone?

Are we envious of them? Do they represent something we secretly desire? Do they remind us of someone who hurt us? Does their demeanor seem to shield them from repercussions we (and others) cannot avoid?

Even if we do not find the most specific answer, we know then what we are to do.

We seek to understand them. We search for validity in what they say. We try to find areas of agreement. We don't engage in areas of conversation we know would arouse them. We behave in a civil fashion. We even *avoid* areas certain to provoke them, if necessary.

We give them the same respect and common courtesy we would a stranger who has had only limited contact with us.

Is there even anything at stake for us in this, except perhaps a fleeting and temporary state-of-mind?

Yes.

How easy it has become for someone to provoke the worst in us by declaring the worst about someone else.

We cannot both be right, so therefore the *other* must be wrong.

We would all be better off if we simply admitted we just don't **like** someone and then elaborate on our reasons instead of puffing ourselves at the expense of others.

And, obviously, an error by another does not make us right. It simply makes them wrong.

As nullifying as it would and should be, internally acknowledging our dislikes about anyone and everyone has infinitely more value than fooling ourselves.

We cannot possibly maintain a spiritual basis while we hold these thoughts and feelings. We cannot possibly claim a spiritual basis (within or without) while we hold these thoughts and feelings. And we cannot hope to create *goodness* in any environment while we hold these thoughts and feelings.

Those who cannot be honest about bias cannot be trusted with any decision which has the potential for bias.

We will never like everyone. There will always be those who more easily annoy us. Nor should we punish ourselves for this, as long as we recognize the shortcoming is **ours.**

Some people *are* more likeable than others. Some people can become fast friends while others never will. However, the spiritually-based person is required to go beyond this to some greater level of comprehension and operation. If we do not learn to view all, to accept all, and to

provide for all the same, we allow our core deficiencies to dilute our approaches to God.

It is the same as with all limitations. We become like Sisyphus, pushing the stone of our constraints toward God, often without realizing it, only to have it roll away from us. And rather to leave it behind, we retrieve it again and again.

Common sense dictates we should treat others the way we would like to be treated. Yet one of the major obstructions to the causes of grace is that we cannot seem to help but define others. We categorize people so we do not have to delve deeper. We like things neat and tidy. We do not want to dwell on anything that requires a greater depth of understanding.

There is no greater indication of this than when we trivialize the feelings of someone else. Things that are important to some people seem so insignificant to us. We look at what we perceive to be the essence of someone and believe they are shallow, or overly emotional, or that their priorities are askew. We disagree about a lot of things.

More, we tend to lessen our understanding or our desire to understand by these differences.

When confronted by something contrary to what we find important, our *natural* inclination is usually one of two responses:

First, we denigrate the emphasis another places upon such things. Someone who misses work because of a sick child is different from someone who misses work because of a sick cat. Someone who creates a schedule around a child's activity is different from someone who creates a schedule around a certain television program.

How often do we view people with worship practices different from ours, or alien to us, as something other than children of God?

We *know* there is no spiritual basis for this, but we do it anyway. Our minds declare *much ado about nothing*, and so we exempt ourselves from the process of deeper understanding, which is necessary, and service, which is required.

Feelings *are* important. Some may be poorly controlled, or overly zealous or even irrational, but that's what feelings are. Feelings are responses to stimuli, both internal and external. Feelings are signs of what's really going on. We are not required to become psychologists, but we *are* required to understand. An angry person may be hurt or afraid. An emotional person may be depressed. The same applies to an exceptionally quiet person. A boisterous person may be hiding other feelings they do not want to share.

The feelings of others are always important because they speak to us the same as words, even if the accompanying words are different. But feelings are also important because each of us has the right to have them. Each of us has the right to feel, even in the absence of immediate resolution.

How easy or desirable it is to ignore someone who wears their feelings on their sleeve.

Whatever instinctive reason we may have, we find ways to avoid asking *Are you okay?* or *How can I help?*

Our failure to first address all symptoms in a loving, caring, spiritually-based manner allows such things to rise in the first place, and our prejudices and proclivity toward judgment creates detrimental consequences.

Just as we are the earthly emissaries of God, so are we the implements of *bad karma*. People do reap what they sow, in a general sense. People are responsible for the results of poor decisions, in a general sense. And people are prone to allow their emotions overcome them, in a general sense.

But it is not our function to judge or punish, just as it is not our function to allow suffering, regardless of how much some part of us may believe it is *deserved*.

The very dismissal of such ideas and conduct helps make up the spiritual basis of our lives. When we are able to serve first, able to treat the symptom without such notions, **then** we are able to aid in the causes.

Why is this important? Because we cannot alter how a person thinks or feels or behaves without his/her permission, and as such, we cannot make this a condition of our service. We can no more rightfully withdraw our loving actions from an addict who has not yet found the impetus to stop than we can withdraw our loving actions from an *innocent* victim of an unexpected setback.

To the spiritually-based person, such attitudes are vital, even as we struggle to come to terms with the limitations of our own mortal thought processes. It is better to feed the sixth child of a destitute woman, even if we have to hold our noses and keep our mouths shut during the process, than to speak a single word of dissension until the immediate task is discharged.

When we cease to *trivialize* the *trivial,* and can validate the feelings of others no matter how we perceive them at first glance, we help create a more whole environment.

Secondly, acknowledge any problem we create with a solution. If we're running late, we call ahead. If we have to retrace our steps, we do this. Any problem we have a hand in requires us to be a part of a solution, whether it's a quick stop for gasoline because we procrastinated, or reducing the carbon emissions poisoning our planet.

We are responsible.

Thirdly, do not criticize or denigrate anyone or anything without a solution. Adding more toxicity to the fray is not only a detachment from the spiritually-based life, it's counter-productive. Do not comment at all without a solution in hand, or a willingness to be a part of a solution.

Author's Note

If we complain about being stuck in traffic because of a disabled car and do nothing, we are hypocrites. If we do not vote, we cannot complain about the outcome. If we see someone litter and don't pick it up, our words mean nothing. If we are intolerant, we have no right to grumble about dissension.

The spiritually-based life requires us to *act*. Often it is better to act in error than not at all, especially if we understand what is required of us.

Complex solutions to complex problems are much the same as simple solutions to simple problems. Offering a ride is not the same as preventing a war, but the concept is the same. Wars are prompted by people who are lazy in their thinking and quick to take offense. If spiritually-based people feel required to act positively, to provide solutions, then conflicts are slower to arise.

We cannot avoid difficulties. But we can learn to face difficulties with a bent toward solution rather than idle criticism. There are always going to be people who influence situations and events more than we do. There are always going to be people who create problems that affect us, or create environments that can affect us negatively. And, we can only do so much.

Yet we must confront every inconvenience we face, regardless of its source, with a true, deep, committed and spiritually-based tendency to do all we can to provide a solution.

Do good in all things,
M A Street

Made in the USA
Charleston, SC
28 April 2013